Searching for
Christian Unity

Searching for Christian Unity

John Paul II, Cardinal Walter Kasper
Metropolitan Ioannis Zizioulas
Reverend Professor Geoffrey Wainwright
Bishop Kurt Koch, Monsignor Eleuterio Fortino, Bishop Brian Farrell
Cardinal Ivan Dias, Cardinal Cormac Murphy-O'Connor
Chiara Lubich, Enzo Bianchi

New City Press
Hyde Park, New York

Published in the United States by New City Press
202 Cardinal Rd., Hyde Park, NY 12538
www.newcitypress.com
©2007 Cardinal Walter Kasper

Cover design by Leandro de Leon

ISBN: 978-1-56548-265-4

Printed in the United States of America

Contents

Presentation 9

    Attendance at the meeting 10
    Meeting programme 13
    Support of Pope John Paul II during the meeting 15
    Initiatives within the context of the meeting 16

The Decree on Ecumenism –
Read Anew After Forty Years 18
    Cardinal Walter Kasper

    Introduction 18
    I. Background to the Decree on Ecumenism 19
    II. Ecumenism – Expression of the
        Eschatological Dynamic of the Church. 20
    III. "Subsistit in" – Expression of an
        Historically Concrete Ecclesiology 24
    IV. Ecumenism Under the Banner
        of Communio Ecclesiology 28
    V. East and West – Two Forms of
        the One Ecumenical Movement 31
    VI. Quanta es nobis via 36

Unitatis redintegratio: An Orthodox Reflection 37
    Metropolitan Ioannis Zizioulas

    Introduction 37
    I. The Importance of the Decree for
        Ecumenism in General 38
    II. The Importance of the Decree for Roman
        Catholic–Orthodox Relations 46
    III. Conclusion 53

Unitatis redintegratio in a Protestant Perspective . . . 55
    Geoffrey Wainwright

    Introduction 55
    I. To Identify and Locate the Church 56
    II. Baptism and the Ecclesial Communities. 58

III." Faith and Order" Efforts toward a
    Definition of Unity. 61
IV. Ecumenism in Time 64
V. Ut unum sint 66
VI. The Topography of Unity 69
VII. A Universal Ministry of Unity? 73
VIII. Unity "in Via"? 74

Ecumenical Developments and New Challenges.
Where Do We Stand Forty Years after
Unitatis redintegratio? 77
    Kurt Koch

Introduction 77
I. Developments within the Ecumenical Movement 78
II. Ascertaining the Origins of Ecumenism 85
III. The Contentious Goal of Ecumenism 95
IV. Ecumenical Restoration of Unity 100

The Action of the Pontifical Council for Promoting
Christian Unity from the Promulgation of
Unitatis redintegratio Until Today 105
    Eleuterio F. Fortino

Introduction. 105
I. Promotion of Ecumenism Within the
    Catholic Church 107
II. Relations and Theological Dialogue with
    Other Churches and Ecclesial Communities 129
III. Towards the Future 145
Conclusion 154

Ecumenism Today: The Situation in
the Catholic Church 156
    Brian Farrell

Introduction. 156
I. The Advance of Ecumenical Awareness
    within the Catholic Church. 158
II. The Practice of Ecumenism 162
III. Catholic Ecumenical Action at the Local Level 164

IV. Some Thoughts on what you can do
   for the Future of Ecumenism 165
Conclusion 167

The Missionary and Ecumenical
Task of the Church. 168
   Cardinal Ivan Dias

   Introduction. 168
   I. The Missionary Mandate. 169
   II. The Future Ecumenical Perspectives of the Church . . 171
   III. Dialogue of Life, Ideas, Action and Experiences . . . 172
   IV. Ecumenical Challenges 175
   Conclusion 178

Concrete Steps in the Ecumenism of Life 180
   Cardinal Cormac Murphy-O'Connor

A Spirituality of Unity Within Diversity 190
   Chiara Lubich

A Spirituality of Communion: Unity in Diversity. . . 204
   Enzo Bianchi

Concluding Observations 211
   Cardinal Walter Kasper

Appendix

Unitatis redintegratio
[Text of the Conciliar document] 219
   Introduction. 219
   Chapter 1: Catholic Principles on Ecumenism 220
   Chapter II: The Practice of Ecumenism 227
   Chapter III: Churches and Ecclesial Communities
      separated from the Roman Apostolic See 232

Separated Churches and Ecclesial
    Communities in the West 238
Notes. 243

Directory for the Application of
Principles and Norms on Ecumenism 245
    Preface 245
    I. The Search for Christian Unity. 249
    II. The Organization in the Catholic Church of the
      Service of Christian Unity 263
    III. Ecumenical Formation in the Catholic Church 276
    IV. Communion in Life and Spiritual Activity
      among the Baptized. 300
    V. Ecumenical Cooperation Dialogue and
      Common Witness. 326
Notes. 359

Presentation

The Decree on Ecumenism of the Second Vatican Council was promulgated on 21 November 1964 in the Basilica of St Peter, with 2137 *placet* votes and only 11 *non placet*. With this solemn act, the Catholic Church committed itself irreversibly to the search for full and visible communion of all the baptised. In so doing it responded by the grace of the Holy Spirit to the growing tendency that had started increasingly to develop among separated Christians towards an interior reappraisal and a desire to re–establish unity (cf. Decree on Ecumenism *Unitatis redintegratio,* Introduction).

The Pontifical Council for Promoting Christian Unity[1] has taken the initiative to commemorate the fortieth anniversary of the promulgation of *Unitatis redintegratio* by convening from 11–13 November 2004 at Rocca di Papa (in the vicinity of Rome) a meeting on the theme: *The Decree on Ecumenism of the Second Vatican Council Forty Years After the Council – Developments and Lasting Significance – Present Situation and Future Perspectives.*

---

1. Established on 5 June 1960 by Blessed John XXIII in preparation for the Second Vatican Council and confirmed by Pope Paul VI at its conclusion, the Pontifical Council is the office of the Holy See responsible for promoting Christian unity.

Attendance at the meeting

The meeting was held at the Congress and Spirituality Centre of Mondo Migliore and was also attended by other Churches and Ecclesial Communities which have worked together with the Catholic Church during these forty years. There was a significant presence of their fraternal delegates at the meeting.[2]

The meeting also fell within the framework of the periodical meetings convened by the Pontifical Council for Promoting Christian Unity in order to provide an update and an exchange of information with the ecumenical bodies of the Bishops' Conferences, the International Federations of Episcopal Conferences, and Synods of the Eastern Catholic Churches.[3]

---

2. The meeting was attended by: a] *for the Orthodox Churches:* the Ecumenical Patriarchate of Constantinople, the Greek Orthodox Patriarchate of Alexandria and All Africa, the Patriarchate of Moscow, the Orthodox Church of Belarus of the Patriarchate of Moscow, the Orthodox Church of the Ukraine of the Patriarchate of Moscow, the Patriarchate of Serbia, the Patriarchate of Romania, the Orthodox Church of Greece, the Orthodox Archdiocese of Cyprus, the Orthodox Church of Poland; b] *for the Eastern Orthodox Churches (Ancient Churches of the East):* the Coptic Orthodox Church, the Syrian Orthodox Catholicossate of Antioch, the Armenian Apostolic Church (See of Ethcmiadzin), the Catholicossate of Cilicia of the Armenians (Antelias, Lebanon), the Orthodox Church of Ethiopia, the Assyrian Church of the East; c] *for the Churches and Ecclesial Communities of the West:* the Anglican Communion, the World Lutheran Federation, the World Methodist Council, the Christian Church–Disciples of Christ, the Pentecostal Church, the World Mennonite Council; d] *for the international Christian organisations:* the World Council of Churches of Geneva, the Conference of European Churches [CEC], the Christian World Communions.

3. The last of these meetings was convened in 1993 on the publication of the updated version of the *Directory for the Application of Principles and Norms on Ecumenism,* approved by the Holy Father in

The response of the Bishops' Conferences and the Eastern Catholic Churches was well beyond our expectations, with a wide episcopal representation:

Europe[4]	36 participants	[73% of the episcopal and synodal bodies][5]
Africa[6]	38 participants	[62% of the episcopal bodies]
Asia	39 participants	[87% of the episcopal bodies][7]
Americas	24 participants	[100% of the episcopal bodies of North America; 66% of Central America; 90% of South America]
Oceania	2 participants	[out of a total of 3 episcopal bodies]

---

order to guide and develop the ecumenical commitment within the norms of the Catholic Church.

4. This data is based on the geographical distribution of the ecclesiastical territories. The European continent includes Eastern and Central Europe; Asia includes the Middle East.

5. Of particular interest is the extensive representation of the Bishops' Conferences of European countries in which religious freedom had been limited for many years or in which there had been a tragic experience of war, such as Belarus, Bosnia and Herzegovina, Bulgaria, Croatia, Russian Federation, Poland, Czech Republic, Romania [Latin and Eastern Catholics], Serbia and Montenegro, Slovenia, Ukraine [Greek Catholics], Hungary.

6. Particularly noteworthy for Africa is the extensive participation of the Federations of the Episcopal Conferences: *Association des Conférences Episcopales de la Région de l'Afrique Central* [ACERAC], *Inter-Regional Meeting of Bishops of Southern Africa* [IMBISA]; *Conférence Episcopale Régionale de l'Afrique de l'Ouest francophone* [CERAO], *Association of Episcopal Conferences of Anglophone West Africa* [AECAWA], *Association of Member Episcopal Conferences in Eastern Africa* [AMECEA]. Some Bishops' Conferences of Africa were unable to attend due to difficult local situations.

7. Among others, the meeting was attended by the Patriarch of Cilicia of the Armenians and the Greek-Melkite Catholic Patriarch of Antioch and All the East, as well as by high-level delegations of the Assembly of the Catholic Patriarchs and Bishops of Lebanon, the Assembly of the Catholic Hierarchy in Syria, the Synod of the Bishops of the Syrian Catholic Church of Malabar, the Conference of Catholic Bishops of India [Eastern rite]. There was an almost unanimous attendance on the part of Asia, with only four Bishops' Conferences not attending.

Other representatives responded positively to our invitation to commemorate the anniversary of the promulgation of the Decree: the *Members* of the Plenary of the Pontifical Council and its *Consultors* [Cardinals, Archbishops, Bishops and theologians from various parts of the world]; the Catholic *Presidents* of the Joint International Commissions for bilateral theological dialogue with the main Christian Communions;[8] some *special guests* who have been particularly close to the Pontifical Council over the last forty years, offering their service in a multitude of ways;[9] and also representatives of the universities and pontifical faculties.

The inauguration ceremony was attended by a delegate of the Secretariat of State. As well, various offices of the Holy See took part in the meeting. All staff members of the Pontifical Council for Promoting Christian Unity were present at Mondo Migliore.

8. These are the bilateral dialogues commenced either at the time of or since the Second Vatican Council with the Orthodox Churches, the Eastern Orthodox Churches (Ancient Churches of the East), the Anglican Communion, the main Christian Communions originating in the Reformation (World Lutheran Federation, World Methodist Council, World Assembly of Reformed Churches, Disciples of Christ, Pentecostals, etc.).

9. These include Cardinal Edward Idris Cassidy, who guided the Pontifical Council for Promoting Christian Unity from 1990 until 2000, and the former Secretary of the Council, Bishop Pierre Duprey. Cardinal Walter Kasper also extended a warm invitation to Cardinal Johannes Willebrands, the second President of the Council, who declined due to his advanced age. The special guests also included Orthodox representatives working on special collaborative projects supported by the *Catholic Committee for Cultural Collaboration* within the ambit of the Eastern Section of the Pontifical Council for Promoting Christian Unity, as well as the *Fidel Götz Foundation* and the *Iniziative Unità dei Cristiani – Einheit der Christen Foundation*, which also made a financial contribution to the meeting.

Meeting programme

The meeting focused on the theme *The Decree on Ecumenism of the Second Vatican Council Forty Years After the Council — Developments and Lasting Significance — Present Situation and Future Perspectives.*

11 November 2004

Lasting and Crucial Significance of Unitatis redintegratio *was the theme of the introductory paper of the President of the Council.*

Cardinal Kasper's paper was developed in an ecumenical and dialogical key by the two following speakers, the first offering reflections from the Orthodox perspective [Iohannis, Metropolitan of Pergamon — Ecumenical Patriarchate of Constantinople], the other from the perspective of the Churches issuing from the Reformation [Geoffrey Wainwright — World Methodist Council].

During the afternoon, regional and language — based working groups [Italian, English, French, Spanish] discussed the implementation of the Decree and the problems, needs and achievements of the ecumenical commitment at various levels. As well, participants were presented with a project for a *Vademecum œcumenicum,* which will be eventually distributed to the Bishops' Conferences with a view to promoting spiritual ecumenism.

12 November 2004

Retrospective on the Ecumenical Commitment and Present Situation

This theme was developed by Bishop Kurt Koch of Basle (Switzerland), who spoke of ecumenical developments and new challenges. The Secretary of the Pontifical Council, Bishop Brian Farrell, outlined the results of the survey carried out by the Council in preparation for the meeting providing recent data on the current situation. The Under Secretary of the Pontifical Council, Monsignor Eleuterio F. Fortino, spoke of the action of the Council in the forty years since the promulgation of the Decree.

During the afternoon, regional and language–based groups presented their recommendations and suggestions.

13 November 2004

Future perspectives

This theme was examined in the papers by the Archbishop of Bombay, Cardinal Ivan Dias [on the ecumenical and missionary commitment], the Archbishop of Westminster, Cardinal Cormac Murphy–O'Connor [concrete steps in the ecumenism of life], Ms Chiara Lubich,[10] President of the Focolare Movement, and by Brother Enzo Bianchi, Prior of the Bose Monastery [spirituality within diversity].

---

10. Chiara Lubich was unable to attend due to ill health. Her paper was presented by Dr Gabriella Fallacara, staff member of *Centro Uno per l'Unità dei Cristiani* of the Focolare Movement.

Support of Pope John Paul II
during the meeting

The afternoon of the last day of the meeting was dedicated to prayer, the *soul of the whole ecumenical movement (cf. Unitatis redintegratio,* 8). Participants attended vespers presided by Pope John Paul II in the Vatican Patriarchal Basilica. As well as representatives of the Churches and Ecclesial Communities of Rome, the ceremony was attended by the parish priests and faithful of the Diocese, and movements and associations working for Christian unity.

The celebration of vespers in St Peter's gave spiritual sustenance and solemnity to the Pontifical Council in its commitment to what is fundamental in the search for the visible unity of all Christians: *gratitude* to the Lord for the many gifts bestowed on the journey to the full realisation of his prayer to the Father, *ut unum sint;* the *understanding* that "on Jesus's prayer and not on our own strength that we base the hope that even within history we shall be able to reach full and visible communion with all Christians"; the *conviction* that the "invocation *ut unum sint* is, at one and the same time, a binding imperative, the strength that sustains us, and a salutary rebuke for our slowness and closed–heartedness".[11]

---

11. John Paul II, Apostolic Letter *Novo millennio ineunte*, 48.

Initiatives within the
context of the meeting

On 11 November, participants viewed a screening of a documentary entitled *Ut unum sint: Forty Years of Ecumenism*. The documentary, which created great interest, presented the key events of the ecumenical journey. Its production was made possible through the commitment of the Centro Televisivo Vaticano, and the contribution of the Pontifical Council for Social Communications, the Bose Community and many other individuals and institutes.

After the celebration of vespers on 13 November, the programme of the meeting included a musical presentation organised by the Artistic Section of the *Rondine Cittadella della Pace* Association of Arezzo,[12] directed by Maestro Giorgio Albiani. This part of the programme was entitled *A Thread of Voices Between East and West* and included works from various popular traditions, as "together with the magnificent liturgical traditions, the popular song entwines diverse strands in surprising ways and nurtures the different religious traditions, and accordingly it has been appreciated by men and women of different traditions who often sing it together".[13] The songs and music were presented by the *Viulàn* group and the *Slavey Quartet* (Bulgaria). The last musical piece entitled *Unità sul filo di voce*

---

12. This Association is active in the Diocese of Arezzo and focuses on initiatives for promoting a culture of peace. It has established an international student house that welcomes young people from conflict zones throughout the world and enables them to live side by side together. The Association also has a 'Peace School' which works on the resolution of interconfessional conflicts and the promotion of dialogue and collaboration among Christians at the level of formation.

13. Taken from the programme distributed during the concert.

was composed by Maestro Albiani for the anniversary of *Unitatis redintegratio*. The words of the song were liberally inspired by verse 37 of the Book of Ezechiel. During the meeting, participants also visited a book display of various works on the theme of ecumenism. The display was prepared by the generous and competent assistance of the Daughters of St Paul, and included works in Italian, English, French, Spanish and German. The Sisters also especially prepared an ecumenical bibliography which was distributed among the participants. A section of the display featured publications currently being prepared in conjunction with the Orthodox Churches, as well as a number of Catholic theological texts translated into Russian and Ukrainian.

An architect from Arezzo, Chiara Braconi, designed a commemorative logo for the anniversary. The circular image depicts a baptismal font, symbol of the common belonging to Christ, which is illuminated by the light of the Resurrection; different paths radiating from and returning towards the font are taken by people who following different itineraries, both personal and shared, walk towards their unity.[14]

14. The anniversary celebration of *Unitatis redintegratio* was also made possible by the generosity of a number of benefactors who assisted the Holy See in covering expenses: Missio, Misereor, CNEWA, Fidel Götz Foundation, 'Iniziative Unità dei Cristiani – Einheit der Christen', Kirche in Not, Renovabis, Adveniat. The Daughters of St Paul financed the book display. Banca Intesa financed the documentary.

The Decree on Ecumenism –
Read Anew After Forty Years[1]

Cardinal Walter Kasper

Introduction

On 21 November 1964 the Decree on Ecumenism *Unitatis redintegratio* (UR) was solemnly proclaimed by the Second Vatican Council. Already in the introduction we find the statement: "Christ the Lord founded one Church and one Church only.... division openly contradicts the will of Christ, scandalizses the world and damages the holy cause of preaching the Gospel". "The restoration of unity among all Christians is one of the principal concerns of the Second Vatican Council."

Forty years have passed since that day, and the influence exerted by this document in that time constitutes an incomparable record. Forty years represent a Biblical time-span, so we have good grounds for asking: What was the intention of this document? What effect has it had, and where do we stand today in regard to ecumenism? What is the future direction of ecumenism? *Quo vadis* ecumenism?

The Council is the Magna Charta for the pathway of the church into the 21st century (*Tertio millennio adveniente, 18*). The Pope has repeatedly said that the path of ecumenism is irreversible (*Ut unum sint [UUS] 3 and passim*); ecumenism is one of the pastoral priorities of his pontificate (*UUS, 99*). So the question arises: What are the Catholic principles of ecumenism as formulated by the Decree *Unitatis redintegratio*?

---

1. Translated from the original German text.

Thank you for choosing this book.
If you would like to receive regular information
about New City books, please fill in this card.

Title purchased: ....

Please tick the subjects
that are of particular interest to you:

❑ Fathers of the Church
❑ Classics in Spirituality
❑ Contemporary Spirituality
❑ Theology
❑ Scripture and Commentaries
❑ Family Life
❑ Biography / History

Other subjects of interest: ....

....

BLOCK CAPITALS PLEASE

NAME: ....
ADDRESS: ....

.... POSTCODE ....

New City
Unit 17, Sovereign Park
Coronation Road,
London NW10 7QP
ENGLAND

I. Background to the Decree on Ecumenism

The Decree on Ecumenism did not fall readymade from heaven. It forms a part of the ecumenical movement which had arisen outside of the Catholic Church during the 20th century (*UR, 1, 4*) and which achieved a decisive breakthrough with the formation of the World Council of Churches in 1948. This movement was for a long time regarded with suspicion by the Catholic Church. But its reception by the Second Vatican Council has roots reaching back to the Catholic theology of the 19th century. Johann Adam Möhler and John Henry Newman in particular should be mentioned as forerunners and pioneers.

The way was also prepared by the Holy See. Even prior to the Second Vatican Council the Popes fostered the Prayer for Unity and the Week of Prayer for Unity. Popes Leo XIII and Benedict XV prepared the way for openness towards ecumenism; Pope Pius XI gave express approval of the Malines Conversations with the Anglicans (1921 - 1926).[2]

Pope Pius XII went a step further. In an Instruction of 1950 he expressly welcomed the ecumenical movement and attributed it to the influence of the Holy Spirit. In addition, this Pope also paved the way for the Council with a series of groundbreaking encyclicals. It would therefore be erroneous to overlook this fundamental continuity and see the Council as a radical breach with tradition and the advent of a new church.

---

2. On the pre-history of the ecumenical movement in the Catholic Church: H. Petri "Die römisch-katholische Kirche und die Ökumene" in *Handbuch der Ökumenik*, Bd. 2 (Paderborn 1986), pp.95-135.

II. Ecumenism – Expression of the
Eschatological Dynamic of the Church

But something new did in fact begin with the Council, not a new church but a renewed church. It was Pope John XXIII who initiated this renewal. He can rightly be called the spiritual father of the Decree on Ecumenism. He wanted the Council, and he set its goals: the renewal inside the Catholic Church and the unity of Christians.

It is not my intention to outline here the eventful history of the genesis of *Unitatis redintegratio* as it overturned the narrow post-Tridentine Counter-Reformation outlook of the church.[3] This was not "Modernism", rather it was a return to the Biblical, patristic and early-medieval tradition, opening the way for a renewed understanding of the church.

The Council was able to embrace the ecumenical movement because it understood the church as a whole as movement, namely as the people of God on the move *(Lumen gentium 2, [Conclusion], 8, 9, 48-51; UR, 2, [Conclusion and passim])*. Or to formulate it another way: the Council ascribed new relevance to the eschatological dimension of the church and described the church not as a static but as a dynamic entity, as the people of God undertaking a pilgrimage between "already" and "not yet". The Council integrated the ecumenical movement into this eschatological dynamic. Understood in this sense, ecumenism is the way of the church *(UUS, 7)*. It is not an addendum or an appendix but forms an integral part of the very essence of the church and its pastoral activity *(UUS, 20)*.

---

3. Cf. W. Becker in LThK Vat. II, Vol. 2 (1967), pp.11-39; L. Jaeger, *Das Konzilsdekret über den Ökumenismus* (Paderborn 1968), pp.15-78; *Storia del Concilio Vaticano II*, G. Alberigo (ed.), Vol. 3 (Bologna 1998), pp.277-365; Vol. 4 (Bologna 1999), pp.436-446.

From this eschatological perspective, the ecumenical movement is intimately connected with the mission movement. Ecumenism and mission belong together like twins.[4] Mission is an eschatological phenomenon in which the church takes up the cultural riches of the peoples, purifies and enriches them, and is thereby itself enriched and endowed with the full expression of its catholicity (*Ad gentes 1ff., 9 and passim*). Similarly, in ecumenism the church enters into an exchange of gifts with the separated churches (*UUS, 28, 57*), enriches them, but also reciprocally makes their gifts its own, adds them to its catholic fullness and thus fully realises its own catholicity (*UR, 4*). Mission and ecumenism are the two forms of the eschatological pathway and the eschatological dynamic of the church.

The Council was not so naïve as to underestimate the danger inherent in this integration of the ecumenical movement into the eschatological dynamic of the church. The eschatological dynamic could — as so often in the history of the church — be misunderstood as a progressive movement in which the deposit of older traditions is felt to be outdated and is discarded in the name of a so-called progressive understanding of the faith. Where this occurs, there is a real danger of relativism and indifferentism, of a 'cheap ecumenism' which in the end makes itself redundant. In this way ecumenism has on occasion fallen prey to movements which have been critical of the church and have been instrumentalised against the church.

Any such softening of dogma fails to recognise the essence of the eschatological character of the church. The

---

4. J. Le Guillou, *Mission et unité. Les exigences de la communion* (Paris 1959); Y. Congar, *Diversités et communion* (Paris 1982), pp.239ff. Pope John Paul II also stressed this connection in the Encyclical *Redemptoris missio* (1990, Nos. 36 and 50).

Eschaton does not refer to an historically unrealised future reality. With Jesus Christ and the outpouring of the Holy Spirit it has entered into history once and for all and is present in the church. The church itself is an eschatological phenomenon; unity as an essential characteristic of the church is not a future, or much less an eschatological goal; the church is already the *"una sancta ecclesia" (UR, 4; UUS, 11-14)*. The ecumenical path is not a mystery tour. Through history the church becomes what it already is, what it always was and what it forever remains. It is on the way towards the concrete realisation of its essential nature within the reality of life in its fullness.

The Catholic principles of ecumenism, as formulated by the Council and later by Pope John Paul II, are therefore clear and unequivocal in their rejection of the irenicism and relativism which reduce everything to banality *(UR, 5, 11, 24; UUS, 18, 36, 79)*. The ecumenical movement does not throw overboard anything which has been valued and cherished by the church in its previous history, it remains faithful to the truth that has been acknowledged in history and defined as such; nor does it add to it anything absolutely new. The ecumenical movement and its avowed goal, the unity of the disciples of Jesus Christ, remain inscribed within the furrow of tradition.

The tradition is, however, in the sense of the two great precursors of the Council, J. A. Möhler and J. H. Newman, not a petrified entity; it is a living tradition. It is an event in the Holy Spirit, who according to the promise of the Lord guides the church into all truth *(Jn 16:13)*, again and again elucidating the Gospel which has been handed down once and for all, and granting growth in understanding of the truth which has been revealed once and for all *(Dei verbum [DV] 8; cf. DSDH 3020)*. According to the martyr bishop

Irenaeus of Lyon it is the spirit of God who keeps the apostolic heritage, handed down once and for all, young and fresh.[5]

In this sense the ecumenical movement is a charismatic phenomenon and "an undertaking of the Holy Spirit". The church has not only an institutional but also a charismatic side, as the Council demonstrated (*LG, 4, 7, 12, 49; Apostolicam actuositatem 3; AG, 4, 29*). So ecumenism is a new beginning, set in motion by the Holy Spirit and led by him (*UR, 1, 4*). The Holy Spirit as it were the soul of the church (*LG, 7*), grants unity as well as the multiplicity of gifts and services (*LG, 7; UR, 2*). Thus the Council was able to say that spiritual ecumenism is the heart of ecumenism. Spiritual ecumenism means inner conversion, a change of heart, the sanctification of personal life, love, self-denial, humility, patience, but also renewal and reform of the church; and not least, prayer is the heart of the ecumenical movement (*UR, 5-8; UUS, 15ff., 21-27*).

As a spiritual movement the ecumenical movement does not annul tradition, rather it grants a new and more profound insight into what has been handed down once and for all; it blazes the trail for the renewed Pentecost which Pope John XXIII predicted in his opening address to the Second Vatican Council; it paves the way for the new historical form of the church, not a new church but indeed a spiritually renewed and spiritually enriched church. Together with mission, ecumenism is the way of the church into the 21st century and into the third millennium.

---

5. Ireneaus of Lyon, *Adversus haereses* III, 24, 1 in *Sources chrétiennes*, 211 (Paris 1974) p.472.

III. "Subsistit in" – Expression of an Historically Concrete Ecclesiology

The eschatological and pneumatological dynamic demanded conceptual clarification. This was in fact achieved by the Council in the Constitution on the Church, with the much-debated formulation that the church of Jesus Christ "subsists" in the Catholic Church (*LG, 8*). The principal editor of the Church Constitution, G. Philips, was far-sighted enough to predict that a lot of ink would be spilt over the significance of this "*subsistit in*".[6] Indeed, the flow of ink has not subsided to this day, and it is likely that much more printer's ink will be needed to clarify the issues it raises.

In the course of the Council the "*subsistit in*" took the place of the previous "*est*".[7] It contains *in nuce* the whole ecumenical problem.[8] The "est" claimed that the church of Christ Jesus "*is*" the Catholic Church. This strict identification of the church of Christ Jesus with the Catholic Church had already been represented most recently in the encyclicals *Mystici corporis* (1943) and *Humani generis* (1950).[9] But even according to *Mystici corporis* there are people who, although they have not yet been baptised, are subsumed under the Catholic Church because that is their express desire (DSDH 3921). Therefore Pius XII had condemned

---

6. G. Philips, *L'Église et son mystère aux deuxième Concile du Vatican*, tome 1 (Paris 1967), p.119.
7. Overview in *Synopsis historica*, G. Alberigo-F. Magistretti (ed.) (Bologna 1975), p.38; pp.439ff; pp.506ff.
8. G. Philips, op.cit.
9. *Acta Apostolicae Sedis [AAS]* 35 (1943) 199; 42 (1950) 571.

an exclusive interpretation of the axiom *"Extra ecclesiam nulla salus"* already in 1949.[10]

The Council went a decisive step further with the aid of the *"subsistit in"*. It wished to do justice to the fact that there are found outside of the Catholic Church not only individual Christians but also "elements of the church",[11] indeed churches and ecclesial communities which, although not in full communion, rightly belong to the one church and possess salvatory significance for their members (*LG, 8, 15; UR, 3; UUS, 10-14*). Thus the Council is aware that there are outside of the Catholic Church forms of sanctification which even extend as far as martyrdom (*LG, 15; UR, 4; UUS, 12, 83*). The question of the salvation of non-Catholics is now no longer answered personally as in *Mystici corporis* on the basis of the subjective desire of single individuals, but institutionally on the basis of objective ecclesiology.

The concept *"subsistit in"*, according to the intention of the Theological Commission of the Council, means: the church of Christ Jesus has its concrete location in the Catholic Church; it is there that it is found.[12] It is not a purely Platonic entity or a prospective future reality, it exists in a concrete historical form, it is located in the Catholic Church.

---

10. Letter of the Holy See to the Archbishop of Boston (1949), in *Denzinger-Hünermann [DH]* (Herder 1999) 3866-3873.

11. This concept originates in the first instance with J. Calvin, but while it there refers to the miserable remnants of the true church, within ecumenical discussion it is understood as positive, dynamic and future-oriented. It was first brought into play in an extension of the anti-Donatist position of Augustine by Y. Congar (cf. A. Nichols, *Yves Congar*, London 1986, pp.101-106). In the Toronto Declaration (1950) it also entered into the usage of the World Council of Churches.

12. *Synopsis historica*, op.cit. p.439; G. Philips, op.cit. p.119; A. Grillmeier, LThK, Vat. II, Vol.1, 1966, p.175; L. Jaeger, op.cit. pp.214-217.

Understood in this sense *"subsistit in"* encompasses the essential thrust of the *"est"*. But it no longer formulates the self-concept [self-image] of the Catholic Church in "splen- did isolation", but also takes account of churches and ecclesial communities in which the one church of Jesus Christ is effectively present (*UUS, 11*), but which are not in full communion with it. In formulating its own identity, the Catholic Church at the same time establishes a relationship of dialogue with these churches and ecclesial communities.[13]

Accordingly it is a misunderstanding of *"subsistit in"* to make it the basis of an ecclesiological pluralism or relativism which implies that the one church of Christ Jesus subsists in many churches, and thus the Catholic Church is merely one among many other churches. Such theories of ecclesiological pluralism contradict the self-concept which the Catholic Church — like the Orthodox Churches, incidentally — has always had of itself and which the Second Vatican Council also wished to maintain. The Catholic Church continues to claim, as it always has, to be the true church of Christ Jesus, in which the entire fullness of the means of salvation are is present (*UR, 3; UUS, 14*), but it now sees itself in a context of dialogue with the other churches and ecclesial communities. It does not propound any new doctrine but establishes a new outlook, abandons triumphalism and formulates its traditional self-concept in a realistic, historically concrete — one could even say, humble — manner. The Council is aware that the church is on a journey through history towards a concrete historical realisation of what its most profound essence "is" (*"est"*).

This realistic and humble view is found above all in *Lumen gentium 8*, where the Council with the words *"subsistit in"*

---

13. Pope Paul VI demonstrated the principle of this dialogic nature of the church in his first Encyclical *Ecclesiam suam* (1964).

allows not only for elements of the church outside of its visible boundaries but also for sinful members and sinful structures within the church itself.[14] The people of God also incorporates sinners within its fold, with the result that the spiritual essence of the church does not rightly shed its light upon the separated brethren or the world. Thus the church bears some of the guilt for the divisions, and slows down the growth of the Kingdom of God (*UR, 3ff.*). On the other hand, the separated communities have on occasion better developed individual aspects of the revealed truth, so that the Catholic Church, under the circumstances of division, is unable to fully accomplish its intrinsic catholicity (*UR, 4; UUS, 14*). Therefore the church is in need of purification and renewal, and must constantly walk the path of penance (*LG, 8; UR, 3ff., 6ff.; UUS, 34ff., 83ff.*).

This self-critical and penitent view forms the basis for the path of the ecumenical movement (*UR, 5-12*). That includes conversion and renewal, without which there can be no ecumenism, and dialogue, which is more than an exchange of ideas but rather an exchange of gifts.

From this eschatological and spiritual perspective the goal of ecumenism cannot be described simply as "the others" returning to the fold of the Catholic Church. The goal of full unity can only be achieved through conversion, when all are impelled by the spirit of God to turn to the one head of the church, Christ Jesus. To the degree that we are one with Christ we will all be one with one another and thus realise the intrinsic catholicity of the church in its concrete fullness. Theologically the Council defined this goal as *communio* unity.

---

14. On the concept of "structures of sin" cf. the Apostolic Letter of Pope John Paul II *Reconciliatio et Paenitentia* (1984) 16 and the Encyclical *Ut unum sint [UUS]*, 34.

IV. Ecumenism Under the Banner
of Communio Ecclesiology

The fundamental idea of the Second Vatican Council and especially of the Decree on Ecumenism is: *communio*.[15] This is essential to the correct understanding of the talk of *"elemente ecclesiae"*. This expression gives a quantitative, almost materialistic impression, as though one could count these elements and check whether the number is complete. This "ecclesiology of elements" was criticised already during the Council and even more so after the Council.[16] But *Unitatis redintegratio* did not stop at this point; the Decree on Ecumenism does not view the separated churches and ecclesial communities simply as entities which have retained a limited stock of elements, different in each instance, but able to be quantitatively determined; rather, it sees each as an integral whole which gives expression to those elements within the totality of its ecclesiological understanding.

That occurs with the aid of the concept of *"communio"*. With this concept drawn from the Bible and the early church the Council circumscribes the most profound mystery of the church, which is formed as it were as an icon of the trinity in the image of the trinitarian *communio* (*LG, 4; UR, 2*). *communio* and *communio sanctorum* originally meant not the *communion* of Christians with one another but sharing (*participatio*) in the goods of salvation, in the *sancta*

---

15. See the Extraordinary Episcopal Synod of 1985 (II C 1). The Pontifical Council for Promoting Christian Unity dealt with this issue in detail at the 2001 Plenary. Cf. the introduction by W. Kasper, "Present Situation and Future of the Ecumenical Movement" in *Information Service* N. 109, 2002/I-II, pp. 11-20.

16. Cf. above all H. Mühlen, *Una mystica persona* (Münich-Paderborn 1968) pp.496-502; pp.504-513.

or the *sacramenta*. Fundamental to this is baptism. It is the sacrament of faith, whereby those who have been baptised belong to the one body of Christ which is the church. Non-Catholic Christians are therefore not outside of the one church, they already belong to it in a most fundamental way (*LG, 11, 14; UR, 22*). On the basis of the one common baptism ecumenism goes far beyond simple goodwill and friendliness, it is not a form of church diplomacy; it has an ontological foundation and an ontological depth, it is an event of the Spirit.

Baptism is of course only the point of departure and the foundation (*UR, 22*). Becoming a member of the church reaches its fulfilment in the eucharist; that is the source, centre and summit of Christian and ecclesial life (*LG, 11, 26; Presbyterorum ordinis 5; AG, 39*). Thus eucharistic ecclesiology forms the foundation of the Constitution on the Liturgy and the Constitution on the Church (*Sacrosanctum concilium 47; LG, 3, 7, 11, 23, 26*).

Unitatis redintegratio states that the eucharist both signifies and brings about the unity of the church (*UR, 2*). Later it says of the celebration of the eucharist by the Orthodox Churches: "Through the celebration of the eucharist of the Lord in each of these churches the church of God is built up and grows in stature, and through concelebration their communion with one another is made manifest" (*UR, 15*). Wherever the eucharist is celebrated is the church. This axiom has — as I will demonstrate shortly — fundamental significance for the understanding of the oriental churches and the distinction between them and the Protestant ecclesial communities.

This means: Every local church celebrating the eucharist is church in the full sense, but it is not the whole church

(*LG, 26, 28*). Since there is only one Christ Jesus and only one eucharist, each church celebrating the eucharist necessarily stands in communion with all other churches. The one church exists in and of the local churches (*LG, 23*), and the local churches exist vice versa in and of the one church (*Communionies notio, 9*).[17]

If we transfer this concept of unity to the ecumenical problematic, the ecumenical unity we strive for is more than a network of church denominations which mutually recognise one another by establishing altar and pulpit fellowship. The Catholic understanding of ecumenism takes as its starting point the already existing unity and the already existing partial *communio* with the other churches and ecclesial communities, in order to progress from this incomplete fellowship to full communion (*UUS, 14*) which includes unity in the faith, in the sacraments and in church ministry (*LG, 14; UR, 2ff.*).

Unity in the sense of full *communio* does not mean uniformity but unity in diversity and diversity in unity. Within the one church there is a legitimate multiplicity of mentalities, customs, rites, canonical orders, theologies and spiritualities (*LG, 13; UR, 4; 16ff.*). We can also say: the essence of unity understood as *communio* is catholicity, not in the denominational sense but in its original qualitative meaning; it means the realisation of all the gifts which the local and denominational churches can contribute.

The contribution which *Unitatis redintegratio* makes towards the solution of the ecumenical problem is accordingly

---

17. Congregation for the Doctrine of the Faith, *Communionis notio*, Letter to the Bishops of the Catholic Church on Some Aspects of the Church Understood as Communion, (28 May 1992) in *AAS 85* (1993) 840.

not an "ecclesiology of elements" but the distinction between full and imperfect communion (*UR, 3*).[18] The consequence of this distinction is that the aim of ecumenism is not directed towards amalgamation but has as its goal a *communio* which does not mean either reciprocal absorption or fusion.[19] This formulation of the ecumenical problem is the most important theological contribution of the Council towards the question of ecumenism.

V. East and West – Two Forms of the One Ecumenical Movement

Integrating ecumenical theology into the *communio* ecclesiology permitted a distinction between two kinds of church division: the division between East and West and the divisions within the Western church since the 16th century. Between the two kinds there is not only a geographic and chronological distinction; the two divisions are different also in nature. While in the case of the split with the Eastern church the fundamental ecclesial structure which had developed since the second century remained intact, in the case of the churches which emerged from the Reformation we are dealing with a different type of church.[20]

The Eastern schism encompasses both the ancient oriental churches which separated from the imperial church in the 4th and 5th centuries and the schism between Rome

---

18. In the Council documents themselves this distinction is not yet fully developed terminologically. In UR 3 the terms *"plena communio"* and *"quaedam communio, etsi non perfecta"* are used.
19. John Paul II, Encyclical *Slavorum apostoli* (1985) 27.
20. J. Ratzinger, "Die ökumenische Situation – Orthodoxie, Katholizismus und Reformation" in *Theologische Prinzipienlehre* (München 1982) pp.203-208.

and the Eastern Patriarchates, frequently linked symbolically to the year 1054.

The Council is far removed from reducing the difference to cultural and political factors. From the start East and West received the one Gospel in different ways and developed different forms of liturgy, spirituality, theology and canonical law. But in the basic sacramental-eucharistic and episcopal structure, however, they are in agreement. The national and international dialogues initiated following the Council have confirmed this profound communion in the faith, in the sacraments and in the episcopal structure.

Therefore the Council speaks of relationships like those between local churches as sister churches (*UR, 14*). This formulation, which is left rather vague in the Decree on Ecumenism, was taken up and further developed by Pope Paul VI and the Ecumenical Patriarch Athenagoras in *Tomos Agapis.*[21]

Restoration of full communion presupposes careful consideration of the various factors involved in the division (*UR, 14*) and recognition of the legitimate differences (*UR, 15-17*). The Council determines that the differences are more often to be considered mutually complementary rather than in fact conflicting (*UR, 17*).[22] Therefore it declares that the "entire heritage of spirituality and liturgy, of discipline and theology, in the various traditions, belongs to the full apostolic and catholic character of the church" (*UR,*

---

21. *Tomos Agapis, Vatican–Phanar* (Rome–Istanbul, 1971), pp.386-392 (No. 176). In the joint declaration of Pope John Paul II and the Ecumenical Patriarch Bartholomew of 1995 the turn of phrase was taken up once more.
22. *The Catechism of the Catholic Church* (No. 248) also numbers the question of the *Filioque* among the problems which signify a complementary rather than a contradictory difference.

17).[23] In order to restore unity one must therefore not impose any burdens beyond that which are is strictly necessary (*Acts 15:28; UR, 18*).

The essential problem in the relationship between East and West is the Petrine office (*UUS, 88*). Pope John Paul II has issued an invitation to a fraternal dialogue on the future exercise of the Petrine office (*UUS, 95*). It is not possible in this context to enter into the complex historical questions raised here or the current possibilities for reinterpretation and re-reception of the dogmas of the First Vatican Council. It must suffice to mention that a symposium conducted by the Pontifical Council for Christian Unity in May 2003 with the Orthodox churches resulted in openings on both sides.[24] We hope that the international theological dialogue can soon be resumed and that it can give priority to addressing this question.

The Western schism which originated in the 16th century Reformation is of a different kind. As the Decree on Ecumenism clearly recognises, this constitutes a complex and subtly differentiated phenomenon in both the historical and the doctrinal sense. We are linked with the Reformation communities too by many important elements of the true church. These include in particular the proclamation of the Word of God, and baptism. In many post-Conciliar dialogue documents these commonalities have been extended and intensified.[25]

---

23. See also the Decree *Orientalium ecclesiarum* 1, and the Encyclical *Orientale lumen* (1995) 1.
24. Cf. *Il ministero Petrino. Cattolici e ortodossi in dialogo*, W. Kasper (ed.), (Rome 2004).
25. Particularly noteworthy are the Lima documents *Baptism, Eucharist and Ministry* (1982), the ARCIC Documents with the Anglican Communion, the Convergence Documents with the Lutherans

But there are also "very weighty differences" which are not only of a historical, sociological, psychological or cultural nature, but are in fact based primarily on differing interpretations of revealed truth (*UR, 19*). According to the Council these differences concern in part the doctrine of Jesus Christ and redemption, and in particular the Holy Scriptures in their relationship to the church and the authentic teaching office, the church and its orders, the role of Mary in the work of salvation (*UR, 20f; UUS, 66*), in part also moral questions (*UR, 23*). The latter have particularly in recent times come to the forefront and are creating problems both within the Reformation communities and in their relationships with the Catholic Church.

In contrast to the Eastern schism, the Reformation communities of course involve not only individual doctrinal differences but also a different fundamental structure and a different type of church. Regardless of the differences between the Reformers — often considerable — their understanding of the church is grounded not on the eucharist but primarily on the Word of God as *creatura verbi*.[26]

The distinction becomes more marked in the question of the eucharist. The ecclesial communities which emerged from the Reformation have — as the Council says — "not preserved the original and complete reality (*substantia*) of the mystery of the eucharist" (*UR, 22*) because of the absence of the sacrament of orders.

In the sense of eucharistic ecclesiology this lack of eucharistic substance results in the distinction between churches and ecclesial communities. The declaration *Dominus*

(*The Lord's Supper; Spiritual Office in the Church*, etc.) and especially the *Joint Declaration on Justification* (1999).

26. M. Luther, *De captivitate Babylonica ecclesiae praeludium* (1520): WA pp.560ff.

Jesus (DJ) added conceptual sharpness to this distinction *(DJ,16)*, and this has often been the subject of harsh criticism on the part of Protestant Christians. Doubtless the intended meaning could have been expressed in a more understandable way; but in regard to the facts of the matter it is impossible to overlook the real difference in the concept of the church. Protestant Christians do not wish to be a church in the same way as the Catholic church understands itself as a church; they represent a different type of church and for this reason they are not a church in the Catholic meaning of the word.

Because of these differences the Council warns against frivolous and imprudent zeal. "Ecumenical activity cannot be other than fully and sincerely Catholic, that is, loyal to the truth we have received from the Apostles and the Fathers and in harmony with the faith which the Catholic Church has always professed" *(UR, 24)*. The Council however also warns against polemics. It is significant that the word "dialogue" recurs repeatedly at the conclusion of the different paragraphs, almost as a refrain *(UR, 19, 21, 22, 23)*. That expresses once more the new spirit in which the Council addresses the task of surmounting the differences.

VI. *Quanta es nobis via?*

The Decree was a beginning. Nevertheless it has exerted an enormous influence both within the Catholic Church and ecumenically, and has profoundly transformed the ecumenical situation in the course of the last forty years.[27]

Doubtless *Unitatis redintegratio* has also left some questions open, as well as encountering objections and undergoing further development. But we should not on account of these problems overlook the rich fruits which this Decree has borne. It has initiated an irrevocable and irreversible process to which there is no realistic alternative. The Decree on Ecumenism points us on the way forward into the 21st century. It is the command of the Lord to follow this path, with moderation, but also with courage, with patience and above all with unshakeable hope.

In the end ecumenism is an adventure of the Holy Spirit. Therefore I finish with the words which also conclude the Decree: "And hope does not disappoint, for God's love has been poured forth in our hearts through the Holy Spirit, who has been given to us" (*Rom 5:5*) (*UR, 24*).

---

27. Cf. *Il Concilio Vaticano II. Recezione e attualità alla luce del Giubileo*, R. Fisichella (ed.), (Rome 2000), pp.335-415, with papers by E. Fortino, J. Wicks, F. Ocáriz, Y. Spiteris, V. Pfnür.

Unitatis redintegratio:
An Orthodox Reflection[1]

Metropolitan Ioannis Zizioulas
of Pergamon

Introduction

It is a great honour and a privilege for me to be invited to address this august assembly which is gathered here to celebrate the 40th anniversary of one of the most important documents of the 20th century for the life, not only of the Roman Catholic Church, but of Christianity as a whole. I have been asked to offer some comments on the document of the Second Vatican Council on ecumenism and its significance from the point of view of the Orthodox Church to which I belong. My comments will be, of course, personal in character but they will, I hope, reflect the feelings, hopes and expectations of the Orthodox Church as a whole. For, although there has been no official reaction of the Orthodox Church to this document, or for that matter to any of the Decrees promulgated by the Second Vatican Council, the influence that this Council has exercised on Orthodox theology and the discussion it has provoked have been considerable. In addition to that, this document has opened the way for great historical events to happen which started a new chapter in the relations between the Orthodox and the Roman Catholic Churches. The lifting of the anathemas of 1054 AD between Rome and Constantinople, the meeting of Pope Paul VI with Patriarch Athenagoras in Jerusalem,

---

1. Original English text.

the exchange of visits on a regular basis of delegations from both Churches on their respective official Feasts, and, above all, the establishment of the official theological dialogue between the Roman Catholic and the Orthodox Churches are among the most important consequences of the Decree on Ecumenism. There is no doubt that this Decree has made history and opened new avenues for the restoration of Christian unity.

In the lines that follow I shall offer some personal reflections and comments on the following points:

(a) The importance of the Decree on Ecumenism for the promotion of Christian unity in general;
(b) The importance of the Decree for Roman Catholic-Orthodox relations;
(c) Questions and problems that continue to be open and expectations and hopes for the future.

I. The Importance of the Decree for Ecumenism in General

The late Professor Oscar Cullman, a Protestant observer at the Council, is reported to have said of the Decree: "This is more than the opening of a door; new ground has been broken. No Catholic document has ever spoken of non-Catholic Christians in this way". What is so new and so open to non-Catholics in this Decree?

First and foremost, there is the *theology of the Church* which lies behind the Decree on Ecumenism that strikes the non-Catholic Christian. In order to appreciate this one has to read the Decree in close relationship with the Decree *Lumen gentium*, for it is only then that the deeper significance of the Decree will become evident. The Decree on Ecumenism presupposes a concept of the Church which is different from the traditional Roman Catholic identification of the ecclesial reality solely and exclusively with the canonical limits of the Roman Catholic Church. In *Lumen gentium* the Church is presented as a *Mystery*. This implies that the Church in her essence is a divine reality implanted in history and therefore greater than its actual historical and institutional form. As Pope Paul VI put it in his opening address at the second session on September 29, 1963, "The Church is a mystery. It is a reality imbued with the hidden presence of God. It lies, therefore, within the very nature of the Church to be always open to new and greater exploration".

This opening up of the boundaries of the Church beyond her canonical limits was not a radical departure from the genuine Patristic tradition, indeed of the West itself, since it was in fact a return to St Augustine's ecclesiology which, contrary to that of St Cyprian, distinguished clearly between the canonical and the charismatic limits of the Church. The presence of the Holy Spirit is operative outside the canonical Church, and the Decree on Ecumenism did not hesitate to stress this:

> "For men who believe in Christ and have been properly baptized are brought into a certain, though imperfect, communion with the Catholic Church ... [A]ll those justified by faith through Baptism are incorporated into Christ. They therefore have a right to be honoured by the title of Christian, and are properly regarded as brothers in the Lord by the sons of the Catholic Church.
>
> Moreover some, even very many, of the most significant elements or endowments which together go to build up and give life to the Church herself *can exist outside the visible boundaries of the Catholic Church*: the written word of God; the life of grace; faith, hope and

charity, *along with other interior gifts of the Spirit and visible elements"* (UR, 3).

All this echoes *Lumen gentium* (15): the non-Catholic Christians "in some real way ... are joined with us in the Holy Spirit, *for to them also He gives gifts and graces, and is thereby operative among them with His sanctifying power"*.

This opening up of the boundaries of the Church was also due to the ecclesiology of the "People of God" promoted by *Lumen gentium*. This profoundly Biblical idea suggests that instead of emphasizing, as it was the case in the past, the hierarchical and institutional aspects of the Church, the stress is put on the *communal* aspect, which recognizes the importance of the lay members of the Church, as well as on the *pilgrimage* character of the Church which moves through history to the Kingdom. If my interpretation of this image is correct, the "pilgrim" character of the Church implies that on her way to the Kingdom she is loaded with faults and mistakes which call for admission of guilt. This is particularly applied in the Decree to the division of Christians which in a remarkable way the Council regards as the result of sin *on all sides* (UR, 3). It is noteworthy that concerning the blame for the division of Christians the Council makes a distinction between those who were involved in the appearance of the divisions, and who are guilty of that, and the Christians that were born in a state of division. This liberates history from its bondage to the past, which is what the spirit of Christian forgiveness demands from the Church. Ecumenism, therefore, must be built on charity if it is to bear fruit.

Now, this opening of the boundaries of the Church and the recognition of the presence of the Spirit outside its canonical borders, together with the admission of guilt for the division of Christianity by all sides, ground ecumenism on a solid ecclesiological basis. Ecumenism is not conceivable as an effort to unite Christians simply as believers in Christ but *as members of the Church*. Ecumenism is about the unity *of the Church*, not about Christian unity as such. This is something the Orthodox would not only subscribe to but strongly insist upon.

Having said this, one wonders what ecclesial unity the Council has in mind in speaking of *Unitatis redintegratio*. The following points may serve as illustrations of some difficulties that the non-Catholic reader of the Decree may have in understanding the Council's mind.

Both the Constitution of the Church and the Decree on Ecumenism refer to the non-Catholics as "separated" Christians. But what does "separated" mean? Reading the documents one gets the impression that this expression means separated *from the Catholic Church*. Does this means separation from the *institutional* Church or from the Church in the wider sense implied in the definition of the Church as "mystery" and as "the people of God" which we discussed earlier? This is crucial for the proper understanding of the nature of division in ecclesiology: is division something that affects only the realm outside the canonical or institutional borders of the Church, or is it something that jeopardizes the fullness and catholicity of the Church *from* which separation takes place? In other words, does division occur *inside* or *outside* the Church?

There is a paragraph in the Decree on Ecumenism that is somewhat ambiguous with respect to this question. It reads:

> "Nevertheless, the divisions among Christians prevent the Church from effecting the fullness of catholicity proper to her in those of her sons who, though joined to her by baptism, are yet separated from full communion with her. Furthermore, the Church

herself finds it more difficult to express in actual life her
full catholicity in all its aspects" (*UR*, 4).

From a careful reading of this paragraph one is led to the
idea that the Church [i.e. the Roman Catholic Church] is the
one and only fully "catholic" Church which, however, is
prevented from fully effecting her catholicity so long as there
is division. If this interpretation is correct, one may conclude
that the realisation of the full catholicity of the Church
presupposes unity, *Unitatis redingratio*. Such a conclusion
would be of immense significance both ecclesiologically and
ecumenically. It would make the restoration of unity an
ecclesiological necessity, not only for the fullness of catholicity, but also for the Church herself who, according to the
same source, does not lack such a fullness. In this case the
expression "separated from" may not be an ecclesiologically
accurate expression. Division affects the fullness of catholicity on *both sides,* albeit on the one side more than on the
other.

"For men who believe in Christ and have been properly
baptized are brought into a certain, though imperfect,
communion with the Catholic Church". A number of points
emerge from the interpretation of this quotation from *Unitatis
redintegratio* (3).

1.   Baptism in Christ is the *sine qua non conditio* for the
restoration of the unity of the Church and for the recognition of any degree of "communion" with the Catholic
Church. This implies the *recognition of the Baptism of all Christians* provided that it is "properly" done. ("Properly" must
mean its performance in the name of the Trinity; not by a
validly ordained minister or with any similar conditions,
since this would make the recognition of Baptism in this case
impossible). If that is the case, the Decree on Ecumenism has

made an extremely important ecumenical step which must be fully implemented and applied. Considering the fact that for Roman Catholic as well as Orthodox theology Baptism belongs to the sacramental order of the Church the recognition of non–Catholic baptism implies a recognition of sacramentality outside the Catholic Church.

2. Baptism outside the Catholic Church leads to "a certain though imperfect" communion with her. We have again the problem whether the "Catholic Church" in this context is the institutional canonical Roman Catholic Church, which I believe it is. Why then avoid saying that these baptized Christians are (imperfect) *members* of the Church? Is being in communion, albeit imperfect, a weaker state than membership? Why does the Council use communion, which is the ecclesiological concept *par excellence*, as such an ecclesiologically weak and secondary notion?

3. The employment of the adjective "imperfect" in connection with communion raises some questions of a theological nature to my mind. The intention of the Council is clear: it wants to indicate that division has not brought about a *complete* separation (although there is talk of "separated" brothers) but only a partial one, since many elements from the previous unity have survived. This is an extremely valuable idea for ecumenism. For it means that the ecumenical work must always begin from what unites us already and not from what divides us. This intention must be noted with appreciation. In this case the employment of an expression like "imperfect relationship" or something similar would save the term "communion" from its association with the adjective "imperfect".

4. In addition to grounding ecumenism on ecclesiology, which I regard as extremely important, the Council produced

justifications for ecumenical involvement on two other grounds which are worth our attention:

(a)   The idea of "hierarchy of truths". In § 11 the Decree on Ecumenism states: "when comparing doctrines, they (i.e. the Catholic theologians) should remember that in Catholic teaching there exists an order or 'hierarchy' of truths, since they vary in their relationship to the foundation of the Christian faith". This reflects the famous distinction between tradition with a big T and traditions in plural, which has been so widely discussed since Faith and Order at Montreal (1963). This liberates the ecumenical discussion from rigoristic and fundamentalistic approaches to the Truth. At the same time it reminds ecumenists of the importance that the question of Truth must enjoy in our search for unity. For there are many among those working for ecumenical progress who would regard doctrinal questions dividing the Christians as secondary and irrelevant for the unity of the Church, and discussions about such matters as undesirable obstacles for the restoration of unity. The criteria, however, for what is essential and fundamental and what is lower in the scale of "hierarchy of truths" are extremely difficult to establish in ecumenical dialogue. We need to develop a *hermeneutic* of tradition and doctrine in the ecumenical dialogue, and we have not done that.

(b)   The distinction between the deposit of faith and the formulation of doctrine (*Unitatis redintegratio,* 6). This idea was already presented by Pope John XXIII in his address at the beginning of the Council: "the deposit of faith is one thing; the way that it is presented is another. For the truths preserved in our sacred doctrine can retain the same substance and meaning under different forms of expression".

The ecumenical significance of this distinction hardly needs to be emphasized. On the one hand it makes it possible for a re-interpretation and re-reception of previous conciliar decisions in accordance with their *intention* rather than their formulation (e.g. Vatican I in relation to Vatican II). On the other hand it can go as far as to recognize the possible deficiency of doctrinal formulations of the past, as in fact it does in the Decree when it states: "therefore, if the influence of events or of the times has led to deficiencies in conduct ... or even in the formulation of doctrine ... these should be appropriately rectified at the proper moment" (*UR*, 6). Such a statement makes an Orthodox admire its boldness, for it would be difficult for the Orthodox to say such things in relation to the decisions of the Ecumenical Councils. Perhaps the distinction made by Pope Paul VI between an "Ecumenical Council" and a "General Council or Synod" would be necessary in order to apply this possibility of "deficiency" to the Roman Catholic-Orthodox dialogue. But the principle of re-interpretation and re-reception cannot be denied by the Orthodox, even with regard to the Ecumenical Councils.

5. In addition to ecclesiology and doctrine the Decree on Ecumenism is extremely significant for the *spirit* it brought into ecumenism. It gave a decisive blow to *polemics* in theological debate (*UR*, 10), so common in the past. It instructed Roman Catholics to learn as accurately as possible the traditions and theological teachings of other Christians (*UR*, 9), and even to be ready to learn from them (*UR*, 4). It called for a spiritual ecumenism, which involves humility, charity, holiness of life and above all *prayer* (*UR*, 8). The insistence of the Decree on the practice of prayer for unity is remarkable not only in terms of spirituality but even theologically

and ecclesiologically, since such prayers are regarded as "a genuine expression of the ties which even now bind Catholics to their separated brethren. 'For where two or three are gathered together in my name there am I in the midst of them' (*Mt* 18, 20)".

Finally, the exhortation to Roman Catholics to cooperate with the other Christians in the world on practical and social matters, particularly in order to protect the dignity of the human person, the promotion of peace, etc. (*UR*, 12) adds to ecumenism the dimension that would make unity visible to the world, which is so important for the mission of the Church.

II. The Importance of the Decree
for Roman Catholic–Orthodox Relations

The Decree on Ecumenism devotes a special chapter (Chapter 3) to "Churches and Ecclesial Communities separated from the Roman Apostolic See". Within this chapter a large section (*UR*, 14-18) bears the title "The Special Position of the Eastern Churches". The title is in itself significant.

The reservation of a "special position" to the Orthodox Church is not simply a matter of courtesy, and it is not due only to historical reasons. A careful reading of the text of the Decree suggests some extremely significant considerations which I shall try to sum up in the following observations.

There is no hesitation to call the Orthodox Churches by the name of *Church* in the full sense. There is full sacramental reality and life in these Churches so that nothing may be said to be lacking for the salvation of their members. The Eucharist receives special mention in the Decree, probably because of the eucharistic theology and ecclesiology which Orthodox theology promoted in the 20th century as a distinctive characteristic of Orthodoxy. In connection with the Eucharist the Council does not hesitate to declare the full validity and saving power of the celebration of this Sacrament by the Orthodox Churches: "In this celebration (of the Eucharist) the faithful, united with their bishop and endowed with an outpouring of the Holy Spirit, gain access to God the Father through the Son, the Word made flesh, who suffered and was glorified. And so made 'partakers of the divine nature' (2 *Pet* 1,4), they enter into communion with the most Holy Trinity. Hence, *through the celebration of the Eucharist of the Lord in each of these Churches, the Church of God is building and grows in stature,* while through the rite of concelebration their bond with one another is made manifest" (*UR*, 15, my emphasis). As a result, the Council declares that the Orthodox Churches "possess true sacraments, above all — by apostolic succession — the priesthood and the Eucharist" (*ibid.*). This is interpreted as implying "a very close relationship" with the Roman Catholic Church, and makes the participation of Roman Catholics in the Eucharist of the Orthodox "not merely possible but ... recommended", "given suitable circumstances and the approval of Church authority".

The existing "separation" between the two Churches is attributed to "external causes, and to mutual failures in understanding and charity" (*UR*, 14). For this reason the Synod urges the Roman Catholics involved in relations with the Orthodox to give due consideration to the character of the relations which obtained between the Orthodox and the Roman Catholics *before the separation.* This in a sense sets the agenda for the theological dialogue between Roman Catholics and Orthodox: a return to the first millennium of the undivided Church should be the basis of ecumenical *rapprochement* in this particular case.

With regard to differences that arose after the separation, the Council proposes to approach them with the view that there is always a difference between the faith itself and its theological expression and that for this reason many of the differences that appeared after the separation between East and West may be regarded as *complementary* rather than contradictory. This is a very helpful proposition to the extent that it can apply to all cases of difference between the two traditions. For there have been, alas, several conflicts during the second millennium between the two Churches (e.g. conciliar decisions in the East in connection with the Palamite controversy, promulgation of new dogmas unilaterally in the West, etc.) that make "complementarity" difficult to work as a means of convergence. A profound discussion and above all hermeneutic would be required before these differences can be overcome. A re-interpretaion of these unilateral decisions is necessary in order to show that they do not constitute obstacles to unity. In addition to that, a more *positive* approach should be applied whereby these differences may be shown to contain important elements that one tradition may contribute to the other. This would lead to a *synthesis* between the two traditions and re-affirm the view expressed already by the late Father Georges Florovsky that true catholicity of the Church requires the coming together and interpenetration of both the West and the East.

A crucial question is what the Council expects from the Orthodox Churches in order to remove entirely the separation that exists between them. It is noteworthy that the Decree says nothing explicit about that. There are, however, some very important hints that we must bring up in order to capture the mind of the Council on this matter.

In *UR* 16 the Council "solemnly declares that the Churches of the East, while keeping in mind the necessary unity of the whole Church, have the power (*facultatem*) to govern themselves according to their own disciplines, since they are better suited to the temperament of their faithful and better adapted to foster the good of souls. Although it has not always been honoured, the strict observance of this traditional principle is among the prerequisites for any restoration of unity".

This quotation is significant because it seems to suggest that the canonical structure of the Orthodox Churches does not have to change in order to arrive at full unity with the Church of Rome. How far can this freedom of canonical independence go? The answer lies in this sentence: *"while keeping in mind the necessary unity of the whole Church"*. Given that the unity of the whole Church is from the Roman Catholic point of view safeguarded and maintained through the Petrine office, the implication is that this office must be recognised by the Orthodox Churches in order to have unity restored. But it is noteworthy that this is not explicitly said by the Council. This is done for the first time in many many centuries. And this in itself is significant.

The significance of this silence of the Council on an issue that divided the East and the West for so long lies in the fact that *the way* of fulfilling the condition of "the necesary unity of the whole Church" is left open to dialogue and not pre-defined by the Council. The Orthodox are called to state in what way they think universal unity can be maintained and what in their view the role of the Petrine ministry is for this unity. This is the most critical question that the Roman Catholic and Orthodox dialogue must face. After the present Pope's encyclical *Ut unum sint* we are embarking on the discussion of this problem as the most important one in the relations between Roman Catholics and Orthodox.

We cannot and should not prejudge the way this discussion will go. The Decree on Ecumenism gives us freedom of movement. The fact, however, that the Council, as we have seen, strongly speaks of the right and "power" of the Orthodox Churches to maintain their present canonical structure clearly implies that the intention to *subject* the Orthodox to the rule of Rome — an intention which the Orthodox always suspected behind the Pope's claims to universal jurisdiction — does not seem to emerge from the Decree we are honouring these days. This is most encouraging for the progress of Roman Catholic-Orthodox relations.

Related to this is the description of the Orthodox Churches as "sister Churches". There is more in this expression than has been understood, appreciated and made use of in the relations between Roman Catholics and Orthodox so far. The deeper implication of this description is that of an *essential equality* between the Roman Catholic and the Orthodox Church. This equality, which is of an ecclesiological nature, precludes any domination and superiority of power and authority of one Church over the other. The implications of this idea have not yet been worked out ecumenically. There may be potential for solving the problem of primacy in this idea. Certainly it would be worth pursuing further this idea in the theological dialogue between Roman Catholics and Orthodox.

Finally, a word must be said about the Eastern Churches united with Rome, since this subject has always been crucial for Roman Catholic-Orthodox relations. The Decree on Ecumenism says very little, practically nothing, on this matter. In *UR* 17 we read: "While thanking God that many Eastern sons of the Catholic Church, who are preserving this heritage and wish to express it more faithfully and completely in their lives, are already living in full communion with their brethren who follow the tradition of the West, this sacred Synod declares that this entire heritage of spirituality and liturgy, of discipline and theology, in their various traditions, belongs to the full catholic and apostolic character of the Church". The intention behind these words seems to be an emphasis on the idea that the variety of forms of spirituality, liturgy, discipline, and even theology is not only legitimate but an aspect of the catholicity and apostolicity of the Church. It is because of this that the existence of the Eastern Churches united with Rome is justified in the eyes of the Council. The Orthodox have always looked at these Churches as means of proselytising them to Roman Catholicism, or as models of the future unity of the Orthodox Church with the Roman see. Nothing of this, however, is implied in the decision of the Council on ecumenism.

In order to get a fuller appreciation of the Council's understanding of the nature and role of these Churches, which cause so much uneasiness to the Orthodox, one should go to the Decree on Eastern [Catholic] Churches, which was promulgated on November 21, 1964. This Decree falls outside the scope of the present meeting and will not be considered directly in this paper. Its aim is mainly to re-establish and secure the privileges and customs of these

Churches, but in addition to that, it manifests the hope of the Council for a corporate reunion of the Eastern Churches currently not in union with Rome. It is this last point that brings to the Orthodox "suspicions" of proselytistic intentions. Particularly the encouragement of *communicatio in sacris,* which is a painful and complex problem in the Orthodox presence and involvement in ecumenism as a whole, bilateral decision and action is preferable to any unilateral action.

Recent experience in Roman Catholic-Orthodox relations has shown how sensitive the Orthodox remain to this problem. Common statements at Freising and Balamand on Uniatism in the context of the official theological dialogue between the two Churches have aimed at dispelling the fears of the Orthodox that these Churches exist in order to proselytise them and to be used as a model for union with Rome. The past is still throwing its shadow on the present and the future. We must try more to free ourselves from it.

More than the fear of proselytism this issue belongs to the realm of ecclesiology. It must be placed and discussed in this context and not as an isolated subject. It is to be hoped that the official theological dialogue between the Roman Catholic and the Orthodox Church will proceed with ecclesiological subjects and place all such differences in this context.

Conclusion

It has been said that the Decree on Ecumenism is not an end but a new beginning. Its significance, therefore, must be judged from what it *can still* contribute to the unity of the Church.

Speaking as an Orthodox, I cannot but rejoice in the fact that the kind of ecumenism that *Unitatis redintegratio* proposes takes seriously two concerns which have marked Orthodox participation in the ecumenical movement since the beginning. The one is that unity should not bypass the question of *truth*. The other is that unity must be *visible* and be based on a common understanding *of the Church*. Ambiguities about the essential content of the faith, and the question what it means to be a Church cannot constitute a firm basis for any attempt to restore Christian unity. It is important, therefore, that ecclesiology in its relation to the basic doctrines of our faith, such as the Holy Trinity, Christology, pneumatology, etc., has been the main subject in the official theological dialogues between the Roman Catholics and the Orthodox, and that the same agenda has been also adopted by the dialogues between the Anglicans and the Orthodox. Ecumenism must aim at *Church* unity, not simply at a unity of Christians.

Viewed in this perspective the Decree on Ecumenism has placed the ecumenical problematic on the right basis. But it has made only a beginning. Thus, two fundamental problems still remain open. One is the recognition of Baptism, and the other is the relation between the local and the universal Church. The problem of unity, in the sense of *Church* unity, hangs on these two questions which Vatican II stated but left open. The question of the recognition of

Christian baptism by all Christians is a *sine qua non conditio* for an ecumenism of *Church* unity. And the question of the relation between the local and the universal Church will decide *what kind* of Church unity we are seeking. This last question inevitably involves the problem of universal primacy, which will mark the ecumenical debate in the future. The question to which the Orthodox would eagerly await an answer is this: how far can the Roman Catholic Church go with a reformation of the way in which papal primacy is exercised? How far can eucharistic ecclesiology be accepted by the Roman Catholics and applied to ecumenism? And how far can the idea of *communion* affect the concept and practice of primacy?

This ecclesiocentric ecumenism should be placed in the context of issues preoccupying humanity in our time. The Church does not live in isolation from the world, and its unity must have an existential significance for humanity, indeed for creation as a whole, especially in our time. This is something that has emerged as a necessity in the 40 years that have elapsed since the promulgation of *Unitatis redintegratio*. An enrichment of the ecumenical agenda in this direction may be now necessary.

The Decree of which we celebrate the 40th anniversary is a gift to all Christians who seek fervently the restoration of the Church's unity. It is with deep appreciation that we offer our modest comments on its ecumenical significance.

Unitatis redintegratio in a Protestant Perspective[1]

Geoffrey Wainwright

Introduction

I am honored by the invitation to speak on behalf of the churches and ecclesial communities stemming from the Reformation, although as a historically late-coming Methodist I accept the honor with some trepidation. That Metropolitan John Zizioulas has agreed to address the topic of *Unitatis redintegratio (UR)* from the Orthodox perspective inevitably brings to my mind the occasion when he and I, together with Fr. Jean Tillard (of blessed memory), were seated on the platform at Lima, Peru, in January 1982, and had to deliver our judgment on whether or not to accept last-minute proposals for amendments to the text of *Baptism, Eucharist and Ministry* ("BEM"). Such proposed changes were to pass into the document if, and only if, all three of us, after a fifteen-seconds consultation among ourselves, approved them. Happily, the document was then voted upon and unanimously adopted by the Faith and Order Commission as ready for transmission to the churches for their evaluation. Cardinal Kasper also participated in that meeting as Professor Walter Kasper of Tübingen, occupying one of the places allotted to Catholics on the Commission from 1968 onwards. My personal interest in *Unitatis redintegratio* reaches further back still. In 1966-67

---

1. Original English text.

I spent a year in Rome during my doctoral studies at a time when foreign Protestants were still something of a rarity in the city, and I profited in many ways from the generous hospitality which the recent promulgation of the ecumenical decree by the Second Vatican Council seemed to unleash. Such memories help to constitute the human history of the movement in favor of Christian unity, and so they are not alien to our theme; but I will now pass, in the capacity of a professional theologian, to a more systematic consideration of the conciliar decree and its effects.

I. To Identify and Locate the Church

A fundamental assumption of ecumenism is that Christianity in some form exists beyond the boundaries of the institution to which oneself belongs in the divided state of Christendom. Under the guidance and empowerment of the Holy Spirit, the aim of the Ecumenical Movement is then the "reintegration of unity" among Christians and their communities — out of obedience to Christ, for the sake of witness before the world to Christ and his divine mission, and all to the glory of God. Consequently, the major ecclesiological question of the twentieth century was to identify and locate "the one Church"— holy, catholic, and apostolic — to which all Christians really or ideally belong. The ecclesial claims typically made on their own behalf by what — for simplicity's sake — may be called the Protestant churches will gradually emerge in my address. I shall hint at some critical and constructive interactions between them and the positions expressed in Vatican II's ecumenical decree, with a view to noting any convergences that may have occurred as well as proposing possible future developments.

The basic ecclesiological claim of the Roman Catholic Church was stated in the Dogmatic Constitution on the Church: "The sole Church of Christ" — professed in the Creed to be one, holy, catholic and apostolic — "subsists in the Catholic Church, which is governed by the successor of Peter and by the bishops in communion with him" (*Lumen gentium [LG]*, 8). The Decree on Ecumenism explicated that "it is only through Christ's Catholic Church ... that the fullness of the means of salvation can be attained," and the belief is expressed that "it was to the one apostolic college of which Peter is the head that our Lord entrusted all the blessings of the new covenant, in order to establish the one Body of Christ on earth into which all should be fully incorporated who belong in any way to the people of God" (*UR*, 3). Ecclesial unity "subsists in the Catholic Church as something she can never lose" (*UR*, 4). Nevertheless, *Lumen gentium* recognized, "many elements of sanctification and of truth" are to be found outside the visible structure (*compages visibilis*) of the Catholic Church, and since these are "gifts properly belonging to the Church of Christ," they "impel towards Catholic unity" (*LG*, 8). It fell to the Decree on Ecumenism to specify the ecclesial "elements and endowments" that "can exist outside the visible boundaries (*visibilia saepta*) of the Catholic Church," and to discern the dynamism by which those features make for unity — which it did thus: "All of these, coming from Christ and leading back to him, properly belong to the one Church of Christ" (*UR*, 3).

II. Baptism and the
Ecclesial Communities

Regarding the precise formulations of *Unitatis redintegratio,* let us look especially at two short, and related, passages. First, there is the case of individuals "who believe in Christ and have been rightly baptized" and thus put "in a certain communion, albeit imperfect, with the Catholic Church (*in quadam cum ecclesia catholica communione, etsi non perfecta*)" (*UR*, 3). Next, given that such individuals are for the moment found in their respective "churches and communities," it will follow that "the sacred Christian rites" performed in these latter "can truly engender a life of grace" and "give access to the communion of salvation." Thus "the separated Churches and communities as such ... have by no means been deprived of meaning and importance (*significatio et pondus*) in the mystery of salvation," for "the Spirit of Christ has not refrained from using them as means of salvation which derive their efficacy from the very fullness of grace and truth entrusted to the Catholic Church" (*UR*, 3).

First, then, the ecclesial scope of baptism and of the faith that it signifies. According to the Lima text of Faith and Order in 1982, "Our common baptism, which unites us to Christ in faith, is thus a basic bond of unity" ("Baptism," 6).[2]

Undoubtedly, many churches have regarded a "common baptism" as the foundation of ecumenism, and the Ecumenical Movement has fostered a mutual recognition of baptism among them. *BEM* itself recorded convergences on "the meaning of baptism." The World Conference on Faith and Order at Santiago de Compostela in 1993 encouraged the spread of a common baptismal certificate such as had al-

---

2. *Baptism, Eucharist and Ministry*, Faith and Order Paper No. 111 (Geneva: World Council of Churches, 1982) abbreviated as *BEM*.

ready come into use in some places. But mutual recognition of baptism is by no means completely achieved, since Churches in the Baptist line continue to question the propriety of infants as baptismal subjects, and various Orthodox Churches still raise the matter of which bodies have authority to administer baptism. Moreover, the Lima text spoke of "the actual dividedness" of churches continuing even "in spite of mutual baptismal recognition" and thus giving "dramatic visibility to the broken witness of the Church" ("Baptism," 6, commentary). Thus, despite the welcome mutual baptismal recognition that now exists between the Roman Catholic Church and the Churches of Methodism, the fact that I was "baptized Methodist" and remain in a Methodist Church means that I cannot partake of communion in the Catholic Church, while (in the other direction) a "baptized Catholic" cannot receive communion in the Methodist Church without infringing the discipline of his or her own Church. The individual cases instantiate the "imperfection" of the communion existing at the level of ecclesial community to ecclesial community. That is why the goal of the bilateral dialogue between, say, Catholics and Methodists cannot and dare not stop short of "full communion in faith, mission, and sacramental life."[3]

---

3. For the Joint Commission for Dialogue between the Roman Catholic Church and the World Methodist Council, see *Towards a Statement on the Church* (Nairobi Report, 1986), paragraphs 20 and 28, and *The Word of Life: A Statement on Revelation and Faith* (Rio de Janeiro Report, 1996), sections 2-5, as well as the Prefaces to the Singapore Report of 1991 (*The Apostolic Tradition*) and the Brighton Report of 2001 (*Speaking the Truth in Love: Teaching Authority among Catholics and Methodists*). Texts of the first three of these reports in *Growth in Agreement II: Reports and Agreed Statements of Ecumenical Conversations on a World Level 1982-1998*, J. Gros, H. Meyer and W. G. Rusch (eds.), (Geneva: WCC; Grand Rapids: Eerdmans, 2000); of the fourth, in *Information Service* of the

What, then, about the "meaning and importance" of churches and ecclesial communities "in the mystery of salvation"? Confident in its own ecclesiality, the Roman Catholic Church is here speaking about *other* — "separated" — bodies. While the positive intention and specific address of the phraseology of the Vatican II decree are clear and much appreciated, the question is not a new one; and it can, *mutatis mutandis*, be put by others from their own standpoints. In reflecting on the significance of their membership in the World Council of Churches that had been established in 1948, the member churches stated — in the Toronto Declaration of 1950 — that such membership "does not imply that a church treats its own conception of the Church as merely relative"; nor does it imply "the acceptance of a specific doctrine concerning the nature of Church unity," nor "that each church must regard the other member churches as churches in the true and full sense of the word." Rather, the member churches "recognize in other churches elements of the true Church," which "obliges them to enter into a serious conversation with each other in the hope that these elements of truth will lead to the recognition of the full truth and to unity based on the full truth"; these "traces" are "to be followed" as each church performs its "simple Christian duty" to "do its utmost for the manifestation of the Church in its oneness, and to work and pray that Christ's purpose for his Church should be fulfilled."[4]

Pontifical Council for Promoting Christian Unity, N. 107, 2001/II–III, pp.94-117.

4. Text cited from *The Ecumenical Movement: An Anthology of Key Texts and Voices*, Michael Kinnamon and Brian E. Cope (eds.), (Geneva: WCC; Grand Rapids: Eerdmans, 1997), pp.463-68.

III. "Faith and Order" Efforts
toward a Definition of Unity

In the course of the 1950s, the Faith and Order Commission of the WCC worked towards a provisional definition of what the report of the section on unity at the New Delhi Assembly of 1961 described as the unity for which "we believe we must pray and work."[5] It ran thus:

> We believe that the unity which is both God's will and his gift to his Church is being made visible as all in each place who are baptized into Jesus Christ and confess him as Lord and Saviour are brought by the Holy Spirit into one fully committed fellowship, holding the one apostolic faith, preaching the one Gospel, breaking the one bread, joining in common prayer, and having a corporate life reaching out in witness and service to all and who at the same time are united with the whole Christian fellowship in all places and all ages in such wise that ministry and members are accepted by all, and that all can act and speak together as occasion requires for the tasks to which God calls his people.

The Orthodox representatives welcomed the statement but considered it to belong in a "Protestant world" characterized by "denominationalism": "The Orthodox cannot accept the idea of a 'parity of denomination' and cannot visualize Christian reunion just as an interdenominational adjustment. The unity has been broken and must be recovered. The Orthodox Church is not a confession, one of many, one among many. For the Orthodox, the Orthodox Church is just the Church." From the Catholic side, Avery Dulles wondered whether the New Delhi description did not depend on a dichotomy whereby a "spiritual" unity already

---

5. *Ibid.*, pp.88-93.

existed that then "merely" needed to be "made visible."[6]
More positively, it should be noted that the chief drafter of
the key New Delhi paragraph was Lesslie Newbigin, a bishop
in the Church of South India. That Church had in 1947
brought together in an "organic union" the fruit of Anglican,
Methodist, Presbyterian, and Congregationalist missionary
labors and, by its adoption of an episcopate in the Anglican
line, had signaled its intention in favor of that "ecumenism
in time" for which the Orthodox called and which was at
least touched on in the New Delhi references to "the one
apostolic faith" and "the whole Christian fellowship" in "all
ages."

True, for the two decades after New Delhi the attention
of Faith and Order in the matter of unity was fixed on "all in
each place," expanded by the Uppsala and Nairobi Assemblies in 1968 and 1975 to a complementary stress on "the
unity of all Christians in all places."[7] The Uppsala Assembly
called on the member churches of the WCC to "work for the
time when a genuinely universal council may once more
speak for all Christians, and lead the way into the future."
The Nairobi Assembly adopted from Faith and Order meetings at Louvain and Salamanca the terminology of "conciliar
fellowship":

> The one Church is to be envisioned as a conciliar
> fellowship of local churches which are themselves truly
> united. In this conciliar fellowship, each local church
> possesses, in communion with the others, the fullness
> of catholicity, witnesses to the same apostolic faith,
> and therefore recognizes the others as belonging to the
> same Church of Christ and guided by the same Spirit.

---

6. Avery Dulles, "The Church, the Churches, and the Catholic
   Church" in *Theological Studies* 33 (1972), pp.199-234.
7. See Kinnamon and Cope (eds.), op.cit., pp.93-97 and 110-13
   respectively.

It was emphasized that this description was not meant as an alternative to New Delhi's organic unity of all in each place, but rather as "a further elaboration of it." Nevertheless, the phrase "conciliar fellowship" became used by proponents of a vision of unity as a "reconciled diversity" among continuing "confessional families" whose global assemblies were already at least (in Nairobi's terms) "a true foretaste" of "full conciliar fellowship." "Unity in reconciled diversity" was the language favored by Lutherans; Anglicans characteristically envisaged the goal as a "communion of communions." The Canberra Assembly of the WCC in 1991 enlarged the horizons of unity to the cosmic:

> The purpose of God according to holy scripture is to gather the whole of creation under the Lordship of Christ in whom, by the power of the Holy Spirit, all are brought into communion with God (Ephesians 1). The church is the foretaste of this communion with God and with one another.

The elements from New Delhi and Nairobi were reworked into a statement on "The Unity of the Church as Koinonia: Gift and Calling":

> The goal of the search for full communion is realized when all the churches are able to recognize in one another the one, holy, catholic and apostolic church in its fullness. This full communion will be expressed on the local and the universal levels through conciliar forms of life and action. In such communion churches are bound in all aspects of their life together at all levels in confessing the one faith and in engaging in worship and witness, deliberation and action.

The current challenge in the Ecumenical Movement was for "the churches" (not further defined or identified) to act upon the measures of convergence already registered and for "parishes and communities [to] express in appropriate ways locally the degree of communion that already exists."[8] I shall return to what may be called the "topogaphy" of unity, in which indeed the synchronic relation between the local and the universal is a crucial matter, rendered more complex by the historical inheritance of confessionally and institutionally divided claimants to ecclesial status.

IV. Ecumenism in Time

Meanwhile, then, we need to return to the question of diachronic unity, of "ecumenism in time." In responding to the Lima text on *Baptism, Eucharist and Ministry,* the churches were asked "the extent to which your church can recognize in this text the faith of the Church through the ages." The Roman Catholic response, while pointing to some inadequacies in the document, offered a predominantly positive evaluation and applauded the authors' use of both Scripture and early Tradition. In the 1980s, Faith and Order expanded its attention to a project entitled "Towards the Common Expression of the Apostolic Faith Today." The structure was provided by the Nicene-Constantino-politan Creed of 381, whose historical formulations were expounded in relation, on the one hand, to the biblical witness and, on the other hand, to contemporary questions both between the churches and in face of the world. The resultant document, *Confessing the One Faith* (1991),

---

8. For Canberra 1991, see *ibid.*, p.124 ff. Here, and at the World Conference on Faith and Order at Santiago de Compostela in 1993, the category of "koinonia/communion," flexibly understood, became totally dominant; see Thomas F. Best and Günther Gassmann, *On the Way to Fuller Koinonia: Official Report of the Fifth World Conference on Faith and Order,* Faith and Order Paper No. 166 (Geneva: WCC, 1994).

somehow stalled in the machinery of the WCC and failed to get brought before the churches in the manner of *BEM.*

An important thread in the matter of "ecumenism in time" was highlighted in the work of a small group at the Bangalore meeting of the Faith and Order Commission in 1978, although it took a while before being picked up. A single sentence in *Unitatis redintegratio* had declared it "right and salutary (*aequum et salutare*) to recognize the riches of Christ and the virtuous deeds in the lives of others who bear witness to Christ, sometimes even to the shedding of their blood" (4). The short text from Faith and Order at Bangalore on "Witness unto Death" pointed to the ecumenical significance of martyrdom, where the ultimate testimony to Christ in the power of grace is widely recognized to transcend divisions among Christians and — precisely on that account — may (one would think) reflect positively on the community in which the martyr has learned and lived the faith.[9] Pope John Paul II extends the thought in paragraph 84 of his 1995 encyclical *Ut unum sint:*

> Albeit in an invisible way, the communion between our Communities, even if still incomplete, is truly and solidly grounded in the full communion of the Saints – those who, at the end of a life faithful to grace, are in communion with Christ in glory. These Saints come from all the Churches and Ecclesial Communities which gave them entrance into the communion of salvation.

As a Methodist, I suggest that a great step would be taken towards the manifestation and completion of communion between our communities if the Roman Church

---

9. See "Witness unto Death" in *Bangalore 1978: Sharing in One Hope* (Geneva: WCC, 1978), pp.195-202.

could officially and liturgically recognize the place which
we know John and Charles Wesley to enjoy in the Communion of the Saints. In the process of liturgical revision in the
latter half of the twentieth century, several Protestant
churches introduced a type of *sanctorale* which included
figures from the "other side" in cases of schism.[10] If our
saints in heaven, in whose united worship we join, are
praying for our unity on earth, then perhaps we are not so
far from attaining the goal as may immediately appear.

V. Ut unum sint

With the mention of *Ut unum sint* and its vigorous reaf-
firmation of the Catholic Church's commitment to the
ecumenical cause we come to the third of the three or four
most important ecumenical documents of the second half
of the twentieth century, together with *Unitatis redintegratio*
itself, *BEM*, and the *Joint Declaration on the Doctrine of Justification* between Lutherans and Catholics. How does Pope
John Paul there deal with our questions of the identification
and location of "the Church," and what does he see as the
"dynamism" for the attainment of full communion between the separated brothers and sisters and their communities, on the one side, and "the Catholic Church," on the
other? Naturally, the Pope maintains the claim of Vatican
II that the one Church of Christ "subsists in" the Catholic
Church that is "governed by the successor of Peter and by
the bishops in communion with him." But he introduces
what is, to my eyes, a fresh nuance when he takes up an idea
that had in fact occurred in a *relatio* prior to the adoption of

---

10. See Geoffrey Wainwright, "The Saints and the Departed: Confessional
    Controversy and Ecumenical Convergence" in *Studia Liturgica* 34
    (2004), pp.65-91.

the Decree on Ecumenism; it was there suggested that the one Church of Christ was "in a certain manner active (*aliquo modo actuosa*)" in the separated communities by means of the ecclesiastical elements in them.[11] The pope writes: "To the extent that these elements [of sanctification and truth] are found in other Christian Communities, the one Church of Christ is effectively present in them" (*UUS, 11*). To these living in such Communities, the notion of a "*praesentia efficiens*" of the Church in them sounds more acceptable than the image of a magnetic "return" of iron filings to the original block which is conjured up by the Decree's language of gifts and endowments that "belong by right" to "the one Church of Christ" and "lead back" to him. Members of other churches and ecclesial communities find it difficult to envisage that the "mediation" of the Roman Catholic Church is somehow needed in order to secure their own ecclesiality — even if they are nowadays probably more willing than perhaps they once were to consider the Roman Catholic Church as such, and not just good individual Catholics, to be at least "part of" the universal Church within which communion is to be restored.[12]

---

11. *Acta Synodalia Sacrosancti Concilii Oecumenici Vaticani II*, vol III/2 (Vatican City, 1974), p.335. The importance of this text from the then Secretariat for Promoting Christian Unity has been recovered by Jared Wicks, S.J., in his article "The Significance of the 'Ecclesial Communities' of the Reformation" in *Ecumenical Trends* (December 2001), pp.10-13.

12. In recurrent controversy with the Catholic bishop Richard Challoner on the "marks" and identification of the Church, John Wesley charged "the Romanists" with mistaking "a part" for "the whole." Positively put, Wesley at that point recognized to the Roman Catholic Church what, applying in a reverse direction the language of Cardinal Franz König at Vatican II, we might even dare to call an "*indolem*" or "*characterem vere ecclesialem*" (see again the texts cited in the preceding note) – and this despite some

As was the case already with *Unitatis redintegratio*, Pope John Paul in his encyclical letter insists on the fundamental importance of doctrine, for unity must occur "in the truth" (*UUS,* 18-19; 36-37). The Pope pays warm tribute to the progress so far made in ecumenical dialogues, both in Faith and Order and in the various bilateral conversations in which the Roman Catholic Church is engaged (*UUS,* 59-61, 64-70, 78, 89). In paragraph 79 he lists five "areas in need of fuller study before a true consensus of faith can be achieved." The primary place is occupied by "the relationship between Sacred Scripture, as the highest authority in matters of faith, and Sacred Tradition, as indispensable to the interpretation of the Word of God." That strikes me as the best formulation of the question since the sixteenth century. And that is the question which underlies the Pope's four other topics: the eucharistic presence and sacrifice; sacramental ordination to the threefold ministry; the magisterium of the Church; and the Virgin Mary as Mother of God and Icon of the Church. Doctrinal agreement rightly governs the extent to which practical cooperation can occur in humanitarian service (*UR,* 12 and 23), let alone participation together in liturgical action (*UR,* 4 and 8) and engagement in the common task of evangelization (*UR,* 1, 10, and 20). In the first of those three spheres, controversial questions of fundamental anthropology may be encountered (*UUS,*75). In the second, one may certainly rejoice in

---

erroneous doctrines and superstitious practices. At other points, however, Wesley confined his recognition to "the case of some particular souls" among Roman Catholics as belonging to "the people of God." The question is discussed in some detail, with citation of Wesley's writings, in Geoffrey Wainwright, *The Ecumenical Moment: Crisis and Opportunity for the Church* (Grand Rapids: Eerdmans, 1983), in particular pp.192 and 206-9.

the increased *communicatio in sacris* that has developed since my own undergraduate days in the late 1950s, when the joint recitation of the Lord's Prayer was still a recent concession for Catholics, and even then we never knew whether to continue with "For thine is the kingdom, the power and the glory ..."; John Paul strongly emphasizes the value of common prayer, but the possibility of a shared eucharist still tarries (*UUS*, 21-27). In the matter of common witness, it is regrettable that the degree of shared faith and ecclesiality was apparently insufficient to allow for other Christian communities to be seen by the document *Dominus Iesus* of 2000 as partners with the Catholic Church in the urgent task of witness to the sole Savior of the world.

VI. The Topography of Unity

Neither *Unitatis redintegratio* nor *Ut unum sint* offers a detailed pattern for the institutional structures that might hold together a reunited Christendom. What, in particular, would be the "units" that were joined in full communion? It is, I think, fortunate that one hint in the afore-mentioned *relatio* of early 1964 was not followed. One may read there that in the separated ecclesial communities "the one sole Church of Christ is present, albeit imperfectly, in a way *quasi tamquam in Ecclesiis particularibus.*" A better account is needed of the relation between local and universal which, while in some way recognizing the traditions that have developed in the times of separation, does not allow them such structural gravity in a reunited Christendom as the present "confessional families" or "Christian world communions" bear. A mere "parallelism of communions" would be an inadequate model for the future.[13] The danger in modern Protestantism, even when somewhat ecumenically inclined, is that it would remain content with "interdenominational readjustment," with what the EKD in 2001 called "ein geordnetes Miteinander bekenntnisverschiedener Kirchen" – which might be translated as "unreconciled denominationalism" or, even more rudely, "peaceful co-existence in conditions of Cold War."[14]

The "topographical" question is well sketched in the 1986 Nairobi Report of the Methodist-Roman Catholic dialogue, *Towards a Statement on the Church*.[15] Recognizing that the word "Church" is used in the New Testament with a "spatial" scope ranging from the domestic through a city or region to the universal, the text also notes the rise of other uses, some of them benignly due to diversities of language or rite (such as Syrian Church, Coptic Church, or Latin Church), but others to "fundamental differences in doctrine, faith or ecclesial polity, such as Lutheran Church, Methodist Church, or Roman Catholic Church"; and "as Methodists and Roman Catholics we recognize that the divisions underlying this last usage are contrary to the unity Christ wills for his Church" (18-20). Acknowledging, nevertheless, that "many different gifts have been developed, even in separation," the Commission wondered whether, in the situation of reunion, the needs of the various developed traditions could be provided for "within the framework of the local congregation" or might require "special provisions (parishes,

---

13. On this point, see Geofrey Wainwright, "La confession et les confessions: vers l'unité confessionnelle et confessante des chrètiens" in *Irènikon* 57 (1984), pp. 5-26, in particular pp. 15-17.
14. Evangelische Kirche in Deutschland, "Kirchengemeinschaft nach evangelischem Verständnis" in EKD-*Texte* 69 (2001).
15. See *Growth in Agreement II*, op.cit., pp.583-96.

ministries, other organizations)": "How far would the pastoral care of such groups require separate, possibly overlapping jurisdictions, or could it be provided by one, single, local form of *episkope* (supervision or oversight)?" (23, 26-27). Off my own bat, I have made the suggestion of a "perichoretic episcopate" in the shape of a local college of bishops, perhaps with a rotating presidency, and allowing ample opportunity for spiritual fellowship, sacramental communion, and joint action among the mutually open, confessionally reconciled, and culturally diverse communities represented in the council of bishops "in each place."[16]

The appropriate weight of translocal arrangements for the preservation of features inherited from the confessionally and institutionally separated past would need careful estimation. The Catholic-Methodist Report already cited was ready to entertain, among the possible "ways of being one Church," the notion of "typoi" advanced by Cardinal Johannes Willebrands at the prompting of Dom Emmanuel Lanne: within the one Church marked by basic agreement in faith, doctrine, and government, there would be room for various "ecclesial traditions," each characterized by a particular style of theology, worship, spirituality, and discipline. Another possibility derived from an analogy between John Wesley's Methodist movement and the "religious orders" in the Roman Catholic Church, each charcterized by special forms of life and prayer, work, evangelization, and internal organization, while being related in different ways to the authority of Pope and bishops. The Methodist historian Albert Outler, a promi-

---

16. Geoffrey Wainwright, "In favour of a perichoretic and peripatetic episcopate – perhaps ..." in *Gemeinsamer Glaube und Strukturen der Gemeinschaft*, Harding Meyer (ed.), (Frankfurt am Main: Otto Lembeck, 1991), pp.198-207.

nent observer at the Second Vatican Council, had envisaged Methodism as "*une église manquée*, theoretically and actually," needing "a catholic church within which to function as a proper evangelical order of witness and worship, discipline and nurture."[17]

Other Protestant bodies (and probably some other Methodists) would doubtless make stronger claims for an autonomous ecclesial status, but all should be ready to acknowledge, with Lesslie Newbigin, that there can be no "reunion without repentance," given the baneful character of schism — which the Roman Catholic Church also confesses, together with a share of responsibility on its side (*UR*, 3; *UUS*, 11; cf. 15, 34).[18] In the words of the New Delhi statement, in which Outler also had a hand, "the achievement of unity will involve nothing less than a death and rebirth of many forms of church life as we have known them." There may also be features in the Roman Catholic Church, developed and shaped in the times of separation, that must be surrendered — or at least configured according to new circumstances. With that, we come to the final, and most astonishing proposal made by Pope John Paul in *Ut unum sint*.

---

17. A. C. Outler, "Do Methodists have a doctrine of the Church?" in *The Doctrine of the Church*, D. Kirkpatrick (ed.), (Nashville: Abingdon, 1964), pp.11-28.

18. J. E. L. Newbigin, *The Household of God* (London: SCM Press, 1953) p.22; (US edition, New York: Friendship Press, 1954) p.14.

VII. A Universal Ministry of Unity?

I refer, of course, to the particular responsibility that John Paul acknowledges — in light of "the ecumenical aspirations of the majority of the Christian Communities" for a "universal ministry of Christian unity" — to "find a way of exercising the primacy which, while in no way renouncing what is essential to its mission, is nonetheless open to a new situation" (*UUS*, 89 and 95): "Could not the real but imperfect communion existing between us persuade Church leaders and their theologians to engage with me in a patient and fraternal dialogue on this subject?" (96). I will repeat here the personal suggestion which I first made in 1997 that, as a first step, the Bishop of Rome

> should invite those Christian communities which he regards as being in real, if imperfect, communion with the Roman Catholic Church to appoint representatives to cooperate with him and his appointees in formulating a statement expressive of the Gospel to be preached to the world today. Thus the theme of the "fraternal dialogue" which John Paul II envisaged would shift from the *theory* of the pastoral and doctrinal office to the *substance* of what is believed and preached. And the very *exercise* of elaborating a statement of faith might – by the process of its launching, its execution, its resultant form, its publication, and its reception – illuminate the question of "a ministry that presides in truth and love." *Solvitur ambulando.*[19]

---

19. Geoffrey Wainwright, "'The Gift Which He on One Bestows, We All Delight to Prove': A Possible Methodist Approach to a Ministry of Primacy in the Circulation of Love and Truth" in *Petrine Ministry and the Unity of the Church: "Toward a Patient and Fraternal Dialogue". A Symposium Celebrating the 100th Anniversary of the Foundation of the Society of the Atonement, Rome, December 4-6,*

John Paul generously recognizes that in other ecclesial communities "certain features of the Christian mystery have at times been more effectively emphasized" than in the Catholic Church (*UUS*, 14); and he insists that dialogue entails not only an exchange of ideas but also an "exchange of gifts" (*UUS*, 28). It is permissible to think that the Petrine ministry claimed and offered by the see of Rome may be such a gift, whose very reception in other historic Churches and ecclesial communities may affect its future shape.[20] Perhaps that is also the providentially provided framework for what has been called "the next Christendom," in which the "global South" will figure prominently and the style of Christianity is likely to be markedly "Pentecostal."[21]

VIII. Unity "in Via"?

In conclusion, let me dare to offer a thought from my own Methodist tradition as to how the "unity" confessed of the "holy catholic" Church in the Creed may be conceived. I am emboldened to do so by a couple of points made towards the end of paragraph 4 in *Unitatis redintegratio*. First, holiness:

1997, James F. Puglisi (ed.), (Collegeville, Minnesota: Liturgical Press/Michael Glazier, 1999), pp. 59-82.

20. See Geoffrey Wainwright, "A Primatial Ministry of Unity in a Conciliar and Synodical Context" in *One in Christ* 38, no. 4 (October 2003), pp. 3-25.

21. See Philip Jenkins, *The Next Christendom: The Coming of Global Christianity* (New York: Oxford University Press, 2002). For the ecumenical potential and problematic of "classical Pentecostalism," see Geoffrey Wainwright, "The One Hope of Your Calling? The Ecumenical and Pentecosal Movements after a Century" in *Pneuma: Journal of the Society for Pentecostal Studies* 25 (2003), pp. 7-28.

> All Catholics must aim at Christian perfection and,
> each according to their situation, play their part, that
> the Church, bearing in her own body the humility
> and dying of Jesus, may daily be more purified and
> renewed, against the day when Christ will present her
> to himself in all her glory without spot or wrinkle.

Now John Wesley preached and taught "Christian perfection," and he considered it, though still short of the heavenly finality, by the grace of God attainable in this life, in the sense of wholehearted love toward God and neighbor. I am wondering whether, like the universal call to holiness (cf. *LG*, 39-42), unity also may be viewed as a vocation, which allows for degrees in its attainment without calling into question its reality when it exists in an as yet imperfect state.

The second point to be drawn from the very end of the fourth chapter of *Unitatis redintegratio* concerns catholicity. The text declares that:

> the divisions among Christians prevent the Church
> from realizing in practice the fullness of catholicity
> proper to her in those of her sons and daughters who,
> though joined to her by baptism, are yet separated
> from full communion with her. Furthermore, the
> Church herself finds it more difficult to express in
> actual life her full catholicity in every respect (*UR*, 4).

If the "note" of catholicity may receive less than full (dare one say?) "embodiment" in a Catholic Church, might not the same be said of unity?

My intention in posing those questions is not to dismiss unity, any more than holiness or catholicity, into invisibility or postpone it into an indefinite future (such as *Dominus Iesus* warns against). Rather, I wish to suggest that a genuinely eschatological tension allows all the notes of the

Church to be confessed in a dynamic sense that fosters their perfect and tangible attainment, albeit within the limits of a pilgrim existence. In that way, other authentically trinitarian churches and ecclesial communities — marked by the Gospel, the Scriptures, baptism, the Lord's Supper, and active faith (cf. *UR*, 20-23) — could be regarded as *part of* the "one holy catholic Church" while praying and working towards the fullness that would come to them — and to the Roman Church — on the establishment of communion with the apostolic Petrine see in structures that still demand elaboration.[22]

---

22. The intrinsic relations delineated in John 17:17-23 among truth, holiness, unity, catholicity and apostolic witness were perceived by the nineteenth-century Methodist ecclesiologist and proto-ecumenist Benjamin Gregory. In his *The Holy Catholic Church, the Communion of Saints* (London, 1873), Gregory makes much of the *processive* verb in John 17:23 ("that they may be perfected into one") and the *growth into maturity* implied in connection with unity in Ephesians 4:11-16. In terms of another debate: my own proposal favors a *"partim-partim"* understanding – rather than a radically paradoxical view – of the *"simul iustus et peccator"*; see my chapter "The Ecclesial Scope of Justification" in *Justification: What's at Stake in the Current Debates,* M. Husbands and D. J. Treier (eds.), (Downers Grove, Illinois, and Leicester, England: InterVarsity Press, 2004), pp. 249-75.

Ecumenical Developments and New Challenges. Where Do We Stand Forty Years after *Unitatis redintegratio*?[1]

Kurt Koch

Introduction

The ecumenical movement, which has been exerting influence within the Catholic Church since the promulgation of the Decree on Ecumenism by the Second Vatican Council on 21 November 1964, can perhaps be most adequately compared with a plane journey. After lengthy and intensive preparations such a journey begins with a rapid take-off along the runway and an equally steep lift-off into the air. As soon as the plane has reached cruising altitude and is flying through the skies, we can easily gain the impression that all movement has ceased, or at least that we are making very little headway. But in spite of that, each passenger is borne along by the certain hope that the plane will reach its destination safely. With regard to the ecumenical movement in the Catholic Church, the Second Vatican Council was the rapid take-off along the runway. Forty years later we are even today cruising along as though still airborne, or at least that is how it may seem. But even so we cling to the justifiable hope that the ecumenical plane will land safely. This is particularly true since Pope John Paul II

---

1. Translated from original German text.

77

unequivocally declared in his path-breaking ecumenical encyclical *Ut unum sint* that the ecumenical process represents an unrivalled pastoral priority within his pontificate, and that it is irreversible.[2] The comparison of the ecumenical movement with a plane journey is appropriate not only for determining our present position, but also calling to mind its starting point and at the same time reaffirming our destination. For we can only look to the future if we take the tradition seriously and also discern the signs of the times.

I. Developments within the Ecumenical Movement

The ecumenical plane journey which our church started forty years ago invites us first of all to an overview of the ecumenical landscape, which has changed greatly over the past years and decades. In the first place we can establish/ affirm with joy and satisfaction that in many areas of our church ecumenism is no longer a foreign word or a subject which causes anxiety. Instead, in many local churches, parishes, church communities and spiritual movements it is a lived reality. This ecumenism of daily life is of fundamental significance because without it all theological efforts towards a workable consensus between the various Christian churches and ecclesial communities on the elementary questions of faith remain as though hanging in the air. They are also left up in the air when, on the other hand, the pleasing results of the theological ecumenical work are not acknowledged within the faith community of the church.

---

2. Cf. W. Kasper, "Ökumene – menschlich, charismatisch, spirituell" in *Die Kraft des Augenblicks. Begegnungen mit Papst Johannes Paul II*, W. Bartoszcwski (ed.), (Freiburg, 2004), pp.186-191.

The subject heading "Reception" points to one of the first and indeed most elementary challenges to which even greater attention must be paid in the ecumenical education of the faithful and in the training and professional development of the clergy, as the Ecumenical Directory rightly demands.[3]

On the theological level we have many ecumenical successes to report, above all in view of numerous and in some instances comprehensive efforts to achieve convergence and consensus, which have in the past led to genuine "documents of growing agreement"[4] and have reached a certain climax in the *Joint Declaration on the Doctrine of Justification* signed by the Lutheran World Federation and the Pontifical Council for Promoting Christian Unity on 31 October 1999 in Augsburg. This declaration was able to establish a "consensus on the fundamental questions" of the doctrine. At the same time of course, this formula also gives expression to the fact that as yet no full consensus has been reached on the doctrine of justification or on the consequences of this doctrine for — above all — the concept

---

3. Pontifical Council for Promoting Christian Unity, *Directory for the Application of Principles and Norms of Ecumenism* (Vatican City, 1993), Chapter III: Ecumenical Formation in the Catholic Church. Cf. also the study document of the same Council: *The Ecumenical Dimension in the Formation of Those Engaged in Pastoral Work* (Vatican City, 1998).

4. Cf. *Dokumente wachsender Übereinstimmung. Sämtliche Berichte und Konsenstexte inter-konfessioneller Gespräche auf Weltebene,* H. Meyer, H. J. Urban and L. Vischer (eds.). *Band 1* (Paderborn 1983), *Band 2* (Paderborn 1992), *Band 3* (Paderborn 2003).English: H Meyer and L. Vischer (eds.), *Growth in Agreement. Reports and Agreed Statements of Ecumenical Conversations on a World Level* (New York: Paulist Press; Geneva: WCC, 1984) and J Gros, H. Meyer and W Rusch (eds.) *Growth in Agreement II. Reports and Agreed Statements of Ecumenical Conversations on a World Level, 1982-1998* (Geneva: WCC Publications, 2000).

of the church and the question of ministry. The *Joint Declaration* itself referred to those issues which still require clarification. These questions "involve the relationship between the word of God and church doctrine, as well as the doctrine of the church, of authority within the church, of the unity of the church, of ministry and the sacraments, and finally of the relationship between justification and social ethics".[5]

The *Joint Declaration* can be seen as a milestone along the difficult path towards the restoration of unity among Christians. But a milestone is still very far short of the destination.[6] Apart from the open questions on the exact interpretation of the doctrine of justification itself,[7] the remaining questions can be bundled together as the more precise understanding of what the church is, as Cardinal Kasper quite properly emphasises: "Following the clarification of the fundamental questions of the doctrine of justification, in dialogue with the churches of the Reformation tradition priority must be given to ecclesiological questions. According to Catholic and Orthodox understanding they are the key to progress in the pastorally urgent question of Eucharistic communion. That defines the point at which we

5. *Joint Declaration on the Doctrine of Justification*, (Grand Rapids/Cambridge: William B. Eerdmans, 2000), p.43.
6. "Avec la signature du Document, nous avons atteint une pierre milliaire mais nous ne sommes pas parvenus au terme du chemin. La pleine unité visible des chrétiens et leur communion n'est pas encore un fait". See W. Kasper, *L'Espérance est possible* (Langres, 2002) p.70.
7. Cf. K. Lehmann, *Einig im Verständnis der Rechtfertigungsbotschaft? Erfahrungen und Lehren im Blick auf die gegenwärtige ökumenische Situation* (Bonn, 1998); J. Ratzinger, "Wie weit trägt der Konsens über die Rechtfertigungslehre?" *in Communio. Internationale Katholische Zeitschrift* 29 (2000) pp.424-437; *Gerecht und Sünder zugleich? Ökumenische Klärungen*, T. Schneider and G. Wenz (eds.) (Freiburg/Göttingen, 2001).

stand today."[8] We will return to this question later. But first it is important to mention the striking changes which have occurred within the ecumenical movement in the past forty years.

The most conspicuous may be the fact that for almost all churches the question of their own individual denominational identity has become virulent once more. The need to affirm one's confessional position is quite understandable and even welcome, because encounter and dialogue presuppose the individual identity of each party, and signify "riches and challenge",[9] since after all the elixir of life of ecumenism consists in the reciprocal "exchange of gifts". It does however present a difficulty at the point where the conviction that what *already* unites us is much greater than that which *still* separates us — a conviction which has steadily grown over the past decades — is replaced by a process which instead emphasises the differences. The intensive search for individual confessional identity is indeed to be considered just as important as the search for Christian unity. But this process can hinder ecumenical rapprochement when old prejudices and animosities still prove a significant burden on the relationships between Christians and Christian churches.

Closely connected with that is the fact that major tensions and divergences have emerged within ecumenism in the field of ethics. These have become visible with particular clarity in the worldwide Anglican Communion, and have almost brought it to the verge of schism. The confessionally differen-

---

8. W. Kasper, "Situation und Zukunft der Ökumene" in *Theologische Quartalschrift* 181 (2001) p.186.
9. Cf. W. Kasper, "Konfessionelle Identität – Reichtum und Herausforderung" in T. Bolzenius et al. (eds.) *Ihr sollt ein Segen sein. Ökumenischer Kirchentag* (Gütersloh/Kevelaer, 2004) pp.428–442.

tiated answers to the ethical problems of homosexuality for
example on the one hand and to bioethical and social ethical
challenges on the other can be found in other Christian
churches too of course, and are in some instances treated
quite controversially within them. Here it seems paradoxical
that while there has been some success in overcoming old
denominational conflicts or at least approaching rapprochement, great differences are becoming apparent today on
ethical questions. If the Christian churches cannot speak with
one voice on the great questions of ethics and social ethics,
this damages the credibility of ecumenism as a whole among
the general public in today's society.

A third factor is that ecumenical encounters no longer
take place only among the major historical churches primarily of the West, as was originally intended. Instead, since
the great political turning-point in Europe, the Orthodox
churches have taken an increasingly prominent position
within ecumenical consciousness. From the perspective of our
understanding of the faith they are very close to our church,
while from the perspective of their historical and cultural
background they seem more remote than the churches and
ecclesial communities which emerged from the Reformation.
Taking the voice of Orthodoxy into consideration however
proves to be indispensable also for progress in coming to
terms with the problems of the divided church in the West.[10]
In this sense one can not but support Cardinal Walter Kasper's
encouragement for an "eastward expansion" of ecumenism
too. Here he has taken up the expectation expressed by Pope
John Paul II that the unity of Europe will only be possible
when the one church in West and East breathes with both

---

10. Cf. W. Kasper, "L'orthodoxie et l'Église catholique. A 40 ans du
    Décret sur l'oecumenisme *Unitatis redintegratio" in La Documentation
    Catholique* 86 (2004) pp.315-323.

lungs. The political unification of Europe can in any case only succeed when a rapprochement between the eastern and western churches is achieved. In that process a special sensitivity must be exercised towards the Ancient Oriental churches which also belong, like the Orthodox churches, to the Eastern Church. It has been possible to attain extensive agreement between them and the Catholic Church regarding Christological confession.

Undoubtedly the most obvious transformation in the ecumenical landscape is the constantly increasing significance of the so-called free churches which have pre-empted that future that will increasingly clearly confront even the historical churches, namely freedom and independence from the state — that is, the end of Christendom as inherited from Constantine. Of particular significance here is the numerical increase of the Pentecostal communities, which represent worldwide the second-largest ecclesial community after the Catholic Church. Even though they often take up anti-ecumenical and anti-Catholic positions, dialogue with them is especially important if only because it involves such an expansionary phenomenon that one has to speak of a current "pentecostalisation of Christianity".[11]

As well as many positive developments in ecumenism there are of course also numerous setbacks which must be mentioned. These have become evident in ecumenical frictions such as the vigorous reaction and discussion in many Lutheran churches before and after the signing of the *Joint Declaration on the Doctrine of Justification* in Augsburg in 1999; the disputes about the document *Dominus Jesus* of the Roman Congregation for the Doctrine of the Faith, the

---

11. B. Farrell, "Der Päpstliche Rat zur Förderung der Einheit der Christen im Jahre 2003" in *Catholica* 58 (2004) p.97.

ecumenically frosty resolution of the Council of the EKD
[Evangelische Kirche Deutschlands – Evangelical / Lutheran Church of Germany]: *Church Fellowship According to
Lutheran Understanding,* which basically amounts to ecumenism without the Orthodox churches and without Rome,[12]
or the atmospheric disturbances between the Roman Catholic and the Russian Orthodox Church, with the latter
making two main criticisms, namely the charge of proselytism among Orthodox believers, particularly in the western
Ukraine, and the question of Uniatism.[13] It is to be hoped
that the friendly gesture of returning the icon of Kazan to
the Russian Orthodox Church has at least improved the
climatic conditions. On the whole it would amount to a
progressive step within ecumenism if all churches and
ecclesial communities could together concede that they are
all conscious of ecumenical frictions, and that these are
determined less by specific denominational factors and
more by original sin, and if they could therefore refrain
from one-sided apportioning of blame.

12. Cf. K. Koch, "Kirchengemeinschaft oder Einheit der Kirche? Zum
    Ringen um eine angemessene Zielvorstellung der Ökumene" in
    *Kirche in ökumenischer Perspektive. Kardinal Walter Kasper zum 70.
    Geburtstag,* P. Walter, K. Krämer, and G. Augustin (eds.), (Freiburg,
    2003) pp.135-162, especially pp.147-159: "Kirchengemeinschaft
    ohne Rom und ohne die Orthodoxie".
13. Cf. W. Kasper, "Theologische Hintergründe im Konflikt zwischen
    Moskau und Rom" in *Ost-West. Europäische Perspektiven* 3 (2002)
    pp.230-239; also W. Kasper, "Katholische Bistümer in Russland.
    Bemerkungen zur Diskussion um das Verständnis des kanonischen
    Territoriums" in *Stimmen der Zeit* 128 (2003) pp.523-530.

II. Ascertaining the Origins of Ecumenism

A journey by plane does not merely allow an overview of the ecumenical landscape. During the flight one can become so accustomed to the cruising altitude that one could be tempted to assume that the runway has been left so far behind that one no longer has need of it. This temptation has become evident within the ecumenical movement in the more recent past and particularly in the present in two respects above all. In view of these developments it proves urgent to call to mind the origins of ecumenism.

1. Reinforcing the theological foundations of ecumenism

The runway of the ecumenical movement in the Catholic Church was the Second Vatican Council. Accordingly the Catholic understanding of ecumenism is grounded inalienably in the theological foundations which *Unitatis redintegratio* developed as the "Catholic principles of ecumenism". Not only have these foundations been exposed to a creeping erosion during the past years, but at the same time knowledge of the fundamental substance of the Christian faith has decreased massively even among the faithful. Both factors have as a consequence that theological dialogue within the ecumenical movement is widely suspected to be working its way through trivial theological subtleties. Closely connected to this is the evocation of a wide-ranging contrast between the ecumenism of the church's congregations and that of theology and the church leadership, which Joachim Wanke, Bishop of Erfurt has condemned as a "self-blockade of ecumenism by splitting it into an 'ecumenism from above' and one 'from below'".[14]

---

14. J. Wanke, "Erlahmt der ökumenische Impuls" Anmerkungen aus der ökumenischen Praxis" in *Catholica* 53 (1999) p.97.

In view of this difficult situation, one of the major tasks
of ecumenism today consists in a new consolidation of the
theological foundations of ecumenism, which the Decree
on Ecumenism sees above all in baptism and baptismal
faith, and which it is urgently necessary to be reminded of
today. For baptism and its mutual recognition forms the
most fundamental given of all ecumenical efforts. Baptism
is the entrance door into the church and into ecumenism.
This elementary acknowledgement is the starting point of
the Decree on Ecumenism. Already in the first chapter on
the "Catholic Principles of Ecumenism" baptism is seen as
the foundation for the membership of all Christians in the
church. "Whoever believes in Christ and has been properly
baptised is brought therewith into a certain, though imperfect, communion with the Catholic Church."[15] The third
chapter "On the Churches and Ecclesial Communities
which are Separated from the Roman Apostolic See" highlights with particular emphasis in its description of those
churches and ecclesial communities in the West — even
before it mentions their ecclesiological deficits such as the
"lack of the sacrament of orders" and the failure to preserve
the "genuine and complete reality of the Eucharistic mystery" — baptism, which, if administered as instituted and
received in faith, incorporates the baptised individual into
the crucified and glorified Lord and effects his rebirth into
sharing in the divine life. Therefore it is stressed that
baptism is the foundation of a "sacramental bond of unity
linking all" who are reborn thereby. Only then, and without
detracting from what has already been said, is it stated that
baptism is "only a beginning and a point of departure",
since it is by its very nature directed towards "attaining full-

---

15. *Unitatis redintegratio*, 3.

ness of life in Christ and is oriented towards a complete profession of faith, a complete incorporation into the system of salvation as Christ himself willed it to be, and finally a complete participation in Eucharistic communion."[16] The fundamental significance of baptism for all ecumenical efforts does not only form the point of departure of the Decree on Ecumenism, for even today ecumenism stands or falls with the reciprocal recognition of baptism.[17] From that fact one cannot of course draw the conclusion that reciprocal recognition of baptism forms at least a sufficient foundation for Eucharistic communion.[18] Instead the Decree expressly emphasises that "in the ecclesial communities separated from us, the full unity which arises from baptism is lacking".[19] The common bond of baptism permits a basic but imperfect communion. Baptism is indeed the bond of unity and the basis of communion, but it is oriented towards the shared profession of faith and the celebration of the eucharist. While baptism is the beginning and the starting point of Christian life and ecclesial existence, the eucharist is its fullness and consummation.

---

16. *Ibid.*, 22.
17. Cf. W. Kasper, "Ekklesiologische und ökumenische Implikationen der Taufe" in *Weg und Weite. Festschrift ür Karl Lehmann*, A. Raffelt (ed.), (Freiburg, 2001) p.599.
18. Cf. Centre d'Études Oecuméniques (Strasbourg)/Institut Für Ökumenische Forschung (Tübingen)/Konfessionskundliches Institut (Bensheim), *Abendmahlsgemeinschaft ist möglich. Thesen zur Eucharistischen Gastfreundschaft* (Frankfurt, 2003), especially pp.35-39: "Thesis 4. Die Taufe ist das Tor zur Gemeinschaft der Kirche, dem Leib Christi, der im Abendmahl je neu konstituiert wird". Cf. also J. Brosseder, "Das Zweite Vatikanische Konzil und der Zusammenhang von Taufe, Eucharistie und Kirche im Blick auf Eucharistische Gastfreundschaft" in *Eucharistische Gastfreundschaft. Ein Plädoyer evangelischer und katholischer Theologen*, J. Brosseder and H.-G. Link (eds.), (Neukirchen-Vluyn, 2003) pp.15-21.
19. *Unitatis redintegratio*, 22

Therefore we welcome the initiative undertaken by the Pontifical Council for Promoting Christian Unity in 2002, when it requested the Episcopal Conferences to re-examine their existing agreements with their individual ecumenical partners on the reciprocal recognition of baptism, and to consolidate them or to arrive at new agreements. This initiative is to be seen as an important step towards securing the theological foundations of ecumenism, a task which has become so necessary today.

2. The parting of the ecumenical ways

The second temptation on this ecumenical flight con-sists in the threat that in the course of the flight we forget what originally triggered and motivated the journey. Within the ecumenical movement that impetus was doubt-less the deeply felt perception of the profoundly abnormal situation of divided Christendom. The fact that Christians who believe in Jesus Christ as their Redeemer and have been baptised into his body live in churches which are sepa-rated from one another is the great stumbling block which the church still offers to the contemporary world today, and which deserves to be called a scandal. Church divisions are at the very least to be diagnosed as the division of that which is essentially indivisible, the body of Christ.

This is perhaps nowhere more strikingly represented than in the wholly intact robe of Christ. Holy Scripture expressly emphasises that it was woven in one piece "with-out seam, woven from the top throughout" (John 19:23b). It has always made a deep impression on me that in the passion story even the Roman soldiers did not dare to cut into pieces this precious garment of the earthly Jesus: "Let us not rend it but cast lots for it, whose it shall be". Thus the robe of Christ has been able to serve as a real symbol of the unity of the church as the body of Christ. The lamentable tragedy of this story of course consists in the fact that Christians themselves have done exactly that which the Roman soldiers did not dare to do. Therefore the robe of Christ appears, as the former President of the Pontifical Council for Promoting Christian Unity, Edward Idris Cardinal Cassidy rightly stated, "today in rags and tatters, in confessions and denominations which have throughout history often battled against one another instead of fulfilling the mandate of their Lord that they be one."[20]

This gives rise to the (self-) critical question directed at all Christians, whether they really still feel this painful scandal of the split within the one body of Christ, or if they have not already come to terms with and even accepted it. It is my profound conviction that we will only arrive at new impulses in ecumenism when we have the courage to look this still persisting offence in the face. What grieves me most in the current ecumenical situation is the fact that so many Christians no longer grieve over this profoundly abnormal state as deeply as befits the situation. For wherever the division within the body of Christ is no longer perceived as an outrage and no longer causes pain, there ecumenism becomes superfluous.

In the current situation of the ecumenical movement one must therefore diagnose a far-reaching paradigm shift, in that its original goal, namely the restoration of the visible unity of the church, has to a large extent been lost from view. Those ecumenical efforts have been replaced by thor-

---

20. E. I. Cassidy, "Welche nächsten Schritte in der Ökumene sind überfällig, realisierbar und wünschenswert?" in *Una Sancta* 51 (1996) p.112.

oughly justified but not directly ecumenical goals and projects of a "secular ecumenism" which has come to the forefront. The loss of significance of the "Faith and Order Commission" within the World Council of Churches is of course just one symptom of this paradigm shift.[21]

This paradigm shift may well have had such a profound effect on many Christians in many churches because it corresponds to the pluralistic and therefore also relativistic spirit of the age which is currently so widely taken for granted. The basic dogma of this mentality claims that one neither can nor should retreat philosophically to a point pre-dating the plurality of contemporary reality, if one does not wish to lay oneself open to the charge of totalitarian thinking; it is said that plurality is the only way that totality is presented to us, if at all.[22] This conviction also forms the basis of the pluralistic religious trends of the present.[23] Their point of departure is that there is not only a diversity of religions but also a plurality of divine revelations, and accordingly Jesus Christ too can only be seen as one among many in the world of bearers of salvation and revelation. This is the reason why many would like to minimise faith in Christ as far as possible, particularly in encounters with other religions.[24] This tendency is given expression for example in the pointed question of the Lutheran theologian Reinhold Bernhardt "Must we disarm christologically in

21. Cf. W. Pannenberg, "Eine geistliche Erneuerung der *Ökumene tut Not"* in *Ökumene. Möglichkeiten und Grenzen heute,* K. Froehlich (ed.), (Tübingen, 1982) pp.112-123.
22. Cf. W. Welsch, *Unsere postmoderne Moderne* (Weinheim, 1987).
23. Cf. R. Schwager, *Christus allein? Der Streit um die pluralistische Religionstheologie* (Freiburg, 1996).
24. Cf. J. Ratzinger, *Glaube – Wahrheit – Toleranz. Das Christentum und die Weltreligionen* (Freiburg, 2003).

order to become capable of inter-religious dialogue?"[25] Transferred to our ecumenical discussion, the critical question in response would be: "Must we disarm as Catholics in order to become capable of inter-church dialogue?" Contemporary religious and denominational pluralism within the ecumenical movement prove to be two sides of the one coin.

This state of affairs is directly related to the contemporary social context. The thoroughgoing process of differentiation within society, which has become so evident and so influential in the dominant tendencies of individualisation and pluralisation, makes any quest for unity — including and above all within ecumenism — look suspect.[26] At most, unity is seen as the tolerant acknowledgement of multiplicity and diversity. Consequently, the in-principle recognition of diversity is already viewed as the realisation of reconciled difference. How the fundamental concern of ecumenism, the search for the visible unity of the church of Christ Jesus, can be discerned in the context of this post-modern mentality of individualistic and pluralistic arbitrariness is doubtless the greatest challenge facing ecumenism today.[27]

---

25. R. Bernhardt, "Desabsolutierung der Christologie?" in *Der einzige Weg zum Heil? Die Herausforderung des christlichen Absolutheitsanspruchs durch die pluralistische Religionstheologie*, M. v. Brück and J. Werbick (ed.), (Freiburg, 1993) pp.184-200.
26. Cf. M. N. Ebertz, *Aufbruch in der Kirche. Anstösse für ein zukunftsfähiges Christentum* (Freiburg, 2003) p.17.
27. Cf. W. Kasper, "Die Kirche angesichts der Herausforderungen der Postmoderne" in *Theologie und Kirche. Band 2* (Mainz 1999) pp.249-264, especially pp.252-255: "Absage an das Einheitspostulat: Der pluralistische Grundzug der Postmoderne". The new factor in Postmodernism is seen in its deliberate abandonment of the postulate of unity: "Postmodernism is not only the acceptance and

Christian ecumenism cannot accept this challenge by completely adapting itself to this paradigm, if for no other reason than that contemporary pluralism drives the individual into that homelessness which is the best breeding ground for diverse forms of fundamentalism. This proves itself to be an arch-reactionary phenomenon[28] which, as the political scientist Thomas Meyer has illuminatingly demonstrated, is a reaction against the inhospitable nature of modernity.[29] Christian ecumenism does contemporary society a great service simply by keeping alive the question of unity with amiable stubbornness — even if one disregards the fact that without the search for unity the Christian faith would be relinquishing itself. For unity is and remains a "fundamental category of Holy Scripture and of tradition"[30] which professes the one God, the one Redeemer, the one Spirit, the one baptism and the one church (cf. Eph 4: 4-6).

The most profound reason for the waning of the originally fiery determination within the ecumenical movement to give expression to the quest for the visible unity of the church of Christ Jesus — with all its indispensable and inalienable diversity — is no doubt to be sought in the context of contemporary society. Many seem to have come to terms with the current state of diversity and are content

tolerance of plurality, but a fundamental option for pluralism" (p.253).
28. Cf. K. Koch, "Fundamentalismus: eine 'katholische' Häresie? Offene, aber nicht ungestaltete Identität des Christentums" in *Verbindliches Christsein – verbindender Glaube. Spannungen und Herausforderungen eines zeitgemässen Christentums* (Freiburg/Schweiz, 1995) pp.65-114.
29. T. Meyer, *Fundamentalismus – Aufstand gegen die Moderne* (Reinbek bei Hamburg, 1989).
30. W. Kasper, *Sakrament der Einheit. Eucharistie und Kirche* (Freiburg, 2004) p.122.

with the factual pluralism of different churches. For them the already prevailing *tolerated* diversity between the churches suffices, and they do not see why this needs to be overcome in favour of a genuinely *reconciled* diversity.[31]

If I am not mistaken, we are today faced with a fundamental parting of the ways between an ecumenism which continues to strive for the visible unity of the church, working and praying for unification, and an ecumenism which considers that what has already been achieved is sufficient. It is therefore interested in upholding the status quo and wishes to affirm this through the practice of Eucharistic communion. Once more it is evident that the real "conservatives" in the sense of "conservers of the status quo" are the so-called "progressives", who want to 'make' the goal of ecumenism themselves already today by taking the path of intercommunion and inter-celebration, contenting themselves with practising Eucharistic communion while otherwise continuing to exist as separated churches. This praxis brings with it the real danger of degenerating into a cheap consolation which ignores the sinful fact of continuing church division, and thus turns out to be nothing more than an ecumenical 'sedative' – just at a time when what we need are ecumenical de-tranquiliser pills, capable of fortifying and intensifying the will of the Christian churches to make the unity implicit in their faith in Christ Jesus visible and fruitful in daily life.

The Catholic ecumenist Peter Neuner rightly complains that in many Lutheran and Reformed churches — as indeed among not a few Catholics — the goal of ecumenism is no longer seen as ecclesial communio but simply as

---

31. B. Neumann, "Nehmt einander an, wie auch Christus uns angenommen hat" (Röm 15. 7). Bausteine zu einer Spiritualität der Ökumene" in *Geist und Leben* 76 (2003) p.183.

inter-communion, and when this is realised "everything else can remain as it is".[32] Accordingly the great ecumenical goal is seen as the shared eucharist, whereby the separated churches can perfectly well continue to exist. As a consequence there is scarcely any more talk of the communio unity of the church but only of inter-communion. This has its basis in ecclesiological pluralism, according to which there is no need for the different churches to be unified, but instead merely to recognise one another in their diversity and naturally also in some cases with all their confessionally based contradictions.

There is naturally a fundamental tension between this view and the Catholic and Orthodox understanding, according to which the goal of all ecumenical efforts cannot in the first instance be inter-communion but "communio, within which communion in the Lord's Supper then has its place".[33] This understanding is also the foundation for the fact that for the Roman Catholic Church — as for the majority of Christian churches — ecclesial communion and Eucharistic communion are considered inseparable.[34] The great majority of Christian churches — together with the Catholic Church primarily the Orthodox Churches, but also the Anglican Ecclesial Communities — therefore hold fast to the conviction of the early church that there can be

---

32. P. Neuner. "Das Dekret über die Ökumene *Unitatis redintegratio*" in *Vierzig Jahre II. Vatikanum. Zur Wirkungsgeschichte der Konzilstexte,* F. X. Bischof and S. Leimgruber (eds.), (Würzburg, 2004) p.139.

33. P. Neuner and B. Kleinschwärzer-Meister, "Ein neues Miteinander der christlichen Kirchen. Auf dem Weg zum Ökumenischen Kirchentag in Berlin 2003" in *Stimmen der Zeit* 128 (2003) p.373.

34. Cf. M. Eham, *Gemeinschaft im Sakrament? Die Frage nach der Möglichkeit sakramentaler Gemeinschaft zwischen katholischen und nichtkatholischen Christen. Zur ekklesiologischen Dimension der ökumenischen Frage. Zwei Bände* (Frankfurt, 1986); G. Hintzen, *Zum Thema 'Eucharistie und Kirchengemeinschaft'* (Paderborn, 1990).

"no true and genuine Eucharistic communion without ecclesial communion", and by the same token, "no full ecclesial communion" without the eucharist.[35]

III. The Contentious Goal of Ecumenism

Here we can obtain a clear view of the destination of our ecumenical plane journey, which can naturally become unclear in the course of the long flight. The more the take-off fades in our memories, the more indistinct the destination threatens to become. The real crux of the current ecumenical situation consists precisely in the fact that we have so far been unable to reach any really workable consensus on the goal of ecumenism, which has instead become increasingly unclear. The fact that the goal of the ecumenical movement is still a matter of debate between the various churches and ecclesial communities can be diagnosed as the real paradox of the present ecumenical situation. More precisely, this consists in the realisation that in the preceding phases of the ecumenical movement on the one hand pleasing and extensive convergence and consensus have been attained on many individual questions, but on the other hand all the outstanding points of difference can be bundled together in the understanding of the unity of the church itself, where the original sharply differentiated profiles still prevail. This most weighty desideratum in the current ecumenical situation must be tackled energetically. Only when we have a clear view of the goal of the ecumenical movement can we adequately pose the question of the next necessary steps.

---

35. P.W. Scheele, "Eucharistie und Kirche gehören zusammen" in *Die Tagespost* 59 (20 May 2003) p.3.

Clarification of the conceptions of the church and of unity must therefore be the main point to be dealt with on the current ecumenical agenda, and the search for an ecumenically responsible understanding of the essential nature of the church must be conducted as a spiritual process.[36] The lack of consensus on the goal of the ecumenical movement is directly related to the denominationally differentiated ecclesiologies. Since each church has and realises its denominationally specific concept of the unity of its own church, and is therefore virtually automatically intent on transferring this denominational concept to the goal of the ecumenical movement too, there are as many differing representations of the goal of ecumenism as there are different churches.[37] This can be demonstrated by a brief comparison of Catholic ecclesiology with the Orthodox and Lutheran ecclesiologies.[38]

The Orthodox understanding of the church can be best characterised as Eucharistic ecclesiology.[39] Accordingly the church is realised in each local church — gathered around its bishop — where the eucharist is celebrated. Since Orthodox faith holds the conviction that the one Christ is present in each local church, no local church can however exist on its own. Each local church stands in living com-

---

36. Cf. W. Kasper, "Kircheneinheit und Kirchengemeinschaft in katholischer Sicht. Eine Problemskizze" in *Glaube und Gemeinschaft. Festschrift für Paul–Werner Scheele zum 25 jährigen Konsekrationsjubiläum*, K. Hillenbrand and H. Niederschlag (eds.), (Würzburg, 2000) pp.100-117.
37. Cf. G. Hintzen and W. Thönissen, *Kirchengemeinschaft möglich? Einheitsverständnis und Einheitskonzepte in der Diskussion* (Paderborn, 2001).
38. Cf. K. Koch, *Gelähmte Ökumene. Was jetzt noch zu tun ist* (Freiburg, 1991), especially pp.166-170.
39. Cf. J. Oeldemann, *Orthodoxe Kirchen im ökumenischen Dialog. Positionen, Probleme, Perspektiven* (Paderborn, 2004).

munio with all other local churches in which the eucharist is also celebrated; this communio is primarily realised through the metropolis and the patriarchate. The unity of the universal church is consequently a communion unity of local churches, metropolises and patriarchates. Since the local church celebrating the eucharist with its bishop is the representation, actualisation and realisation of the one church in its concrete locality, there can in principle be no priority of the whole church over the local church. Apart from an ecumenical council there can also be no visible principle of the unity of the universal church, such as the Catholic Church perceives and recognises in the Petrine office. This independence from the Pope has of course been purchased at the price of making autocephalism — and the national principle, in part connected with it — the central problem of Orthodoxy. Thus the heart of the ecumenical problem consists in the fact "that a national, culture-bound understanding of the church and a catholic, universally oriented understanding of the church have until now confronted one another unreconciled".[40] It has not proved impossible to conduct a productive ecumenical conversation on this problem, particularly if one keeps in mind the fact that even within the Catholic Church the question of the relationship between local churches and the universal church has not been fully resolved.[41]

---

40. W. Kasper, "Ökumene zwischen Ost und West. Stand und Perspektiven des Dialogs mit den orthodoxen Kirchen" in *Stimmen der Zeit* 128 (2003) p.157.
41. Cf. the dispute within the Curia between Cardinals Walter Kasper and Joseph Ratzinger, which was of course able to achieve a far-reaching rapprochement between the different standpoints: W. Kasper, "Zur Theologie und Praxis des bischöflichen Amtes" in *Auf neue Art Kirche sein. Wirklichkeiten – Herausforderungen –*

According to Lutheran understanding the church is creatura verbi, therefore it is the community of believers where the Gospel is preached in its purity and the sacraments administered in accordance with the Gospel.[42] Since this occurs in the concrete local congregation, Martin Luther gave the word congregation unequivocal preference over the "blind and unclear word church".[43] Accordingly the Lutheran understanding of the church has its unequivocal focus and as it were its centre of gravity in the concrete local congregation in its specific locality. The church of Christ Jesus is in the Lutheran view present in its full sense in the concrete congregation at worship, gathered around the word and the sacraments. Since the church of Christ Jesus not only subsists in the concrete individual congregation but is church in the full sense, the congregation is the prototypical realisation of the church. The individual congregations do indeed stand in communication with one another even in the Lutheran understanding, The supra-congregational aspect of the church is implicitly present to that extent, but is in the end secondary. The aspect of the universal church in particular and also the episcopal structure which are so fundamental to the Catholic understanding of the church are largely underdeveloped theologically. This raises the ecumenically difficult question how

---

Wandlungen. Festschrift für Bischof Dr. Josef Homeyer, W. Schreer and G. Steins (eds.), (Münich, 1999) pp.32-48; J. Ratzinger, "Die Ekklesiologie der Konstitution *Lumen gentium*" in *Weggemeinschaft des Glaubens. Kirche als Communio* (Augsburg, 2002) pp.107-131; W. Kasper, "Das Verhältnis von Universalkirche und Ortskirche. Freundschaftliche Auseinandersetzung mit der Kritik von J. Kard. Ratzinger" in *Stimmen der Zeit* 218 (2000) pp.795-804.

42. Cf. G. W. Locher, *Sign of the Advent. A Study in Protestant Ecclesiology* (Fribourg, 2004).

43. *Weimarer Ausgabe* (WA) 50, 625

the Catholic understanding of the church with its unique interweaving of the singular "universal church" and plural "local churches" relates to the Lutheran understanding of the church which sees the prototypical realisation of the church in the concrete congregation, and whether an ecumenical consensus on this point can be possible at all. This diversity of concepts of the church is the real reason for the impossibility of unproblematically deducing a compatible ecumenical model for unity or communion from any individual denominational understanding of the church. This is particularly true if one has not tested the model in ecumenical conversation, but simply treats one's own denominational ecclesiology as absolute, thus exposing oneself to the suspicion of intending to surreptitiously assert one specific denominational typology (namely one's own).[44] As experience has shown more than adequately, this temptation can be found in all churches. For the radically different denominational conceptions of the church and its unity still stand unreconciled alongside one another.

Clarification of the understanding of the church is therefore proving itself ever more clearly to be the main agenda item of the present. The differing concepts of the church remain the crucial reason for the lack of progress in the concrete questions of reciprocal recognition of ecclesial orders and Eucharistic communion. It is therefore extremely urgent that we tackle these questions together ecumenically, so that we can recognise one another as sister churches in the full sense and thus attain the goal of ecumenism. This

44. F. W. Graf and D. Korsch, "Jenseits der Einheit: Reichtum der Vielfalt. Der Widerstreit der ökumenischen Bewegungen und die Einheit der Kirche Jesu Christi" in *Jenseits der Einheit. Protestantische Ansichten der Ökumene*, Graf and Korsch (eds.), (Hannover, 2001) p.25.

consists in the visible communion of Christian churches which according to the concise formulation of Cardinal Joseph Ratzinger "remain churches but yet become one church".[45] All ecumenical efforts should therefore merge in a similar "Joint Declaration on the Church, Orders and the Eucharist" like that on the doctrine of justification.[46]

IV. Ecumenical Restoration of Unity

Such a declaration can only be set in motion if we are conscious in a new and at the same time authentic way of the division of the church of Christ Jesus as the real scandal contradicting the essential nature of the 'una sancta'. This is the fundamental ecumenical aporia, within which all theological attempts at declarations and practical realisations must in the end remain unsatisfactory. The abnormal situation of division cannot be solved by any satisfactory theological theory, because even that would stand under the aegis of the essentially contradictory initial state of lasting division. This cannot be overcome by a convincing theory or by an ecumenical praxis which deviates from church ordinances. "Solutions which are satisfactory in both theory and practice", as Peter Neuner judges, "are

---

45. J. Ratzinger, "Die ökumenische Situation – Orthodoxie, Katholizismus und Reformation" in *Theologische Prinzipienlehre. Bausteine zur Fundamentaltheologie* (Münich, 1982) pp.203-214.
46. Cf. H. Schütte, "Gemeinsame Erklärung zur Rechtfertigungslehre. Die Ursache der westlichen Glaubensspaltung ist behoben" in *KNA-ÖKI* 40, 5 October 2004. Thema der Woche (Weekly Theme), pp.1-4.

only possible when the division has been overcome as a contradiction against the nature of the church".[47]

Here the original goal of all ecumenical efforts becomes visible, as it was formulated already in the first paragraph of the Decree on Ecumenism: "Promoting the restoration of unity among all Christians is one of the chief concerns of the Second Sacred Ecumenical Synod of the Vatican. For the division of the church contradicts the will of Christ, provides a stumbling block to the world and inflicts damage on the most holy cause of proclaiming the good news to every creature".[48] This statement of principle has not lost any of its contemporary relevance today, forty years after the promulgation of the Decree on Ecumenism; on the contrary, its undiminished truth is re-affirmed today more than ever.

The same is true of that fundamental spiritual impulse which inspired the ecumenical movement from the beginning and set it on its way, which the Second Vatican Council characterised as the "soul of the whole ecumenical movement",[49] and which today demands revitalisation, namely the priority of prayer for unity and ecumenism of daily life, the heart of which consists in an ecumenical spirituality.[50] Because ecumenism dies without this soul, the Pontifical Council for Promoting Christian Unity is rightly convinced

---

47. P. Neuner, "Das Dekret über die Ökumene *Unitatis redintegratio*" in *Vierzig Jahre II. Vatikanum. Zur Wirkungsgeschichte der Konzilstexte*, F. X. Bischof and S. Leimgruber (eds.), (Würzburg, 2004) p.140.

48. *Unitatis redintegratio*, 1.

49. *Ibid.*, 8.

50. Cf. W. Kasper, "Spiritualit ed ecumenismo" in *Rivista Teologica di Lugano* VII (2002) pp.117-132; W. Kasper, "Ökumene des Lebens und Eucharistiegemeinschaft. Perspektiven für die Zukunft" in W. Kasper, *Sakrament der Einheit. Eucharistie und Kirche* (Freiburg, 2004) pp.55-79.

"that ecumenism of truth and love, which retains its central position as a matter of course, must be supplemented by a deeply and comprehensively experienced ecumenism of life",[51] and that the ecumenical movement "at the present time is in need of a renewed motivation grounded in the spirit", that is, a renewed spirituality of ecumenism.[52]

What is encompassed by such a spiritual ecumenism or such ecumenical spirituality in concrete terms [53] I would like in conclusion to elucidate through an event in the story of the friendship of Saint Francis of Assisi and Saint Clare. Once when they wished to see one another again they met at a stream, naturally standing on opposite banks. Since the stream was too broad to be crossed, they arrived at the conviction that they should, each on the opposite side, go back to the source of the stream, which becomes steadily smaller and narrower in that direction. At the source of the stream they were able to meet one another without any difficulty and celebrate their spiritual friendship. I see this event as an apt and helpful image of the situation of ecumenism today. Here too one again and again gains the impression that the different churches seem to be at a standstill, distributed on the two banks of a stream which is still relatively broad. Because the stream cannot be crossed they cannot reach one another and have to resort to speaking to one another now and then in relatively loud tones. In this situation ecumenism needs the wisdom of Francis and Clare, which encourages them to return to the source of the stream

---

51. B. Farrell, "Der Päpstliche Rat zur Förderung der Einheit der Christen im Jahre 2002" in *Catholica* 57 (2003) p.83.
52. *Ibid.*, p.106.
53. Cf. K. Koch, "Wiederentdeckung der 'Seele der ganzen Ökumenischen Bewegung' (UR 8). Notwendigkeit und Perspektiven einer ökumenischen Spiritualität" in *Catholica* 58 (2004) pp.3-21.

along the opposite banks. If the different churches find the shared source of the unity which has already been prefigured for us in Christ Jesus, they will also find one another. This is the deepest mystery of the church and of ecumenism, which does not lead to resignation but becomes a challenge to proceed with courage along the ecumenical path, with the clear conviction of Pope John Paul II that the path of ecumenism is irreversible if it is truly a shared conversion to Jesus Christ and to the unity for which we are to pray to him, and which has already been granted in him. Ecumenism urgently needs this greater depth, even if it wishes at the same time to expand in breadth.

Pope John Paul II lays very special weight on one aspect of the ecumenical spirituality required today, namely on the martyrological dimension of ecumenism. In the Holy Year 2000 at the Colosseum — that is at the place in still pagan Rome where Christians gave their testimony in blood for their faith — when he commemorated the ecumenism of the unnumbered martyrs of the 20th century, he gave expression to his deepest ecumenical conviction: While we Christians here on earth still stand in an imperfect communion with one another, the martyrs in heavenly glory are already living in full and complete communion. The blood of the martyrs of our time will one day become the seed of the full unity of the body of Christ. Their ecumenism of blood proves so convincing because in it the meaning of Jesus' prayer for unity among his disciples has been fulfilled: "That they all may be one; as thou, Father, art in me, and I in thee, that they all may be one in us: that the world may believe that thou hast sent me (John 17:21)".

So that the world may believe: that alone is the destination of the plane journey which we began in our church 40 years ago and which will reach its goal because we are convinced that ecumenism is the work of the Holy Spirit,[54] that he will guide this work to its conclusion, and that he will in the process grant us more than we dare to hope or perhaps even to dream. But it is for us to continue our efforts in this work of the Holy Spirit, in that presence of mind and spirit which is demanded from us but is first of all granted to us.

---

54. W. Pannenberg, "Die Ökumene als Wirken des Heiligen Geistes" in *Gottes Geist bei den Menschen. Grundfragen und spirituelle Anstösse*, S. Leimgruber (ed.), (Münich, 1999) pp.68-77.

The Action of the Pontifical Council for Promoting Christian Unity from the Promulgation of *Unitatis redintegratio* Until Today[1]

Eleuterio F. Fortino

Introduction

Three documents were published at the conclusion of the third phase of the Second Vatican Council (21 November 1964), namely the Dogmatic Constitution of the Church (*Lumen gentium*), the Decree on the Eastern Churches (*Orientalium ecclesiarum*) and the Decree on Ecumenism (*Unitatis redintegratio*).

In the allocution of promulgation, Paul VI expressed the hope that the doctrine of the Church "be benevolently and favourably considered by the Christian brothers of Christ separated from us (sejuncti)". He also expressed the desire that this doctrine "complemented by the declarations contained in framework of *De oecumenismo*, also approved by this Council" might have an enlightening influence on other Christians, fostering a revision of "thoughts and attitudes". It was the hope of the Pope that in this way, other Christians "would increasingly become closer to our communion and finally, God willing, join us in full communion (*in hac nobiscum sint pares*).[2]

---

1. Translated from the original Italian text.
2. Cf. *Enchiridion Vaticanuum, Documenti – Il Concilio Vaticano II, Testo ufficiale e traduzione italiana*, 8th edition, (Bologna: EDB, 1970) p.179. (*Ad hoc* English translation provided here).

Two important aspects emerge:

a) the ecumenical question is fundamentally ecclesiological;

b) a doctrinal relationship with other Christians is therefore indispensable for the process of clarification *(consilia et proposita recognoscenda)* in the progressive rapprochement between Christians towards full communion.

Paul VI reiterated the regard for the relationship with other Christians, expressing "on this occasion, our reverent greeting to the observers representing the Christian Churches and Confessions separated from us, our gratitude for their appreciated presence at the conciliar meetings, our vivid prayer for their prosperity".[3]

Immediately after, Paul VI spoke of the influence of the ecumenical commitment within the Catholic Church: "To ourselves this same doctrine — he affirmed — has enabled us to experience the surprising joy in observing how the Church, delineating the outline of its own configuration, does not restrict but widens the borders of its charity and does not arrest the multifarious movement of its catholicity, which is always progressing and always inviting".[4]

Two fundamental concerns regarding the process of application and implementation of *Unitatis redintegratio* (*UR*) were defined:

a) the promotion of the ecumenical spirit and action of the Catholic Church,

b) relations with other Christians.

---

3. *Ibid.*
4. *Ibid.*

These two concerns are systematically defined in the Decree itself and have formed the basis of the action of the Pontifical Council for Promoting Christian Unity.

I. Promotion of Ecumenism Within the Catholic Church

The conciliar debate on ecumenism was of a high theological and pastoral standard. *Unitatis redintegratio* was voted almost unanimously. The theological foundation of the search for unity and the theological guidelines for action were well set out in the decree.

At the conclusion of the Council (1965) the question arose regarding its reception and practical implementation within a heterogeneous cultural context. There remained in the wider Catholic world attitudes of uncertainty, incomprehension, and reservation, also as a consequence of previous warnings by ecclesiastical authorities.[5] Yet at the same time, enthusiastic and sometimes simplistic initiatives were also developing. There was therefore a need for accurate information on the conciliar decisions and their implementation.

---

5. Cf. G. Baum, "L'unité chrétienne d'aprs la doctrine des Papes de Leon XIII Pie XII" in *Unam sanctam*; 35, (Paris: Cerf, 1961); B. Mondin, *L'ecumenismo nella Chiesa cattolica prima, durante e dopo il Concilio*, (Parma: Silva, 1966); C. Boyer-Bellucci, *Unità cristiana e movimento ecumenico*, (Roma: Studium, 1955). The encyclical of Pius XII *Mortalium animos* (1928) was explicit: "It is clear that the Apostolic See cannot in any way take part in their congresses (=pan–Christian, for the unity of the Church) and in no way can Catholics associate with activities of this type, otherwise authority would be given to the claim of a Christian religion, which is a thousand miles away from the one Church of Christ" (*ad hoc* translation). Y. Congar, *Chrétiens désunis principes d'un oecuménisme catholique*, (Paris: Cerf, 1937); G. Thils, *Histoire doctrinale du mouvement œcuménique*, (Tournai: 1960); B. Lambert, *Le problème oecuménique*, (Paris: Centurion, 1962).

The Secretariat for the Unity of Christians (SPCU) — as the current Pontifical Council was then known — undertook a wide range of activities (conferences, documents, visits, contact with theological institutes, creation of structures, contact with bishops in various countries and attention to the norms of application of the Council emanated by organisms of the Roman Curia and the episcopates).

a) Ecumenical Directory

The Secretariat for the Unity of Christians, created by John XXIII in preparation for the Council, was confirmed as an organism of the Curia in the Apostolic Letter *Finis concilii* (1966). This new structure of the Roman Curia was entrusted with the task of promoting the ecumenical action of the Catholic Church,[6] starting from within. One of its first undertakings was the preparation and publication of

---

6. *The Secretariatus ad Unitatem Christianorum Fovendam* was created by John XXIII with the Motu Proprio, *Superno Dei nutu* dated 5 June 1960 within the context of the creation of 11 preparatory conciliar commissions. Subsequently, with the Apostolic Constitution *Humane salutis* of 25 December 1961 convening the Second Vatican Council, John XXIII among other things clarified that the Secretariat for Christian Unity would deal with relations with the entire Christian world (Protestants and Orthodox alike). This clarification was necessary because the Commission for Oriental Churches had previously dealt with relations with the Orthodox. In the *Ordo Concilii* of 6 August 1962, the Secretariat was confirmed as a conciliar commission. A rescript of John XXIII of 19 October 1962 confirmed that the Secretariat *"eadem munera habet"* would comprise the same persons as the previous preparatory stage. However, in the second part of the Council, the number of members was extended, and also included bishops. In 1963, the Secretariat was organised into two sections, one for relations with the Reformed world and the other for the East. With the Apostolic Letter *Finis concilii* of 3 January 1966 Paul VI established that the Secretariat would remain with the same personnel as a permanent organism of the Roman Curia with the principal task of promoting the application of the ecumenical aspects of the Second Vatican Council. With the Apostolic Constitution *Regimini ecclesiae universae*

the Ecumenical Directory. The Directory was organised in two parts. This initiative proved to be very useful, both for formation at the basic level and for the practical guidelines. Its publication had been envisaged during the Council, and was necessary not only from the point of view of practical guidelines but also to gather together the ecumenical perspectives of various conciliar documents.

In *Unitatis redintegratio*, the Second Vatican Council made an appeal to all Catholics to participate in the search for the full unity of Christians. It asks them to participate "skilfully" *(sollerter)*.

> "Today (1964), in many parts of the world, under the inspiring grace of the Holy Spirit, multiple efforts are being expended through prayer, word, and action to attain that fullness of unity which Jesus Christ desires. This sacred Synod, therefore, exhorts all the Catholic faithful to recognize the signs of the times and to participate skilfully in the work of ecumenism *(operi oecumenico)*".[7]

After explaining what is meant by 'ecumenical movement' *(motus oecumenicus)* it outlines those initiatives "started and organized for the fostering of unity among Christians". The Decree does not provide a comprehensive programme, but offers suggestions for embarking upon relations that had never been undertaken in the past. Other aspects emerge throughout the Decree.

(1967) Paul VI reorganised the Roman Curia, but confirmed the role and structure of the Secretariat. The new reform of the Roman Curia – undertaken by John Paul II following the publication of the new Code of Canon Law and contained in the Constitution *Pastor bonus* (1989) – confirmed the organism of the Roman Curia for ecumenical issues, with the same structure and same operative means. With the exception of a new name, *Pontificium Consilium ad Unitatem Christianorum Fovendam.*

7. *Unitatis redintegratio (UR),* 4.

i) Firstly, a call is made within the Catholic Church to eliminate all depictions that do not reflect "with truth and fairness" the condition of other Christians. "In ecumenical work, Catholics must assuredly be concerned for their separated brethren ... making the first approaches to them" (*UR*, 4).

ii) Further on, and more explicitly, the Decree calls for the renewal of the pilgrim Church and the "continual reformation of which she always has need, insofar as she is an institution of men here on earth ... in conduct, in Church discipline or even the formulation of doctrine" (*UR*, 6).

iii) Therefore, in an active way "Catholics must joyfully acknowledge and esteem the truly Christian endowments from our common heritage which are to be found among our separated brethren" (*UR*, 4).

iv) Furthermore, there must be a recognition of the richness of Christ and the virtuous actions in the life of other Christians "who are bearing witness to Christ, sometimes even to the shedding of their blood" (*UR*, 4).

v) In an even more active way, the Decree affirms: "Nor *(Neque)* should we forget that whatever is wrought by the grace of the Holy Spirit in the hearts of our separated *(sejuncti)* brethren can contribute to our own edification" (*UR*, 4).

vi) The ecumenical movement embraces the theme of dialogue, which is mentioned at this point of the Decree, but expanded upon in the third chapter.

vii) In the part that is of relevance to the application of the Decree in the Catholic Church, as well as renewal mention is made of themes of singular importance for the exercise of ecumenism and for Christian life itself, such as interior conversion, unity in prayer and joint prayer, and ecumenical formation.

viii) Lastly, the Decree touches upon an important aspect: "The manner and order in which Catholic belief is expressed should in no way become an obstacle to dialogue with our brethren" (*UR*, 11). And this is relevant within the Catholic Church itself, that is, in the exposition of Catholic doctrine and discipline. "Catholic belief — the Decree states — needs to be explained more profoundly and precisely, in ways and in terminology which our separated *(sejuncti)* brethren too *(etiam)* can really understand" *(ibid.)*.

ix) All this merges in numbers 2-3 of the Decree on the unity and uniqueness of the Church (*UR*, 2) and the relations with other Christians (*UR*, 3). An understanding of the Catholic principles of ecumenism is indispensable in order to participate authentically and faithfully in the search for full unity.

x) This offered the basis for a solid formation in *ecumenical spirituality* and for a correct starting point for the dialogue with other Churches and Ecclesial Communities.

While *Unitatis redintegratio* may well be considered the ecumenical Magna Charta of the Catholic Church, the Council also provided instructions in other documents. The search for unity involves diverse aspects. Consequently, from the point of view of the theological and pastoral reception of the ecumenical guidelines of the Second Vatican Council, consideration was given in the Directory to nearly all the documents of the Council, particularly the Dogmatic Constitution on the Church, *Lumen gentium*; on Revelation, *Dei verbum;* on the relationship between Church and world, *Gaudium et spes;* the Decree on the Catholic Eastern Churches, *Orientalium ecclesiarum;* the Decree on missions, *Ad gentes;* and the Declaration on religious freedom, *Dignitatis humanae.*

This inclusive criteria emerges from the very title of the first part of the document *Ad totam ecclesiam (Directory for the Application of the Decisions of the Second Ecumenical Council of the Vatican Concerning Ecumenical Matters)*[8] and not merely from the Decree on Ecumenism. This was explicitly affirmed in the introduction to the Directory: "The Ecumenical Directory is being published to encourage and guide this concern for unity, so that what was promulgated in this field by the decrees of the Second Vatican Council may be better put into practice throughout the Catholic Church".[9]

---

8. *Acta Apostolicae Sedis [AAS]* 59 (1967) pp.574-592; also published in *Information Service*, N.2, 1967/II, pp.5-12. The Directory of 14 May 1967 is signed by Cardinal Augustin Bea, President of the SPCU, and by Bishop Johannes Willebrands, Secretary. As a conclusion, the document contains the following approval: "In an audience granted to the Secretariat for Promoting Christian Unity, April 28, 1967, the Sovereign Pontiff, Paul VI, approved this Directory, confirmed it by his authority and ordered that it be published. Anything to the contrary notwithstanding". This is important because it provided new guidelines "anything to the contrary notwithstanding" with respect to the past, particularly concerning *communicatio in sacris.*

9. *Ibid.*

b) First part of the 1967 Directory

The first part of the four-chapter *Directory* responded to a number of concrete and immediate urgent situations such as:

- *The creation of diocesan and national ecumenical commissions* (nn.3-8). These commissions were progresively created, forming an efficient network for action on the local level. John Paul II has expressed this positively in his remark: "These initiatives are a sign of the widespread practical commitment of the Catholic Church to apply the Council's guidelines on ecumenism: this is an essential aspect of the ecumenical movement".[10] The SPCU promoted intermittent international meetings of the presidents and secretaries of the ecumenical commissions of the Synods of the Eastern Churches and the Episcopal Conferences in order to provide a forum for exchange and to coordinate the promotion of Christian unity. The meetings prior to the present one were held in 1967, 1972, 1979, 1985 and 1993.[11]

- *The validity of baptism administered by ministers of the other Churches and Ecclesial Communities (9–20).* Consideration of this still open theme was initiated. It was affirmed: "Baptism is, then, the sacramental bond of unity, indeed the foundation of communion among all Christians. Hence its dignity and the manner of administering it are matters of great importance to all Christ's disciples" (n.11). The Directory offered guidelines for "a just evaluation of

---

10. John Paul II, Encyclical letter *Ut unum sint (UUS)*, 31.
11. Cf. Pontifical Council for Promoting Christian Unity, *Information Service*, N.84, 1993/III-IV, pp.117–136.

the sacrament and the mutual recognition of each other's baptisms by different Communities". The criteria of the Catholic Church for the recognition of the validity of baptism administered by other Christians were outlined. Recently, the Pontifical Council for Promoting Christian Unity took up this issue again and made an inquiry into the agreements between the Churches on baptism. The results of this inquiry were discussed in the 2001 Plenary Session.

– *Spiritual ecumenism in the Catholic Church (nn.21–24)*
  a) conforming all Christian life to the spirit of the Gospel (n.21);
  b) strengthening the prayer for unity in the Catholic Church (n.22).

– *The sharing of spiritual activity with separated brothers (nn.25–63).* The following guideline was given: "Fraternal charity in the relations of daily life is not enough to foster the restoration of unity among Christians. It is right and proper that there should also be allowed a certain *'communicatio in spiritualibus'* — i.e., Christians should be able to share that spiritual heritage they have in common, in a manner and to a degree permissible and appropriate in their present divided state" (n.25) The chapter comprised two parts:
  a) common prayers (nn.32–37),
  b) sharing of spiritual activity *(Communicatio in sacris)* comprised a further two sections, namely sharing of spiritual activity with Eastern Orthodox brothers (nn.39–54) and with other separated brothers, that is, protestants (nn.55–63).

i) *Communicatio in sacris and ecclesial communion*

The guidelines of the Directory have promoted local contact among Christians, common prayer — not without some incertitude — partial *communicatio in sacris,* albeit with some tension and transgressions, and practical collaboration. This has all lead to a greater mutual understanding, which is an essential feature for true progress and for the growing life of ecclesial communion.

In the immediate post–conciliar period, ecumenical reflection within the Catholic Church was characterised by an invariable reference to the Council and its decisions. The fundamental question was the understanding of the mystery of the Church and the relationship between Catholic Church and the other Churches and Ecclesial communions in relation to the interpretation of the *subsistit in* of n.8 of *Lumen gentium.*

This clarification of the Second Vatican Council led to thought on the quality and level of relations with other Christians, the regulations on *communicatio in sacris,* and the ecumenical stance in pastoral care. The recognition of the ecclesial dimension of the other Christian communities and the distinction between Orthodox Churches and the communions originating in the Reformation, due to the diversity of degree of communion and vice versa of doctrinal divergence, became the forum for theological dialogue, pastoral action, and the possibilities and limitations of cooperation.[12]

The emerging theological framework that has increasingly become a feature of ecumenical relations is the the-

---

12. Cf. G. Thils, *L'Eglise et les Eglises, Perspectives nouvelles en oecuménisme* (Bruges: Desclée De Brouwever, 1966); F. A. Sullivan, " 'Sussiste' la Chiesa di Cristo nella Chiesa cattolica romana?" in *Vaticano II – Bilancio e Prospettive, venticinque anni dopo, 1962-1987,* René Latourelle (ed.), (Assisi: Cittadella Editrice, 1987), Vol. II, pp.811-824.

ology of communion. The *Relatio finalis* of the Extraordinary Synod of Bishops in 1985, twenty years after the Second Vatican Council, stated that *"the ecclesiology of communion is the central and fundamental idea of the conciliar documents"* (C,1). The ongoing relations with other Christians finds its place within this perspective.[13]

The *partial and imperfect,* yet authentic, communion existing among Christians,[14] differentiated among the various Churches and Ecclesial communions,[15] tends through the ecumenical movement (contacts, theological dialogue, common prayer, cooperation) towards *full* communion. This perspective delineated by the Council has been progressively received both in the theological dialogue and in the disciplinary norms.[16]

The SPCU enabled the Catholic Church to undertake various initiatives such as the publication of guidelines and their response within the Roman Curia, given that ecumenism involves various aspects of the life of the Church.

In the 1970s one question polarised the attention of Christians and created real tension among the Churches, namely the question of *communicatio in sacris* or of *intercom-*

---

13. The Congregation of the Doctrine of the Faith intervened on the theme of communion by issuing a number of clarifications in 1992, cf. Congregation for the Doctrine of the Faith, *Communionis notio,* Letter to the Bishops of the Catholic Church on Some Aspects of the Church Understood as Communion (28 May 1992): *AAS* 85 (1993), 838.
14. Cf. *UR,* 3.
15. Cf. *UR,* 14-18 for the Eastern Churches; *UR,* 19-23 for the separated Western Churches and Ecclesial Communities.
16. *UR,* 3: "For men who believe in Christ and have been properly baptized are brought into a certain, though imperfect, communion with the Catholic Church". However, "the differences that exist in varying degrees between them and the Catholic Church ... do indeed create many and sometimes serious obstacles to full ecclesiastical communion".

munion (as it was then known) or 'eucharistic hospitality'. The SPCU intervened in many ways, in particular with three documents:

- Declaration (7 January 1970) on the position of the Catholic Church on the shared eucharist among Christians of different confessions;[17]
- Instruction (1 June 1972) on particular circumstances of admission of other Christians to the eucharist in the Catholic Church;[18]
- Note (17 October 1973) on some interpretations of the 'Instruction' (1 June 1972) on particular circumstances of admission of other Christians to the eucharist in the Catholic Church.[19]

This rapid succession of documents on the same theme highlights the underlying pastoral, theological and disciplinary problem, and also discloses the passion that the debate instigated. The question, which is substantially clear enough from the Catholic point of view, remains open in relations with other Christians who have different theologies and practices. Nonetheless, these documents have offered a useful theological and pastoral aid.

17. *AAS* 62 (1970) p.184.
18. *AAS* 64 (1972) pp.518-525.
19. *AAS* 65 (1973) pp.616-619.

ii) Prayer for unity and the World Council of Churches

An initiative of the SPCU that has continued uninter-
ruptedly over time, namely the promotion of prayer for the
unity of Christians, should be borne in mind when implementing the guidelines of the Second Vatican Council.

Beyond the guidelines given in the Ecumenical Directory (1967), the SPCU initiated a close collaboration with
the World Council of Churches (WCC) to jointly prepare
and disseminate the prayer for the unity of Christians. This
prayer forms part of the core that the Decree on Ecumenism
defines as the 'soul' of the entire ecumenical movement
(*UR*, 8). However, there has been a slow and steadfast
effort for its reception and realisation. Collaboration with
the WCC in this sphere has been truly fruitful.

1.   A Joint Working Group was established with the
WCC in 1965. From its very first meeting, the group "felt
the need to establish a certain number of principles for
common prayer". The question of "to what degree an agreement could be reached" between the Catholic Church and
the WCC was also evaluated. In this perspective, the SPCU
undertook to clarify within the Catholic Church the status
of collaboration with the WCC. Consultation took place
with Catholic centres of varying types involved in ecumenism and the prayer for unity. For the sake of convenience,
these varying types could be summarised into two major
categories, namely that adhering to Father Paul Wattson
and the other to Abbé Paul Couturier. The meeting was
held in Lyon (13–16 October 1966) and was attended by
15 Catholic experts. An agreement was reached in line with
the guidelines of the Second Vatican Council. The following pledge was made:

"The representatives of the different Catholic organisations dealing in ecumenism, meeting in Lyon on the invitation of H.E. Msgr Willebrands, have expressed the desire to establish a joint working group, under the patronage of the Secretariat for Unity, in order to promote, in the post–conciliar period, the expansion of the prayer for the unity of Christians and the development of spiritual ecumenism in different forms".

The consultation observed that "today spiritual ecumenism has emerged as essential not only for the unity and renewal of Christianity, but also for the progress and advancement of the whole of humanity". There was consensus to establish an agreement with the WCC. The meeting with 15 representatives of the WCC took place immediately after in Geneva (16–20 October) on the theme: *The Future of the Week of Prayer for Unity.* A report of the consultation was forwarded to the Joint Working Group, which in its second report made public (1967) summarised and confirmed the conclusions thus:

a)   A group will be created comprising representatives of the Faith and Order Commission and of the Roman Catholic centres operating in this field;

b)   This group will principally be responsible for preparing on an annual basis the booklet for the Week of Prayer; this booklet will be made available to the Churches and Councils of Churches;

c)   The Churches in the various countries will be invited to adapt the text of the booklet to their own needs. However, this adaptation must be undertaken, whenever possible, in ecumenical cooperation.

d) The Week need not be celebrated on the same date in all countries. While the majority will prefer 18–25 January, some countries (for different reasons) have chosen other dates (namely the period between the Ascension and Pentecost). Neither of these dates need be considered mandatory, but it would be important for all the Churches in the same country to observe the Week of Prayer on the same date.

The agreement became immediately operative. In February 1967 a joint committee of representatives of the WCC and the Catholic Church met in Geneva in order to prepare together for the first time the booklet for 1968 with the theme *To the praise of his glory (Eph 1:14).* Since then the booklets for the annual prayer for Christian unity have always been prepared together.

2. In 1972, the WCC and the SPCU jointly made an inquiry throughout the world on the progress of the Week of Prayer for Christian unity. Positive comments and proposals emerged. The reply to the question *"In what year did the Week of Prayer for Christian Unity commence in your country?"*is particularly relevant: 1908 = 1; from 1920 to 1930 in 7 countries; from 1930 to 1940 in 10 countries; from 1940 to 1950 in 13 countries; from 1950 to 1960 in 27 countries; from 1960 to 1970 in 77 countries; from 1970 to 1971 in 5 countries. The greatest increase occurred between 1960 and 1970, that is, the years of the Second Vatican Council and the agreement with the World Council of Churches.

After evaluating the overall results of the inquiry, a change was made to the workings of the joint committee preparing the prayer. This committee had expanded to the point that it was difficult to work efficiently. At the same time, there was a request that the text be relevant in the real world. Indeed, drawing the members of the committee from representatives of study centres ran the risk of remaining at the abstract level. A decision was made to reduce the number of participants to five for each part. Conversely, it was decided that a local ecumenical group from a different country each year be asked to present a first draft on a theme to be developed together (local group, WCC, Catholic Church) with a view to reflecting a range of issues and forms of expression. There remained nonetheless the request that ultimately each country would adapt the text to its own context, taking into consideration the diversity of liturgical traditions. This framework proved to be fruitful, and it substantially continues to be used to this day with a permanent impact on Christians.

3. There sometimes is an impression that in various places the prayer for unity has become lukewarm. The documentation received by the Pontifical Council for Promoting Christian Unity reveals that the Week of Prayer in its variegated forms has become a permanent ecumenical appointment. It also reveals that if in some parts of a given country there tends to be a sort of apathy, in other parts it is introduced as an innovation. Already in the inquiry held in 1972 it emerged that the prayer for unity was strictly related to the place of prayer in general in a given community and was responsive to the local ecumenical situation.

The fact that the texts are prepared together by the WCC and the Catholic Church and forwarded to member Churches of the WCC and by the Catholic side to the Ecumenical Commissions of the Synods of Eastern Catholic Churches and the Episcopal Conferences throughout the world, has meant that it has had the sort of distribution it would not otherwise have had.

The annual joint mailing throughout the world of the common text by the SPCU and the Faith and Order Commission of the WCC constitutes a *permanent anamnesis,* the most constant plea for the re-establishment of the unity of Christians.

A new initiative has been undertaken for the forthcoming year, namely not simply to prepare the text together but also to undertake *joint publishing* so that this collaboration may be immediately visible. The Secretary of the PCPCU and the Secretary of the WCC in the joint foreword to the 2005 booklet on the theme *"Christ, the one foundation of the Church" (1 Cor 3:1–23)* speak of "the birth of a new era of collaboration ... a further, small step in the direction of Christian unity". This symbolic initiative cannot but affirm the value of collaboration with the WCC in this field.

c) Second part of the Directory (1970)

Successively (16 April 1970) the SPCU published the second part of the Ecumenical Directory on the crucial issue of *Ecumenism in Higher Education.*[20] This issue was carefully prepared with the twofold purpose of promoting ecumenical research and avoiding hasty digressions and solutions. The introduction to this document affirmed: "All Christians should be of an ecumenical mind, but especially those entrusted with particular duties and responsibilities in the world and in society; hence the principles of ecumenism

---

20. *AAS* 62 (1970) pp.705-724. The document "despite anything to the contrary" was approved by the Holy Father in the audience of 16 April 1970. The text is signed by Cardinal Johannes Willebrands and the Secretary, Father Jerome Hamer, OP.

sanctioned by the Second Vatican Council should be appropriately introduced in all institutions of advanced learning (n.1).[21]

The document comprises the following chapters:

- General principles and aids to ecumenical education;
- The ecumenical dimension of religious and theological education;
- Particular guidelines for ecumenical education;
- Institutional and personal cooperation between Catholics and other Christians.

The document provided a useful guide to promoting unity. It has remained relevant due to the fact that the ecumenical perspective has been increasingly important in theological research, curriculum planning, and ecumenical practice, particularly where Catholics and other Christians live side by side with ensuing daily pastoral problems.

d) Ecumenism in the two Codes of Canon Law

The reception of the ecumenical aspects of the Second Vatican Council has taken place in a number of *key situations* that will have a positive influence in the future. The PCPCU has paid constant attention to ensuring that the guidelines on ecumenism be introduced into the norms of the Catholic Church. It should be simply noted, and indeed it is well–known, that the ecumenical perspective has been incorporated into the Code of Canon Law (CCL) for the Latin Church as well as into the Code of Canons of the Eastern Churches (CCEC).

---

21. 'Institutes of higher education' are understood in this document to be university faculties, academic institutes, seminaries for diocesan clergy, institutes, centres and houses for the formation of religious, excluding high schools and secondary education.

The two codes of canon law contain an analogous norm that stipulates that the promotion of Christian unity must be a priority for the college of bishops, for the Holy See and for every individual bishop. Canon 755 of the CCL affirms:

> §1. It is above all for the entire college of bishops and the Apostolic See to foster and direct among Catholics the ecumenical movement whose purpose is the restoration among all Christians of the unity which the Church is bound to promote by the will of Christ.
>
> §2. It is likewise for the bishops and, according to the norm of law, the conferences of bishops to promote this same unity and to impart practical norms according to the various needs and opportunities of the circumstances; they are to be attentive to the prescripts issued by the supreme authority of the Church".

A similar commitment emerges in the CCEC (canons 902-904). To the best of my knowledge, I am not aware that any other Church has introduced the ecumenical commitment in the form of a canonical norm. The two codes of canon law not only provide general instructions on the pastoral commitment, but also introduce in their various chapters the ecumenical aspects relating to specific issues: validity of baptism, *communicatio in sacris,* mixed marriages, use of places of worship, cooperation. We are dealing with the progressive reception of a fundamental tenet according to which the Catholic Church is not completely separated from other Christians, and that together they undertake the search for full unity. The existing partial communion, albeit imperfect, is authentic and the partial communion of sacramental life is based upon it.

e) Ecumenism in the Catechism of the Catholic Church

The PCPCU has given equal importance to the ecumenical dimension in the Catechism of the Catholic Church (CCC). This text incorporates the ecumenical impetus of the Second Vatican Council, but also includes new elements that have emerged subsequently, incorporating them in various parts of the text where relevant. In presenting it, John Paul II affirmed that the catechism, among other things, "is meant to support ecumenical efforts that are moved by the holy desire for the unity of all Christians, showing carefully the content and the wondrous harmony of the Catholic faith".[22] The catechism, therefore, also has the promotion of Christian unity in its sight. On the one hand, the text, founded on the principle of the 'hierarchy of truths', serves not only to present coherently the Catholic faith, but also facilitates an understanding of other Christians in dialogue with the Catholic Church. On the other hand, the support offered by the catechism to ecumenical efforts is clear in the crucial points of the text introducing elements of communion with other Christians.

A number of priorities could be outlined. When the catechism speaks of the profession of the Christian faith it gives the Nicene–Constantinopolitan symbol and affirms: "It remains common to all the great Churches of both East and West to this day". This constitutes the foundation of the existing communion among Christians. Catholics are brothers in faith with other Christians because, despite different interpretations, they affirm the same profession of

---

22. Apostolic Constitution *Fidei depositum* for the publication of the Catechism of the Catholic Church, prepared after the Second Vatican Council, in *Catechism of the Catholic Church*, (Vatican City: Libreria Editrice Vaticana 1992), p.14.

faith. And while communion is only partial, it is not merely of a sentimental kind, but has sacramental bonds: "Baptism constitutes the foundation of communion among all Christians, including those who are not yet in full communion with the Catholic Church."[23] This is the reception of the teaching of the Second Vatican Council, according to which "Baptism ... constitutes a sacramental bond of unity linking all who have been reborn by means of it".[24]

Within this framework, the catechism draws attention to ecumenical aspects by inserting them appropriately in line with the content of the text. This is at once both an original and realistic methodology. Ecumenism is not presented as an added chapter, but as a dimension inherent in the overall picture. When it is mentioned, what we have in common with other Christians and what still divides us becomes evident.

In conclusion, it could be said that the CCC constitutes a key moment in the reception of the ecumenical perspective of the Second Vatican Council in the reality of the Catholic Church. Not only. Given that it deals with the application within a living organism of a movement in constant evolution, the CCC also incorporates the developments that have subsequently taken place in the ecumenical movement. From the overall ecumenical vision, the CCC features various interconnected aspects: theological principles, liturgical repercussions, regulation of participation — both possibilities and limitations — in the sacraments, and ethical implications. The CCC is a crossroads where one can gain one's bearing on the reception of the Second Vatican Council.

23. *Catechism of the Catholic Church* (CCC), 1271.
24. Cf. *UR*, 22.

f) Updated and extended edition of the Ecumenical Directory

According to John Paul II, the Ecumenical Directory was a precious instrument for guiding, coordinating and developing the ecumenical effort".[25] In the meantime the ecumenical movement had widened itself and had confronted new issues. Among other documents, the SPCU published:

- Reflections and suggestions on the ecumenical dialogue;[26]
- Ecumenical collaboration at the national and local levels.[27]

Documents covering ecumenical themes were issued by other authorities:

- Apostolic Exhortation *Evangeli nuntiandi* of 1975;[28]
- Apostolic Exhortation *Catechesi tradendae* of 1979;[29]
- Apostolic Constitution *Sapientia christiana* on ecclesiastical universities and faculties of 1979;[30]
- *Ratio fundamentalis institutionis sacerdotalis* of the Congregation for Catholic Education in 1970;[31]
- Apostolic Constitution *Ex corde ecclesiae* of 1990.[32]

Together with the two Codes and the CCC, these documents offered material for an overall approach to the ecumenical commitment. Against this background, the PCPCU prepared, in consultation with the Episcopal Conferences and other offices of the Roman Curia, the new edition of the Ecumenical Directory, recalling the title of

---

25. *AAS* LXXX (1988) p.1203.
26. SPCU, *Information Service*, 12, 1970/IV, pp.3-11.
27. SPCU, *Information Service*, 26, 1975/I, pp.8-31.
28. *AAS* LXVIII (1976) pp.5-76.
29. *AAS* LXXI (1979), pp.1277-1340.
30. *AAS* LXXI (1979) pp.469-499.
31. *AAS* LXII (1970) pp.321-384.
32. *AAS* LXXXII (1990) pp.1475-1509.

the 1967 publication: *Directory for the Application of Principles and Norms on Ecumenism* (1993).[33] The Directory was followed by the publication of *The Ecumenical Dimension in the Formation of Those Engaged in Pastoral Work* (1997).

The new Directory was arranged in five chapters presenting an organic overview of the ecumenical commitment in its principles and application:

1. The search for Christian unity;
2. The organization in the Catholic Church of the service of Christian unity;
3. Ecumenical formation in the Catholic Church;
4. Communion of life and spiritual activity among the baptised;
5. Ecumenical cooperation, dialogue and common witness.

This new edition of the Directory, extended and updated on the basis of extensive experience, highlighted in particular the theological principles of ecumenism.[34] The new Directory dedicates a chapter to this theme. Indeed, the reception of principles underlying the entire ecumenical search is the most important aspect of the implementation of the Second Vatican Council regarding ecumenism. Whenever this process has not taken place, ecumenism has not been understood and has been misunderstood.

---

33. *AAS* LXXV (1993) pp.1039-1119.
34. *L'Osservatore Romano*, 9 June 1993. For the origin, preparation, structure and content of the Directory, cf. E. F. Fortino, "Nuovo direttorio ecumenico della Chiesa Cattolica" in *Oriente Cristiano*, 2/1993, pp.74-88; idem, "Principi cattolici sull'ecumenismo nel Direttorio Ecumenico" in *Presenza Pastorale*, 11/1993, pp.35-47.

II. Relations and Theological Dialogue with Other Churches and Ecclesial Communities

The crucial ecumenical issue is the relationship with other Christians from the point of view of discussing together matters of divergence and of fostering the growth towards full communion. Establishing relations and dialogue with the other Churches and Ecclesial Communities has been the second task of the PCPCU. It committed itself to this end before the Council by inviting observers, and during it through its work as a Conciliar Commission. After the Council, its abiding concern has been the organisation of theological dialogue.

a) World Council of Churches

The Joint Working Group between the Catholic Church and the World Council of Churches (JWG) was established as far back as 1965. On 18 February 1965,[35] Cardinal Augustin Bea announced in Geneva the establishment of the first working group comprising six members each. The Central Committee of the WCC had approved this initiative in a meeting at Enugu from 12–21 January 1965.[36] It has been an important mediator with the member Churches of the WCC. The Catholic Church, which has never been a member of the WCC, has collaborated regularly through the JWG in various fields. From 1968, twelve Catholic theologians, appointed on the basis of their expertise, yet fully bearing in mind the authority of the Catholic Church, have been full members of the Faith and Order Commission, which is the doctrinal division of the WCC. This Commission has published various documents in collabora-

---

35. Cf. *Information Service*, 3, 1967/III, p.3.
36. Cf. *Ecumenical Review* 17, 1965, pp.171-173.

tion with Catholic theologians. The most well–known is
Baptism, Eucharist and Ministry (BEM).

The JWG has continued its work over the years, and still
coordinates collaboration both in the study phase and in
common action. The publication of three documents currently in their final stage is envisaged for next year:
  – Ecclesiological and ecumenical implications of com-
    mon baptism;
  – Nature and scope of ecumenical dialogue;
  – Inspired by the same vision: Catholic participation
    in national and regional councils of churches.

b) Bilateral dialogues

After outlining the need for dialogue[37] and providing
some essential features in terms of application,[38] the Decree
on Ecumenism pointed in two important directions: the
dialogue with the Orthodox Churches[39] and that with the
Protestants.[40] In fact, in compliance with Conciliar guidelines, relations were established with all the Churches and
world Christian Communions, both of the East and West.
These relations have developed in two forms: the so–called
dialogue of charity and the *theological dialogue*.

The first aspect tended towards creating possibilities for
the theological dialogue. It was difficult to imagine an immediate dialogue with many Churches: the prejudice, misunderstanding, and reservation were such that a free and
trustful dialogue was impossible. Moreover, the political
situation was not favourable given that Eastern Europe was
under communist regime.

---

37. *UR*, 4.
38. *UR*, 11.
39. *UR*, 14-18.
40. *UR*, 19-23.

What was possible and indeed constructive was the establishment of fraternal relations, particularly in given circumstances such as visits for particular feasts in the individual Churches, solidarity in times of disaster, hospitality for study and research, etc. These relations continue to improve mutual understanding among Christians. It has only been successively that theological discussion has been possible with the general aim — albeit in differing stages and time frames — of attaining full unity.[41]

The Catholic Church has entered into bilateral dialogues in the following chronological order:

Anglican Communion (1966)
Lutheran World Federation (1967)
World Methodist Council (1967)
World Alliance of Reformed Churches (1970)
Pentecostal communities and leaders (1972)
Coptic Orthodox Church (1973)
Disciples of Christ (1977)
World Evangelical Alliance (commenced in 1977 with Evangelical–Roman Catholic Dialogue on Mission)
Orthodox Churches as a whole (1980)
Baptist World Alliance (1984)
Syrian Church of India (1989)
Mennonite World Conference (1998)
Ancient Churches of the East (2003)
Old Catholic Church (2004)

With regard to the proposed dialogue with the Orthodox Churches, *Unitatis redintegratio* had specified the need to study "the relations which obtained between them and the Roman See before the separation" and highlighted that if a

---

41. The Plenary Session of the Pontifical Council for Promoting Christian Unity in 1998 reflected upon the ongoing dialogues, cf. *Information Service*, N.98, 1998/III, pp.104–154.

"correct evaluation" was made and if these recommendations were "carefully carried out" with regard also to the
origin and development of these Churches, they would make
a very great contribution to the proposed dialogue itself.[42]

With regard to communions issuing from the Reformation, the Decree observed that at the time of the Reformation many serious doctrinal differences had emerged with
regard to the Church, its sacraments, ordained ministry and
apostolic succession. The Council specified that these issues
must be the object of dialogue.[43]

The SPCU firstly, and the PCPCU later, investigated the
feasibility of dialogue, and discussed its means and forms.
Within a common general framework — the spirit of reconciliation in Christ — each of these dialogues has taken on
individual characteristics. Each confronts in its own order of
priority those issues which directly come between the individual communions and the Catholic Church. Another element, at once methodological and theological, is a common feature in the various dialogues: at the commencement
of dialogue *a common basis is established on the shared features* of
the Catholic Church and the individual Christian communion, moving later to the *discussion on differences.*

The specific aim of each dialogue also varies. Some tend
towards the re–establishment of full communion, others
aim at intermediate stages such as mutual recognition or
the evangelical commitment and the elimination of inap-
propriate forms of proselytism. From the Catholic point of
view, it is clear that the range of dialogues taken together
should move ultimately towards a unity of faith, sacramental life and ministerial communion.

---

42. Cf. *UR*, 14.
43. Cf. *UR*, 19.

The various dialogues are undertaken between the Catholic Church and other Churches, for example, the Orthodox Church, or the Coptic or Syrian Church; or between the Catholic Church and another 'Communion', 'Alliance,' 'Federation', or 'Council'. The latter terminology respects the reality of our interlocutors, yet also highlights the underlying ecclesiological issue. The range of bilateral dialogues, each with its own characteristics in terms of issues and short–term objectives, has produced a variety of outcomes.

i) Relations with the Orthodox Churches

Relations with the Orthodox Churches are complex, although they constitute an essential feature of the entire ecumenical movement. The testimony of these Churches is inestimable, reflecting as it does the wide–ranging extent of the Christian patrimony, and will offer a distinctive dynamism to full ecclesial communion. The Orthodox Church as a whole comprises 15 autocephalous and autonomous Churches united by the same faith and the same fundamental laws. Nonetheless, each governs itself autonomously and each, clearly, has its own distinctive internal problems. All 15 Orthodox Churches participate in the joint theological dialogue.

However, there are a number of Orthodox groupings with their own hierarchies that are not included in the 15 canonical Churches and that are not even involved in the preparation of the Council of the Orthodox Churches, such as the Church of the ex–Republic of Macedonia, the Orthodox Church in America, the so–called Russian Church outside the boundaries.

Depending on specific circumstances, the internal situation of the individual Churches and the relations between themselves can either facilitate or impede overall relations between the Orthodox Church and the Catholic Church.

In order to establish relations with each of these Churches, the SPCU developed from the time of the Council onwards a network of contacts in various contexts that made it possible to organise the dialogue through one joint commission (1979). Within this perspective we can call to mind the visits of the President of the SPCU to various Churches; participation in feasts, ecclesial celebrations, and other cultural events; as well as the welcome in Rome of delegations of the various Orthodox Churches. The Catholic Committee for Cultural Collaboration has made a precious contribution in this way.

Thus, relations with Orthodoxy progress along two paths, *the theological dialogue* between the Catholic Church and the Orthodox Church as a whole, and *the dialogue of charity* with the individual autocephalous and autonomous Churches. The two paths are fundamentally convergent, although not always concurrent.

After a substantial period of relations with the individual Churches, on the 10th anniversary (1975) of the ecclesial act condemning the excommunications of 1054, the SPCU and the Ecumenical Patriarchate were able to evaluate how best to initiate theological dialogue. In 1978 a joint committee was able to agree on a *Plan to set underway the theological dialogue between the Roman Catholic Church and the Orthodox Church.*[44] The commencement of the dialogue

---

44. Cf. E. F. Fortino, "Impostazione del dialogo teologico tra la Chiesa cattolica e la Chiesa ortodossa" in *Divinarum rerum notizia – La teologia tra filosofia e storia, Studi in onore di Cardinale Walter Kasper,* Antonio Russo and Gianfranco Coffele (ed.), (Rome: Studium, 2001).

was announced during the visit of the Holy Father John Paul II to the Ecumenical Patriarchate in 1979.

The theological dialogue that commenced in 1980 (Patmos – Rhodes) produced four documents of convergence:[45]

a) *The mystery of the Church and of the Eucharist in the light of the mystery of the Holy Trinity (Munich, Germany, 1982);*[46]

b) *Faith, sacraments and unity of the Church (Bari, Italy, 1987);*[47]

c) *The sacrament of order in the sacramental structure of the Church with particular reference to the importance of apostolic succession for the sanctification and unity of the people of God (Valamo, Finland, 1988);*[48]

d) *Uniatism, method of union of the past, and the present search for full communion (Balamand, Lebanon, 1993).*[49]

For some years now, old wounds and new difficulties have hindered the theological dialogue. The reorganisation of the Catholic Eastern Churches suppressed during the communist regime has created new tensions with some Orthodox Churches, particularly in the Ukraine.

At its last plenary session (Baltimore, July 2000), the Joint Mixed Commission was not able to agree upon any document on the planned theme of *Theological and Canonical Implications of Uniatism*. Nonetheless, it was able to affirm

---

45. The four documents can be found in *The Quest for Unity, Orthodox and Catholics in Dialogue*, John Borelli and John H. Erickson (ed.), (Crestwood: St Vladmir's Seminary Press, 1996).
46. *Information Service*, 49, 1982/II-III, pp.107–111.
47. *Information Service*, 64, 1987/III, pp.82–87.
48. *Information Service*, 68, 1988/III-IV, pp.173–178.
49. *Information Service*, 83, 1993/II, pp.96–99.

that the dialogue must continue and, at the same time, to declare that the members of the Commission must clarify with their respective authorities on how to 'proceed' in the future.

The PCPCU has intensified relations with individual Churches, and new possibilities in relations have emerged with different Orthodox Churches which had been fairly reticent in the past – for example, the Church of Greece, the Patriarchate of Serbia, but also the Patriarchates of Bulgaria and Romania. An important symbolic gesture was made in Romania, namely in Cluj, where four theological faculties (Orthodox, Greek Catholic, Latin and Protestant) together conferred a doctorate *in honoris causa* to the President of the PCPCU. Albeit slowly and with difficulty, the joint commission in Romania between the Romanian Patriarchate and the Greek Catholic Church continues its work.

After a period of significant tension, the Russian Orthodox Church has also renewed more fraternal contacts. A local joint commission between the Patriarchate of Moscow and the Russian Catholic Church has been established and has initiated its work, and includes a representative of the PCPCU. In August, the Cardinal President of the PCPCU was delegated by the Holy Father to convey the icon of the Mother of God of Kazan to the Russian Church and to the Russian people.

The PCPCU, together with the Ecumenical Patriarchate, which is responsible for the coordination between the Orthodox Churches in theological dialogue, is currently assessing how to resume the theological dialogue. The joint declaration of Pope John Paul II and Patriarch Bartholomew I concluding the visit of the Patriarch to Rome for the feast of Saints Peter and Paul this year affirmed: "It is our duty to persevere in the important commitment to reopen the work as soon as possible. In examining the reciprocal initiatives of the offices of Rome and of Constantinople with this in view, we ask the Lord to sustain our determination, and to convince everyone of how essential it is to pursue the 'dialogue of truth' *(L'Osservatore Romano, English edition, 7 July 2004).*

The concern about how to resume the dialogue is felt in Rome, Constantinople, Antioch, and Bucharest — as was affirmed on the occasion of the visit of Patriarch Theoctist to Rome (7-14 October 2002) — as well as in other Orthodox churches that also agree upon the need to resume the dialogue. The Holy Father has affirmed that this dialogue "has made substantial progress" (*Ut unum sint,* 59).

Symposium on the Petrine ministry

As mentioned, the fact that the Joint International Commission has not been able to hold a plenary session since July 2000 does not mean that the interval since then has been a 'vacuum'. In its wider significance, the search has continued at various levels, in conferences, doctrinal consultations, in the more silent search in faculties of theology and ecumenical institutes, as well as in the exchange of official visits.

Reflection has continued after the publication of the Encyclical *Ut unum sint* on the desire of the Holy Father to study together, Catholics and Orthodox, the issue of the role of the bishop of Rome in the Church with a view to seeking a form of the exercise of primacy that may be recognised by all concerned and that may render fruitful its inherent service of unity.

The PCPCU organised a Catholic-Orthodox academic symposium (21-24 May 2003) on the very issue of the Petrine ministry. The symposium was attended by a number of theologians, each bringing their own expertise and each invited by their respective Churches. The symposium was attended by 25 participants. Four themes were examined in eight papers, two on each theme, by Catholics and Orthodox respectively. The themes were:

    a)   *The biblical foundation of primacy (Msgr Joachim Gnilka, Catholic; Revd Theodore Stylianopoulos, Orthodox);*

    b)   *Primacy in the Church Fathers (Professor Vlassios Phidas, Orthodox; Revd Vittorino Grossi, OSA, Catholic);*

    c)   *The role of the bishop of Rome in the ecumenical councils (Professor Vittorio Peri, Catholic; Revd Nicolae V. Dura, Orthodox);*

    d)   *Recent discussion on primacy in relation to Vatican I and recent discussions on primacy among Orthodox theologians (Revd Hermann J. Pottmeyer, Catholic; Metropolitan Joannis Zizioulas, Orthodox).*

In order to continue this reflection, the proceedings of the symposium have been published.[50] Translated versions will be available next year.

---

50. *Il ministero Petrino. Cattolici e ortodossi in dialogo,* edited by W. Kasper (Rome: Città Nuova, 2004).

ii) Dialogue with the Ancient Churches of the East or pre–Chalcedonian Churches

Dialogue with these ancient Churches originating from the Council of Ephesus (431), namely the Assyrian Church, known in the past as the Nestorian Church, but also those issuing from the Council of Chalcedon (451) has been undertaken without the mediation of joint commissions, but directly between the PCPCU and the Holy Father and the Patriarchs of the individual Churches. The outcomes have been formulated as joint declarations. With regard to the Assyrian Church — which has in the Catholic Church, from the ethnic and liturgical points of view, a counterpart in the Chaldean Church — there remained open the issue of the conception of *the person of Christ*. Is Jesus Christ, who is the Word of the eternal God and yet a true human born in historical time, a single person, or do two persons co-exist, human and divine, juxtaposed in a voluntary union or conjunction? Can Mary who conceived in her womb and gave birth to Jesus be called the 'Mother of God' *(Theotokos)* or only 'Mother of Christ' *(Christotokos)*? The Holy Father and Patriarch Mar Dinkha were able to declare together (1994) the common faith: "Therefore our Lord Jesus Christ is true God and true man ... His divinity and his humanity are united in one person". Furthermore, "That is the reason why the Assyrian Church of the East is praying the Virgin Mary as 'the Mother of Christ our God and Saviour'. In the light of this same faith the Catholic tradition addresses the Virgin Mary as 'the Mother of God' and also as 'the Mother of Christ'. We both recognize the legitimacy and the rightness of these expressions of the same faith". This Church can no longer be defined Nestorian, that is, inspired by Nestorianism, an heresy affirming that two persons co-existed in

Jesus and condemned by the Council of Ephesus (431). This has been a clear and important outcome of our new ecclesial relations.

The other Ancient Churches of the East, those once called pre-Chalcedonian, affirmed an opposing thesis. Not only did they profess that in Christ only one person existed, but that it was of one nature. The human nature was deified and absorbed by the divine nature. Hence the term monophysite. Dialogue has clarified this issue.

This same problem concerns in one form or another most of these Churches (Coptic, Syrian, Ethiopian, Armenian). Relations with each of these Churches has made it possible for the Pope and the respective Patriarchs to proclaim their common faith in solemn declarations. In these declarations they profess together that Jesus Christ is "Perfect God as to his divinity, perfect man as to his humanity, his divinity is united to his humanity in the Person of the Only–begotten Son of God, in a union which is real, perfect, without confusion, without alteration, without division, without any form of separation" (Declaration with the Supreme Catholicos of the Armenians, Karekin I, 1996).

The Holy Father has summarised it thus: "Ecumenical contacts have thus made possible essential clarifications with regard to the traditional controversies concerning Christology, so much so that we have been able to profess together the faith which we have in common" (*UUS*, 63).

A new step was taken in Rome in January last year (27-29 January 2003). A meeting was held of the *Joint Preparatory Committee between the Catholic Church and the Ancient Churches of the East, or pre-Chalcedonian Churches,* in order to organise a joint commission for dialogue involving all the Ancient Churches. After the bilateral relations with each individually, the step is now being taken to undertake theological dialogue between the Catholic Church and those Churches as a whole. The first meeting of the new joint committee took place in January 2004.[51]

iii) Dialogue with the the other Ecclesial Communities of the West

The Ecclesial Communities issuing from the Reformation cover a wide range and have profound differences among themselves, not only with respect to the Catholic Church; these include the Anglican, Lutheran, Calvinist, and Baptist Communions. The Second Vatican Council had clearly delineated the divergences requiring extensive dialogue: "One should recognize that between these Churches and Communities ... and the Catholic Church ... there are very weighty differences not only of a historical, sociological, psychological, and cultural nature, but especially in the interpretation of revealed truth" (*UR*, 19). These differences relate to questions concerning the Church, to the relationship between Gospel and Church, to Sacred Scripture and the Magisterium, and to the sacraments and the ordained ministry. The differences also touch upon ethical and moral issues. "... in moral matters there are many Christians who do not always understand the gospel in the same way as Catholics" (*UR*, 23).

The PCPCU has entered into bilateral dialogues on these issues in line with programmes drawn up with the individual Ecclesial Communities according to their own priorities.

In his Encyclical on the ecumenical commitment, Pope John Paul II provided a thoughtful assessment on the overall situation of the dialogues: "This dialogue has been and continues to be fruitful and full of promise" (*UUS*, 69). In

---

51. Cf. *L'Osservatore Romano*, 29 January 2003.

order to understand the reach of this affirmation, it needs to be considered in the light of other affirmations. In the same Encyclical, the Pope states: "The Lord has made it possible for Christians in our day to reduce the number of matters traditionally in dispute" (*UUS*, 49).

The discussion in various bilateral dialogues has concentrated on the themes suggested by the Second Vatican Council: for example, baptism, eucharist, ministry, sacramentality, the authority of the Church, apostolic succession, the primacy of the bishop of Rome. All the bilateral dialogues are ongoing.

In particular, two of these dialogues can be brought to mind, namely the dialogue with the Anglican Communion and that with the Lutheran World Federation.

Anglican Communion

The first phase of dialogue with the Anglican Communion concluded with the document entitled *The Final Report* on the themes eucharist, ministry, and authority in the Church (1981) and was followed up with discussion, elucidation, and ultimately by an official stance on the part of the authorities of both the Anglican Communion and the Catholic Church. This led to a critical process of reception, which has been a new element in the history of the dialogues.

Another innovative step was taken recently. The *International Anglican-Roman Catholic Commission for Unity and Mission* was recently established. This is a new type of commission with a specific purpose, namely to gather the outcomes of the dialogue and to introduce them into the respective communities. Comprising mainly bishops, the commission aims at preparing a joint declaration delineating the degree of communion achieved by the dialogue. At the same time, the dialogue process continues its investigation in various fields.

In 2003, relations with the Anglican Communion were complicated by a new problem that has made the dialogue more complex. After the ordination of women in the Episcopalian Church of the USA, a member of the Anglican Communion, a declaredly homosexual person was ordained as a bishop. The case has risked creating a schism among Anglican themselves. At the same time, beyond its doctrinal implication, it also raises within the dialogue a serious ethical problem. The PCPCU has continued to maintain relations in this new and difficult situation.

Lutheran World Federation

The first meeting of the joint dialogue commission took place in 1967 and as shortly after as 1972 it published the document entitled *The Gospel and the Church* that outlined the themes to be dealt with: scripture and tradition, justification, ordained ministry, papacy, and Church and the world. This dialogue has been fruitful.

In particular, it should be noted that as well as the documents published by the joint commission, there has also been the *Joint Declaration on the Doctrine of Justification* (1999). The declaration marks the apex of this dialogue. From the methodological point of view, the joint declaration is a step upwards. While usually the various documents of convergence remain under the authority of the commissions publishing them, the joint declaration, embracing and drawing on the fruits of dialogue, has actually incorporated them in a common declaration between the Catholic Church and the Lutheran World Federation.

The declaration also has practical, canonical and spiritual repercussions. In the annex to the declaration we read: "Thus it becomes clear that the mutual condemnations of former times do not apply to the Catholic and Lutheran doctrines of justification as they are presented in the *Joint Declaration*".[52]

With the other Churches and Ecclesial Communities

This is not the context in which to discuss all the other bilateral dialogues entered into by the PCPCU. It is enough to cite the Encyclical *Ut unum sint*: "The hopes and invitation expressed by the Second Vatican Council have been acted upon, and bilateral theological dialogue with the various worldwide Churches and Christian Communities in the West has been progressively set in motion".[53]

For an overview of the dialogue with the Churches and Ecclesial Communities of the West, the Encyclical stated:

> "This dialogue has been and continues to be fruitful and full of promise.... As a result, unexpected possibilities for resolving these questions have come to light, while at the same time there has been a realization that certain questions need to be studied more deeply" (*UUS*, 69).

In conclusion, it can be affirmed that with regard to the ecumenical aspects, the requirements and guidelines of *Unitatis redintegratio* have been implemented in a substantial way within the Catholic Church and with dialogue with other Christians. Clearly, the process is ongoing and the search continues with the aim of deepening the issues raised and of confronting new questions.

---

52. Cf. *Joint Declaration on the Doctrine of Justification*, (Grand Rapids/Cambridge: William B. Eerdmans, 2000) p.43.
53. *UUS*, 69.

III. Towards the Future

The PCPCU maintains its plan of action both within the Catholic Church and with regard to relations with the other Churches and Ecclesial Communities. This is done in full compliance with the *munus* entrusted to it by the Apostolic Constitution *Pastor bonus* (1988), which defines the task of the PCPCU thus:

Art. 136

§1. It sees that the decrees of the Second Vatican Council pertaining to ecumenism are put into practice. It deals with the correct interpretation of the principles of ecumenism and enjoins that they be carried out.

§2. It fosters, brings together, and coordinates national and international Catholic organizations promoting Christian unity, and supervises their undertakings.

§3. After prior consultation with the Supreme Pontiff, the Council maintains relations with Christians of Churches and Ecclesial Communities that do not yet have full communion with the Catholic Church, and especially organizes dialogue and meetings to promote unity with them, with the help of theological experts of sound doctrine. As often as may seem opportune, the Council deputes Catholic observers to Christian meetings, and it invites observers from other Churches and Ecclesial Communities to Catholic meetings.[54]

This norm draws upon the experience since the Second Vatican Council onwards.

---

54. Apostolic Constitution *Pastor bonus*, 136, §3.

a) Within the Catholic Church

Within the Catholic Church the PCPCU promotes ecumenism through the following means:

- Exchange of information with the local Churches through the ecumenical commissions of the Synods of the Eastern Catholic Churches and the Episcopal conferences;
- Visits of the President, Secretary and other staff members to the local Churches for pastoral or cultural initiatives, and to theological faculties and centres of formation for related events;
- Contact with bishops making *ad limina* visits to Rome in order to discuss difficulties and developments in the ecumenical field.
- Ongoing (since 1968) preparation of the booklets for the prayer for Christian unity and distribution to the ecumenical commissions of the synods and episcopal conferences for adaptation and implementation, together with information on the ecumenical situation in the various countries;
- Organisation of regional meetings on local ecumenical formation;
- Occasional encounters in Rome with Presidents of the ecumenical commissions of the synods and episcopal conferences in order to discuss methods and means for promoting ecumenism. Our meeting this week, although on a wider scale, falls within this category;
- Contact and consultation within the Roman Curia in order to provide the Holy Father with updated information on the ecumenical dimension of his ministry of communion.

Reception of the outcomes of the dialogues

At this stage of the ecumenical movement a crucial questions arises for the entire development of ecumenism, namely what should be done with the outcomes of bilateral dialogues? This is a question of the *reception* of the outcomes. Pope John Paul II as affirmed: "These cannot remain the statements of bilateral commission but must become a common heritage" (*UUS*, 80).

The Ecumenical Directory (ED) clearly establishes the status of these documents: "Statements produced by dialogue commissions have intrinsic weight because of the competence and status of their authors. They are not, however, binding on the Catholic Church until they have been approved by the appropriate ecclesiastical authorities" (no.178). The question of *reception* is raised from the moment that a final document is issued by a given joint commission until the moment in which it is *received* as true doctrine of the Churches in dialogue and not only by the Churches, but within the body of the faithful.

Reception is an ecclesiological notion that is very intricate, and it implies a process of differentiated and complex discernment. Speaking at a convention of the Lutheran Church of America (1980) Cardinal Johannes Willebrands stated:

> "[It is] a process thanks to which the People of God, in its differentiated structure and under the guidance of the Holy Spirit, recognises and accepts new understandings, new testimonies, of the truth and its expression, because they consider them to be in the direct line of the apostolic tradition and in harmony with the sensus fidelium of all the Church".

The Ecumenical Directory also took up this thought: "When the results of a dialogue are considered by proper authorities to be ready for submission for evaluation, the members of the People of God, according to their role or charism, must be involved in this critical process" (ED, 179).

It is therefore not a question of passive acceptance, but an active critical process of the members of the People of God according to their roles and particular charisms. For this to take place, there must be a dissemination and understanding of the outcomes of dialogue.

The Ecumenical Directory sharply highlights this prerequisite. Indeed, reception is not possible if there is not an adequate understanding of the element to be received. The Ecumenical Directory affirms:

> "Every effort should be made to find appropriate ways of bringing the results of dialogues to the attention of all members of the Church. In so far as possible, an explanation should be provided in respect of new insights into the faith, new witnesses to its truth, new forms of expression developed in dialogue — as well as with regard to the extent of the agreements being proposed" (ED, 179).

In some contexts the importance of the dissemination of outcomes is so sharply focused, almost in an exclusive way, that one has the impression that reception takes place in the very dissemination. However, this is only a preliminary step. The process of reception implies a critical evaluation of the text, a comparison with the apostolic tradition in order to assess its fidelity and only then its recognition as a reality in tune with the Catholic faith, a reality to be incorporated within the life of faith. The Ecumenical Directory outlines three levels of this process of critical evaluation of the outcomes of the theological dialogues:

i) *At the level of all the faithful.* Beyond the dissemination of the texts, which should reach the widest range of people within the life of the Church, the faithful should be assisted in a comprehensive and analytical pastoral explanation. This will enable an impartial evaluation of the reactions of all, as they "assess the fidelity of these dialogue results to the Tradition of faith received from the Apostles and transmitted to the community of believers under the guidance of their authorized teachers" (ED, 179). The Church is a community and in its totality is the guarantor of the apostolic faith.

ii) *At the level of theologians.* The Ecumenical Directory notes that "important contributions to this process come from the specific competence of theological faculties" (ED, 182). The themes discussed in dialogue are of a specifically theological nature, and take into consideration sensitive and problematic controversies. The competence of the theologians involved is necessary in order to assess the value of the results of dialogue. For this critical doctrinal task, the Church calls upon theologians whose personal expertise can provide insight into the issues of the dialogue within an academic framework, and who are able to avail themselves of an interdisciplinary methodology and inter-confessional cooperation.

iii) At the level of the authority of the Church. "The whole
process is guided by the official teaching authority
of the Church, which has the responsibility of
making the final judgment about ecumenical
statements" (ED, 1982). In real terms, the role of
the authority of the Church is not limited to giving
a final judgment, but also involves assisting the
process of evaluation by proposing, or remembering, or calling to mind, certain essential reference points. These 'provisional' or 'sectional'
interventions enrich the research.

This is what happened on the Catholic side for the BEM
document (Baptism, Eucharist, Ministry) of the Faith and
Order Commission, and also for the *Final Report* of the joint
commission for dialogue with the Anglican Communion.
When the authorities of the Church give their approval on
the results, "new insights that are thus accepted enter into
the life of the Church, renewing in a certain way that which
fosters reconciliation with other Churches and Ecclesial
Communities" (ED, 182).

This is the way of the Catholic Church, and the
Ecumenical Directory trusts that a similar, or at least
convergent, procedure could be adopted by the other
Churches: "It is hoped that this manner of proceeding
would be adopted by each Church or Ecclesial Community
that is partner to the dialogue and indeed by all Churches
and Ecclesial Communities that are hearing the call to
unity. Cooperation between the Church in this effort is
most desirable (ED, 179). This *cooperation* for a *co-reception*
is absolutely necessary as the ultimate aim is the
re-establishment of communion among all Christians.

Elements to be received to date

The process of reception has just begun. Beyond the increasing dissemination of the texts, comments and evaluations of theologians have been solicited, and doctrinal meetings and symposia have been organised. In some cases there has been direct intervention by the authorities of the Church. The process is therefore an open one. Nonetheless, there are some elements that can be already received and indeed are progressively being received:

i)   *Partial or differentiated existing communion* between the Catholic Church and other Churches and Ecclesial Communities. This is a reality that is becoming understood more fully and that has been received in the two Codes of Canon Law and the Ecumenical Directory, and that has entered increasingly in the theological mentality of Catholics.

ii) *The spirit of fraternity* based on partial communion is growing among Christians who are building up an understanding of a communion that is expressed in solidarity.

iii) The *common commitment* towards dialogue and the search for full unity is certainly a fruit of the ongoing dialogues that encourage a conscious opening to the obedience to the will of the Lord for his Church.

iv) The new common visions on longstanding controversial issues are increasingly being introduced in regular theological training in faculties and specialised institutes. This sort of partial reception helps to deepen the entire process upon

which ultimately the authority of the Church will
express itself.

b) Relations with other Churches and Ecclesial Communities

The dialogue has already established a concrete and
deeper Christian fraternity. "A valuable result of the contacts between Christians and of the theological dialogue in
which they engage is the growth of communion" (*UUS*,
49). A positive experience of this is already perceptible.
This fundamental, yet partial, unity must now proceed to
the necessary and sufficient visible unity. John Paul II
urges: "This journey towards the necessary and sufficient
visible unity, in the communion of the one Church willed
by Christ, continues to require patient and courageous
efforts" (*UUS*, 78).

The bilateral dialogues with all the Christian communions must continue according to their own agendas.

New themes to confront

In his Encyclical on the ecumenical commitment, John
Paul II identifies six areas in which theological dialogue
must continue.

With specific regard to the dialogue with Churches and
Ecclesial Communities of the West, five areas are outlined.
The Holy Father draws attention (*UUS*, 79) to "deep-
ening" the following:

  i)   the relationship between Sacred Scripture, as the
         highest authority in matters of faith, and Sacred
         Tradition, as indispensable to the interpretation
         of the Word of God;

ii) the Eucharist, as the Sacrament of the Body and Blood of Christ, an offering of praise to the Father, the sacrificial memorial and Real Presence of Christ and the sanctifying outpouring of the Holy Spirit;

iii) Ordination, as a Sacrament, to the threefold ministry of the episcopate, prebyterate and diaconate;

iv) the Magisterium of the Church, entrusted to the Pope and the Bishops in communion with him, understood as a responsibility and an authority exercised in the name of Christ for teaching and safeguarding the faith;

v) the Virgin Mary, as Mother of God and Icon of the Church, the spiritual Mother who intercedes for Christ's disciples and for all humanity.

In the dialogue with all Christians, and particularly with the Orthodox, the Pope raises a crucial question in terms of hierarchical communion, namely the *exercise of the primacy* of the bishop of Rome.

The encyclical clearly affirms the ministry of unity of the bishop of Rome among all the Churches and Ecclesial Communities. The Catholic Church is conscious that she has preserved the ministry of the *Successor of the apostle Peter, the bishop of Rome* "whom God established as her 'perpetual and visible principle and foundation of unity and that Spirit sustains in order that he may enable all the others to share in this essential good" (*UUS*, 88).

Nonetheless, the question of the primacy remains a great difficulty in relations between the Catholic Church and all other Churches and Ecclesial Communities. The issue is a matter of debate in all the dialogues. The Pope invites ecclesial leaders and their theologians to "engage with me (John Paul II) in a patient and fraternal dialogue on this subject, a dialogue in which, leaving useless controversies behind, we could listen to one another, keeping before us only the will of Christ for his Church" (*UUS*, 96). The theme is presented by the Pope in this form and within these limits: "to find a way of exercising the primacy which, while in no way renouncing what is essential to its mission, is nonetheless open to a new situation" (*UUS*, 95). He invokes the Holy Spirit "to shine his light upon us, enlightening all the Pastors and theologians of our Churches that we may seek — together, of course — the forms in which this ministry may accomplish a service of love recognized by all concerned".

The dialogue remains open on this point both in official bilateral conversations and in particular instances such as the symposium on the Petrine ministry organised in Rome by the PCPCU mentioned above.

Conclusion

Relations with the other Churches and Ecclesial Communities, inspired and guided by *Unitatis redintegratio*, have undergone profound positive transformations. In his Encyclical *Ut unum sint* (1995), the Holy Father speaks of the "fruits of dialogue" (nn.41-76), noting that ecclesial fraternity has been rediscovered (nn.41-42) and that mutual solidarity has been strengthened (n.43) on the basis of a real "growth of communion" (n.49) both with the Churches of the East (nn.50-63) and with the Churches and Ecclesial Communities of the West (nn.64-76). The growth of communion has had a counterpart in a diminution of long-standing polemics, after having made important clarifications. "As a result, unexpected possibilities for resolving these questions have come to light, while at the same time there has been a realization that certain questions need to be studied more deeply" (*UUS*, 69).

While achieving important positive results, the theological dialogue has not yet completed its task. Full unity has not been achieved, and Christians are still not yet able to make a common complete profession of faith and to concelebrate the Eucharist, the one sacrifice of Christ. Their division continues to be a scandal for the world, and is the source of further divisions, and an impediment to the proclamation of the Gospel to all.

The Christian conscience now has two main priorities: on the one hand, we must receive and disseminate the outcomes achieved within the body of the Christian community; on the other, we must confront the remaining open questions. These include those issues in the ecumenical panorama that seem new due to their increased impact (ordination of women, ethical problems, growth of nationalism together with its relationship to the conception of the Churches).

In pursuing its two main objectives, namely fostering the ecumenical spirit and action within the Catholic Church and establishing dialogue with other Christians, the PCPCU remains vigilantly attentive to its commitment. It does this through its daily work, plenary sessions, consultation with members and experts, and through the ecumenical commissions and bilateral theological dialogue.

Forty years after the promulgation of *Unitatis redintegratio*, these objectives — albeit at a more complex level and with new means reflecting the changing situation — remain our ongoing task. This meeting serves also to seek new future perspectives.

Ecumenism Today:
The Situation in the Catholic Church[1]

The results of a survey carried out by the
Pontifical Council for Promoting Christian Unity

Brian Farrell

Introduction

In 1993 the PCPCU organized a meeting of the representatives of the ecumenical commissions of the Bishops' Conferences and of Synods of Eastern Catholic Churches, and prepared for it by sending out a questionnaire, with the purpose of generating a report on the then current experience of ecumenical work in the Catholic Church. This time, eleven years later, we have tried to put together a questionnaire with a slightly different purpose: we wanted to measure the degree of practical application of *Unitatis redintegratio* forty years after its promulgation and of the *Ecumenical Directory* ten years after its publication.

My task here is to describe the picture which emerges from the responses received — I mean a description, a picture, even an impressionist picture! This is not a scientific analysis of the questionnaire and its responses.

The questionnaire sent out had three aims:

---

1. Original English text.

1. To collect information on how the Council's teaching on the quest for Christian unity has spread throughout the Church;
2. To receive information on whether and how the ecumenical commitment of the local Churches is organized according to the guidelines of the 1993 Ecumenical Directory;
3. To obtain suggestions about how our Council should go forward in promoting Christian unity.

163 questionnaires were sent out. Up to a few days ago we received 83 responses, which represent 51% of the total. Looking at the responses by continents and regions, we see the following: from Africa we had 20 answers (44%); from Latin America and the Caribbean 17 (71%); 1 from North America (50%); 12 from Asia (60%); 24 from Europe (60%); 7 from the Middle East (46%); 2 from Oceania (40%).

We are fully aware of the limited nature of our inquiry and of this presentation; the questionnaire was not scientifically formulated; the responses were fewer than we expected and the responses correspond to quantitatively different realities, which makes comparisons and statistics impossible: Brazil cannot be compared with Gibraltar, or Germany with Kazakhstan. Nevertheless we are grateful for the cooperation received and believe that we have a clearer picture of the state of ecumenism in the Catholic Church, a picture which serves as a basis for further reflection and action.

We have summarized our findings under four headings:
1. The advance of ecumenical awareness within the Catholic Church
2. The practice of ecumenism

3.   The Church's efforts in ecumenism at the local
     level
4.   Suggestions for future work.

I. The Advance of Ecumenical Awareness
within the Catholic Church

a) Positive signs

On the basis of responses to the questionnaire we can
affirm that, forty years after the promulgation of the Decree
Unitatis redintegratio, the restoration of unity among Christians is a real concern among the majority of the Church's
members. Catholics have a positive attitude to the ecumenical task. They are eager to know more about the other
Churches and Ecclesial Communities, and they are generally willing to take part in events and meetings, especially in
common prayer for unity.

There is widespread practice of spiritual ecumenism. As
well as the Week of Prayer for Christian Unity, which
continues to be a principal component of ecumenical action, joint celebrations of major liturgical feasts and com-
memorations, as well as on the occasion of civil, national
and local celebrations, are a reality almost everywhere.
There is widespread sharing of church buildings. Many
examples are provided in the responses: among those mentioned are – between Anglicans and Catholics in Australia,
Catholics and Orthodox in Italy, Lutherans and Catholics
in several countries. Two thirds of our respondents mention
ecumenical cooperation at the parish level and the publication of guidelines for their region.

In general we can be assured that efforts and initiatives to apply the ecumenical commitment of the Second Vatican Council continue and grow throughout the Church.

b) Problems and resistance

At the same time we cannot be naive. And although not all the difficulties mentioned in the responses are equally present in all parts of the Church, an overview of these difficulties may be helpful, since they constitute the challenge which those who work for Christian unity face at the level of practical involvement.

The first category of difficulties has to do with the lack of motivation and enthusiasm. It may seem self-evident, but it is interesting to note that the inquiry confirms that there is more interest in ecumenical matters where Catholics are in a minority, and less where they are a majority. In some places the small number of Christians belonging to other churches, especially the historical churches, is offered as a justification for the lack of ecumenical initiative. In addition, the ecclesial nature of the newer communities such as Pentecostals and Evangelicals is not taken seriously enough. The indiscriminate use of the term 'sect' continues to cause problems, especially in the face of aggressive proselytism on the part of some groups. Unfortunately, Conferences on all continents include in the list of sects Ecclesial Communities with which we have theological dialogues and international relations, even for decades (Baptists, Evangelicals, Pentecostals and Adventists).

On the other hand, responses from Latin America frequently indicate a non-recognition of the Christian character of Catholics by some Evangelical and Pentecostal groups. It may help to remember that on this mutual difficulty we already have studies produced by various mixed commissions of dialogue.[2]

Another question to be faced is the apparent dichotomy between the mission to evangelize and the promotion of unity. Some responses show an attitude of suspicion that ecumenism would weaken the evangelizing mission of the Church. There is mention in a few responses of a kind of resigned acceptance of the ecumenical commitment on the part of some groups within the Church. Some Catholics think that ecumenism compromises their faith and is an admission of an insufficiency in the Catholic Church, which they are not ready to accept. Here we may have a kind of inferiority/superiority complex which needs to be dealt with.

At another level we can mention the need for purification of memories. Although much has been achieved in places, some local Churches say that the memory of past events, remote or more recent, impedes or hinders ecumenical relations. The purification of memories is something to which John Paul II has drawn our attention on numerous occasions, and it remains one of the most crucial challenges for those who work for Christian unity.

With regard to the persistence of attitudes of mutual fear, suspicion and mistrust, respondents in all continents

---

2. Catholic–Pentecostal Dialogue, "Evangelization, Proselytism and Common Witness. The Report from the Fourth Phase of the International Dialogue 1990–1997 between the Roman Catholic Church and Some Classical Pentecostal Churches and Leaders" in *Information Service* 97 (1998/I–II) pp.38–56. Consultation Between the Catholic Church and the World Evangelical Alliance, "Church, Evangelization and the Bonds of Koinonia: A Report of the International Consultation between the Catholic Church and the World Evangelical Alliance(1993–2002)" in *Information Service* 113 (2003/II–III) pp.85–101.

mention the fear expressed by other Christians of being absorbed by the more powerful Catholic community, and the mistrust of Catholics towards groups that use the media and public campaigns to criticize Catholic doctrines or to attack us for certain negative and scandalous situations. In a word there is still much suspicion of one another's real intentions and regarding the evangelical inspiration of one another's programmes and actions.

To summarize in some way, we can outline a number of issues among the theological-pastoral questions most often raised in the responses to our questionnaire, including:

- the issue of the mutual recognition of baptism and the rebaptism of Catholics by some Churches and communities, either as a fact or as a policy; on this point, a presentation of the guidelines followed by some Bishops' Conferences was sent to all Conferences after our Plenary Assembly of 2001, and was also published in the official bulletin of our Council, *Information Service;*[3]

- the matter of abuses in *communicatio in sacris;*

- questions regarding mixed-marriages;

- in some places excesses in Catholic Marian devotions are a problem;

- the matter of unifying the date of Easter, which has been debated here and there since the Council, is a concern, especially in the Middle East;

- differences in ecclesial organization and structures make it difficult in some countries for Catholics to

---

3. Cf. Pontifical Council for Promoting Christian Unity, "Mutual Recognition of Baptism. Synthesis of Responses from Episcopal Conferences, Study Document" in *Information Service* 109 (2002/I-II) pp. 20-25.

identify ecumenical partners in some other confessions;
- we also see many and wildly ranged references to
  mutual accusations of proselytism (Latin America,
  Egypt, Russia).

Among non-theological factors causing concern we find
social and political situations (principally in the ex-Soviet
Union), ethnic conflicts (Africa and the Balkans), and the
state of poverty in different parts of the world. In Eastern
Europe many respondents refer to the tensions surrounding
the question of the restitution of Church properties. In
some instances the quest for Christian unity is seen as a
threat by certain Islamic groups. Finally, many Conferences
coincide in indicating as a problem the lack of an ecumenical literature that is accessible to the simple and uneducated faithful.

II. The Practice of Ecumenism

The Second Vatican Council committed the ecumenical task in a special way to the Bishops. The Ecumenical
Directory recommends the setting up of ecumenical commissions in each diocese, and at national and regional
levels, or at least the naming in each diocese of a delegate in
charge of promoting the ecumenical spirit and inter-church
relations. We are very pleased to see that only very few
Conferences do not have a department or commission for
ecumenism. On the other hand, most respondents indicate
that these commissions or delegates work in restricted
conditions, and they mention the lack of continuity in
carrying out projects, and the need for new, younger blood
among those engaged in ecumenical work.

At the level of dioceses, matters are even less satisfying. The lack of personnel, lack of specific training, lack of resources, financial and otherwise, make ecumenical work difficult. In some countries there are flourishing support groups and associations of people well trained in ecumenism, active in ecumenical education in dioceses, parishes, groups and seminaries. More attention needs to be given to finding and training such experts and volunteers.

Regarding Councils of Churches, which in principle are very useful tools for improving mutual knowledge and collaboration among the churches, we see that a substantial change has taken place in the years since the previous inquiry. Forty years ago, the Catholic Church did not belong to any such Council of Churches. Today she is a member of 70 of the existing 120 national councils of churches, and of 3 out of 7 regional councils of churches, and of 7 regional councils associated with the World Council of Churches.[4] An analysis of the forms, implications, and possibilities of Catholic participation in such councils, as well as suggestions as to how to meet the difficulties and challenges which still impede Catholic participation in some places, is contained in a new document of the Joint Working Group between the Catholic Church and the World Council of Churches. It is due to be published in the

---

4. According to data available up to September 2004, the Catholic Church is a full member in three regional Councils of Churches: the Council of Churches of the Caribbean, the Middle East Council of Churches and the Council of Churches of the Pacific. The Church is a member of 14 national Christian Councils or Councils of Churches in Africa, 3 in Asia, 10 in Oceania, 12 in the Caribbean, 25 in Europe, 1 in North America, 5 in South America.

new year, and I wholeheartedly recommend it to your
attention.[5]

III. Catholic Ecumenical Action
at the Local Level

On the basis of the responses received, we can indicate
the following.

Regarding dialogue and the reception of dialogue documents: 42 out of 83 Bishops' Conferences declare that they
have permanent structures of dialogue with other churches
and communities present in their territory. 38 have mixed
commissions of dialogue.

As regards reception, only 35 Conferences say they have
a good dissemination of the results of dialogues, and have
actively promoted discussion and study through the publication of resources. But there are indications that the
ecumenical commitment is slowly but surely becoming
more present in local church literature. Some responses also
indicated that efforts are being made to utilize the internet
to promote ecumenism in their region. There is need for
more effort in this field. The PCPCU would greatly appreciate receiving documentation on national and local di-

---

5. The document entitled *"Inspired by the Same Vision: Roman Catholic
Participation in National and Regional Councils of Churches. AJWG
Study"* will be published as Appendix E of the *Eighth Report
1999–2005 of the Joint Working Group between the Roman Catholic
Church and the World Council of Churches.* The Report will be
published in 2005 and presented at the General Assembly of the
WCC at Porto Alegre (Brazil) in February 2006. The data relating
to the participation of the Catholic Church to the Councils of
Churches in Footnote 4 Have been taken from this document. The
Report concludes the eighth series of conversations of the Joint
Working Group between representatives of the Catholic Church
and the World Council of Churches.

alogues, and the related resource materials. A large number of Conferences in Latin America and in Asia have asked that the Council use its website to make all these resources available in the relative languages — Spanish, Chinese and Hindi, for example. We are examining the matter carefully.

In the field of social concerns, 44 Conferences say they are involved in cooperative efforts with other confessions. Here too we must admit that more can be done.

With regard to ecumenical formation, the situation is not quite rose-coloured and assuring. Our Council's document on formation, *The Ecumenical Dimension in the Formation of Those Engaged in Pastoral Work* (1995), which offers suggestions for a course in ecumenism and gives resources for the same, is not well known and needs to be distributed more widely. Together with the Congregation for Catholic Education we are now carrying out a survey at the world level of all Catholic seminaries and universities and theological faculties to find out exactly what the practice is and whether proper attention is being given to ecumenism in Catholic education. The data is now being collected and we will eventually publish the results.

IV. Some Thoughts on what you can do for the Future of Ecumenism

Our Council gets fairly good marks in the survey. A positive evaluation is given of the role of the PCPCU down the years in facilitating contacts and relations with other Churches and Ecclesial Communities, in clarifying misunderstandings and in helping to resolve local tensions. Here we are referring to such things as contacts with the Bishops' Conferences and discussions with groups of Bishops on the occasion of their *ad limina* visits, meetings between the

Council and the leaders of Churches (Copts, Orthodox), the discussion of particular situations and difficulties during informal talks (Anglicans, Lutherans). We have taken note of the places where closer attention is requested, especially in Africa and Asia.

That ecumenism becomes an integral part of Catholic life is the goal of our service. With this in mind, we are quickly trying to implement one of the decisions of the last Plenary Assembly of our Council. We are drawing up a *Vademecum* for the faithful, a booklet that gathers practical ideas and suggestions for ecumenical activity. You have all received a copy of a draft, and you will hopefully examine it and offer suggestions for its improvement and for its application to your respective continents.

In responding to the questionnaire, many good suggestions for future ecumenical work have emerged. Many of these have to be implemented at the local level of the Churches since they are connected with the ecumenical dialogue and its reception in specific situations and contexts. That is where most of you come in: you are the ones who have direct responsibility for the promotion of ecumenism within your Churches. We sincerely hope that this meeting, commemorating *Unitatis redintegratio* after forty years and bringing so many committed people together to reflect on the present situation of the movement in the Catholic Church and among our partners, will stimulate you and give you new assurance. The exchange of ideas which we hope will take place here is an important part of what we intended in calling this meeting.

The inquiry underlines three areas as needing urgent attention now and in the future: the insertion of ecumenical initiatives in the organic pastoral programmes of dioceses; reflection on how to respond to the problem of aggressive proselytism; and the question of the ecumenical education of the laity, of religious, seminarians, priests and bishops. This last point has been mentioned by practically all the ecumenical commissions responding to our questionnaire. There has to be a place in this education for the input of representatives of the other Churches and communities. Indeed, we hope that more and more such efforts will be cooperative.

Conclusion

Ours has been a survey. I can think of two surveys mentioned in the Scriptures. One is when the Chosen People reach the promised land, and Jonathan sends out scouts to see what the situation is. In the Gospels, Jesus sends out the disciples, two by two, perhaps to test them. The scouts come back dismayed at the challenges facing them. The disciples come back exhilarated at the way they were received and succeeded in their mission. Neither dismay nor exhilaration are enough in themselves. Realism is needed: ecumenism can only be promoted on a solid doctrinal basis, and on serious study and conversation among divided Christians. But it also requires a deep and convincing spirituality, a spirituality of Christian hope and courage. As those most directly responsible for the implementation of the Church's ecumenical commitment, *you* have to inspire hope and courage in your co-workers and the leaders of your local Churches. We hope and pray that this meeting will give you an impulse to do just that.

The Missionary and Ecumenical Task of the Church[1]

Cardinal Ivan Dias

Introduction

The ecumenical movement has made great strides during the 20th century, ever since it received a first decisive impulse from the World Missionary Conference of Edinburgh in 1910 during which — it is reported — the foreign missionaries working in India poignantly remarked that the divisions between Christian Churches were a major obstacle to their missionary activity, for it was difficult for them to proclaim Christ to a people which was puzzled and confused by the multiplicity of Churches present in the country, each claiming to preach the true faith.

The movement gained momentum in the Catholic Church forty years ago with the Decree *Unitatis redintegratio* of the Second Vatican Ecumenical Council, and was marked by historic gestures from many sides: suffice it to mention the meeting of His Holiness Patriarch Athenagoras I with Pope Paul VI in Jerusalem in 1964 and their Common Declaration a year later,[2] Pope Paul VI's ecumenical gift of the relic of St Andrew's head to the Church of Saint Andrew of Patraxos (1966), the exchange of visits between the heads of various Orthodox and Reformation Churches and the Popes, the lighting of a lamp by Pope John Paul II in the Vatican Synod Hall in 2001 with the flame he brought from the

---

1. Original English text.
2. December 7, 1965. Cf. *Tomos Agapis, Vatican–Phanar: 1958–1970* (Rome–Istanbul, 1971), p.278.

tomb of St Gregory the Illuminator in Armenia, and the recent presentation of the icon of the Kazan Madonna to His Holiness Patriarch Alexis II of Moscow and all Russia.

As we now consider the future perspectives of the missionary and ecumenical task of the Church, it will be well, first of all, to recall the common missionary mandate which Christians have received from Christ Himself.

I. The Missionary Mandate

Before Our Lord Jesus Christ ascended into heaven, He commanded His followers to "go out into the whole world and preach the Good News to every creature" (*Mt* 28:19) This commission was the continuation of the one which Jesus Himself received from His heavenly Father "who so loved the world that he sent his only Son so that all those who believe in him may have eternal life" (*Jn* 3:16). Jesus transmitted the mandate to His disciples: "As the Father has sent me, so do I send you" (*Jn* 20:21).

Though the mandate is one and unique,[3] our Holy Father Pope John Paul II has pointed out its three main expressions in his encyclical *Redemptoris missio*: firstly, it is "*missio ad gentes* or first evangelization" of those who have not yet fully received the Good News of Jesus Christ; then, it is the "pastoral care" of those who have accepted Jesus as Lord and Saviour; and, finally, it is a "new evangelization" of those already evangelized who need to refresh and deepen their Christian roots.[4]

Besides these three dimensions of evangelization, the Holy Father has indicated new areas which cross all geo-

---

3. *Redemptoris missio*, 15.
4. *Ad gentes*,6; *Redemptoris missio*, 31.

graphical, cultural and social divisions. He speaks of them
as an "areopagus", and mentions among them the world of
culture and research, of migrants and poverty, of social
communication and international relations underlining the
importance of information technology and the media in all
its forms, commitment to peace, development and the
liberation of peoples, the rights of individuals and groups,
especially of minorities, the empowerment of women and
the education of children, the ecological safeguard of the
created world. All these, says the Pope, need to be illuminated with the light of the Gospel and hence come within
the missionary purview of the Church.[5] In all of them the
Church must continue Christ's divine and salvific mission,
and consequently will always be *in statu missionis.*[6]

The missionary task of the Church is therefore immense, and there is place for every Christian and for all
Christians. This challenge, of course, differs from place to
place, though its essence remains the same everywhere, viz.
not just proclaiming Gospel values, but spreading the sweet
fragrance of the sacred person of Jesus Christ, Son of God
and unique and universal Saviour of all humankind. It is He
who brings to maturity (fulfilment) the seeds of the Word
sowed by the Holy Spirit in world religions and cultures all
down the ages (Cf. *Mt* 5:7). This point is particularly important in today's context of religious pluralism, indifferentism
and relativism, which is prevalent even in some theological
circles, and of a fundamentalist secularism promoted by
well-known secret sects and New Age practices which aim
at making God irrelevant to human beings. Our missionary
mandate would therefore require, first and foremost, a

5. *Redemptoris missio,* 37.
6. *Ibid.,* 20.

sincere appreciation of our Christian roots and a bold affirmation of our ethos and identity. Else, we shall be, in Jesus' own words, like "salt that has lost its savour" or a "light hidden under a bushel" (*Mt* 5:13–14).

II. The Future Ecumenical Perspectives of the Church

In the face of this challenge, we now ask ourselves: what should be the relationship between Christ's mandate to evangelize the whole world and the ecumenical thrust of the Christian Churches? It is obvious that ecumenism must be at the service of the Church's mission to preach the Good News of Jesus Christ.

On the one hand, while the Christian Churches should mutually respect each other's particular traditions which have brought them to this present day, they should consider ways and means to consolidate the ecumenical gains of the past decades, solve any simmering misgivings or misunderstandings, and forge ahead in giving a common witness to their belief in the uniqueness of Jesus Christ and in the universality of His salvation. The key of such a witness is "love". "By this shall all people know that you are my disciples, if you have love one for another" (*Jn* 13:35).

We must therefore seek ways and means to ensure that the dialogue between our Churches leads to a concerted effort to further the missionary mandate of the Church. This could produce some uneasiness because, while the mission vision of the Church's mandate is one and indisputable, there are a variety of approaches to achieve the same.

III. Dialogue of Life, Ideas,
Action and Experiences

What is of paramount importance, of course, is not the numbers of the faithful which the Churches have, but the quality of witness they give. A continued dialogue of life, of ideas, of action and of experiences is essential to the future progress of our ecumenical dialogue.

A *dialogue of life*, in the first place. Wherever Christians find themselves, no matter what Church they belong to, they must give witness to a harmonious conviviality, thus leading those who do not belong to any Church to affirm, as the pagans did of the early Christians: "see, how they love each other". People today, in fact, believe more in what the Christians *are*, than in what they say or do. As Pope Paul VI emphatically observed: "Our contemporaries listen more willingly to witnesses than to teachers, and if they do listen to teachers, it is because they are witnesses". In India, for instance, Christians — who are only 2.3% of the population of over a billion — cater to 20% of all the primary education in the country, 10% of the literacy and community health-care programs, 25% of the care of the orphans and widows, and 30% of the care of the physically and mentally challenged, the lepers and Aids patients. Naturally, all Christians — whatever be their Church allegiance — are welcomed in these institutions, while the vast majority of those cared for belong to faiths other than Christian.

The dialogue of life should lead the Christian Churches to show solidarity with each other and to rejoice with those who rejoice, and weep with those who weep. A few years ago, such solidarity was shown when an Australian evangelical missionary, Dr Graham Staines, who was working among lepers, was burnt to death with his two little sons by some Hindu fundamentalists who accused him of converting the lepers to Christianity. Christians joined in prayer for those who were killed and for a change of attitude in their murderers. Dr Staines' wife, Gladys, publicly forgave the perpetrators of the hideous crime. Such a genuinely Christian gesture was widely praised all over the country, even by those of other faiths. Mrs Staines was given many awards, even from the Catholic community.

A dialogue of ideas should help purify the memory of the past and to bring out the common heritage which Churches have had from the time the Church was born in the Cenacle in Jerusalem. It could also mean collaboration among their missionary institutes, scientific research centers and universities on missiological matters. So far the exchange of ideas between Christian Churches has been restricted to matters theological, and this was indeed necessary to clarify notions which in the past had led to polemical confrontation. Looking towards the future, themes so far undiscussed will have to be tackled frankly, e.g. those concerning ethical and moral principles. The Popes, for instance, have been outspoken in their defence of human life from conception to its natural end, in opposing the disintegration of family values through contraception, abortion and divorce, and the modern-day aberrations of homosexuality, same-sex unions, euthanasia, etc. It would rebound to the benefit of our common witnessing if all the Christian Churches would be of one mind and heart, and speak with one voice in matters moral and ethical.

As for *dialogue of action,* there should be no dearth of initiatives which could be taken on all sides. In the Archdiocese of Bombay, for example, there are seven churches (including the Orthodox, Roman Catholics, Anglicans and Methodists) who have formed a public Cemeteries Trust to take care of the properties given it by the State authorities for the burial of the deceased. There is a deep sense of fellowship and unity among the leaders of these Churches who meet regularly to discuss and to decide on the management of the land allotted to the Trust: e.g. the building of an enclosure wall, the allocation of plots for burial and the method of burial, the maintenance of the property, the administrator to whom the Churches should refer for the burial, etc. The meetings normally begin with a prayer and end with a friendly *agapé*. This is indeed a practical ecumenism where, paradoxically, the deceased brethren are uniting their living counterparts. Such a fellowship facilitates the yearly common celebration of the Week of Prayer for Christian Unity and makes interpersonal relationships truly pleasant and wholesome.

As far as *dialogue of experiences* is concerned, there is much to be learnt from the spiritualities of the Christian East and West. The famous Jesus Prayer of the Russian Pilgrim, for instance, and the examples of the 4th century Desert Fathers are today being increasingly appreciated and used in the practice of Christian Meditation. In fact, they encourage humility, patience, prayer, introspection and love, and show how the practice of contemplation opens the door to eternal wisdom. Such spiritualities could be encouraged as ecumenical initiatives, and could be proposed as a powerful antidote to the New Age practices that are making inroads into our secularized society with promises of worldly prosperity and propagating superstitions which serve as palliatives for stress and other modern-day ailments of the spirit. On the other hand, the rich Christian spiritualities, both of the East and the West, offer means to achieve the true and abiding peace of Christ, which the world cannot give and which no one can take away.

IV. Ecumenical Challenges

As we look to the future, we cannot ignore the delicate question often raised with regard to the transfer of the Christian faithful from one Church to another. The Decree *Dignitatis humanae* of the Second Vatican Council proclaimed that religious liberty was a right of all individuals, who should be entitled to "both psychological freedom and immunity from external coercion".[7] Speaking of the demands of conscience, the same document says that a person "must not be forced to act contrary to his conscience, nor be prevented from acting according to his conscience, especially in religious matters".[8] In this context, it must be noted that sometimes conversions are erroneously linked with "proselytism" which has a negative connotation, and rightly so, since it very often implies force, allurement and enticements. The Catholic Church considers such proselytism-conversions as invalid, since conversion does not mean a purely external adhesion to a given Church, but implies a voluntary and radical change of life from within. We must therefore denounce those Christian groups which entice people to join them by means reputed to be non-spiritual and cause embarrassment to other Christian Churches. On the other hand, one cannot strictly speak of "proselytism" when a person already converted to Christ by reasons of conscience wants to pass from one Church to another, nor can one deny Chris-

---

7. *Dignitatis humanae*, 2.
8. *Ibid.*, 3.

tians the right to worship in the Church of their own choice or constrain them to do so only in the one they were born into.

India prides itself to have had the ministry of two Apostles, Thomas and Bartholomew. There are large groups which call themselves Saint Thomas Christians and belong to many Churches: we have the Catholic Syro-Malabar and Syro-Malankara Churches, the Mar Thomas Christians, two Churches which call themselves Syrian and Jacobite, each headed by a Catholicos. Besides these, there are the Churches of the Reformation: the Anglican Communion, the Evangelicals, the Methodists, the Presbyterians and others. This could have posed a challenge to the ecumenical thrust launched by the Second Vatican Ecumenical Council. But, *de facto,* there are no serious problems as far as changing one's membership of a particular Church is concerned. Problems, however, do arise when it comes to the behaviour of non-denominational Christian sects who resort to unconventional methods to increase their num- bers.

As for the Roman Catholic Church *ad intra,* the Code of Canons in the Eastern Churches envisages the hypothesis of a person wishing to transfer from one Church *sui iuris* to another. While it asserts the general principle that "no one can validly transfer to another Church *sui iuris* without the consent of the Apostolic See", it adds: "In the case of Christian faithful of an eparchy of a certain Church *sui iuris* who petition to transfer to another Church *sui iuris* which has its own eparchy in the same territory, this consent of the Apostolic See is presumed, provided that the eparchial bishops of both eparchies consent to the transfer in writing".[9]

---

9. *Code of Canons of the Eastern Churches,* Canon 32, § 1-2.

It may interest you to know about the happy relationships existing between the Archdiocese of Bombay, which is of the Latin Rite, and the Syro-Malabar Eparchy of Kalyan which covers the same territory and much more. There have been no insurmountable problems whatsoever in the matter of transfers from one Church *sui iuris* to another, thanks to the positive and constructive attitude of the two Ordinaries concerned. The Holy See also granted an Indult on September 18, 1993 whereby the faithful of the Syro-Malabar Church *sui iuris*, who used to frequent the Latin Church in the past, could continue doing so also in the future, if they so desired. This would be in line with the mind of St Paul as expressed in his letters to the Corinthians (cf. 1 *Cor* 1:12) who were quarrelling as to whether they belonged to Paul, to Apollos, to Cephas: Christ is not divided, he says, and when one is in Him, he is a new creation (cf. 2 *Cor* 5:17), and there is no distinction between Jew nor Greek, slave nor freeman, male nor female, for all are one in Christ Jesus. The same could be said of the Church. The Second Vatican Council solemnly affirmed that "Christ the Lord founded one Church and one Church only".[10] Whatever be our Church denomination, we "belong to the one Body of Christ and have the same Spirit; we have one Lord, one faith, one baptism, one God and Father, who is above all, through all and in all" (*Eph* 4:5-6).

---

10. *Unitatis redintegratio*, 1.

Conclusion

Christian Churches must needs work hand-in-hand in order to bring to fulfilment Christ Our Lord's mandate to preach the Good News to the whole of creation, especially in today's world marked by secularist trends, doctrines and practices seeking to make God irrelevant in people's lives. Divisions among the Churches are a scandal to people of other faiths, especially in countries where Christians are a tiny minority. The Father of the Indian Nation, Mahatma Gandhi, speaking of Christianity, which he greatly admired, once said: "I love Christ, but I do not like Christians, because they do not do what Christ has said". Today, more than ever, we must be convinced that "if Christians do not hang together, they will hang separately".

Christian Churches should therefore further the ecumenical process bearing in mind that Christian unity is a sign of mission proclamation. At the Last Supper, Jesus prayed that His disciples may be one, so that the world could believe that the Father had sent Him (*Jn* 17:21). The process may be slow and long, but it is worth the prize we are striving for. St Paul's words in his letter to the Philippians can inspire and encourage our ecumenical endeavours: "Not that we have already obtained the prize (of Christian unity) or are already perfect, but we press on to make it our own ... Forgetting what lies behind and straining forward to what lies ahead, we press on toward the goal for that prize" (*Phil* 3:12-15).

There is a Chinese proverb which says: *Instead of cursing the darkness, light a candle.* This should be our common attitude when facing the tremendous missionary challenge in a world marked by growing religious apathy and indifference towards God and neighbour. If the Christian Churches would light many candles of Christian solidarity among themselves, the Holy Spirit — who is the prime agent of both, mission and Christian unity — will quickly dissipate the dark shadows of their past differences which led to *divisions,* and transform them into *diversities.* The one Church of Jesus Christ will then present itself as a beautiful, seamless and many-coloured garment, as it was on the day it was born at Pentecost when peoples of diverse races and nations sang praises to the mighty works of the Lord, each in its own tongue (cf. *Acts* 2:1-11). The Holy Spirit is, in fact, a God of unity in diversity.

We are all aware that an iceberg can be destroyed the hard way, i.e. by chiselling it to bits slowly, or, more easily, by warming up the waters around it. So also the iceberg of a divided Christianity: it will be more easily dissolved by allowing the Holy Spirit to warm up the relationships between the Churches, than by strong stokes of arguments and discussions.

May the Holy Spirit quicken the completion of the unfinished symphony of Christian unity with chords of harmony, so that all the Christian Churches may experience in unison the new Pentecost for which Blessed Pope John XXIII prayed when he convoked the Second Vatican Council, and may witness the birth of a new world order, a *"civilization of love"*, which was Pope Paul VI's cherished dream and which is Pope John Paul II's prophetic vision for the new millennium we have just begun.

Concrete Steps in
the Ecumenism of Life[1]

Cardinal Cormac Murphy-O'Connor

I once had an uncle, a priest, who at family gatherings would always quote, during his speech, a phrase from Isaiah: "Remember the rock out of which you were hewn". He was really referring to the family tradition, rooted in the Catholic Faith, in prayer, in unity, loyalty to each other, to the Church and to society. How often do I remember, in my own family, the focus or our life being prayer together, the Mass and Sacraments, and being part of the community of the living Church. I am reminded of this because, in speaking to you about ecumenism I am not essentially speaking to you about doctrinal or other Church matters on which we disagree with fellow-Christians — rather I am talking to you about what essentially we share. There is a wonderful passage in the Decree on Ecumenism of the Second Vatican Council which says, "We should not forget that anything wrought by the grace of the Holy Spirit in the hearts of our separated brethren can contribute to our own edification. Whatever is truly Christian is never contrary to what genuinely belongs to the faith; indeed, it can always bring a more perfect realisation of the very mystery of Christ and the Church". So in beginning this address to you, I am speaking about what already unites us with our fellow-Christians — unites us through our common baptism, through our belief in Jesus Christ as Lord, our common acceptance of Holy Scripture and many other gifts of

---

1. Original English text.

180

the Holy Spirit. I also wish to speak about what has the potential to deepen and extend our unity so as to draw it closer to that fullness which is the desire of our Lord for his Church.

The key word that underpins the renewal of our friendship and collaboration with fellow-Christians is the word *communio,* or *koinonia,* which is the Greek for *communion. Koinonia,* of course, is to share, to participate and to have something in common. All the theological dialogues between the Catholic Church and other Christian churches *are* based on *communio* or *koinonia.* It really means union with God in Jesus Christ through the Holy Spirit, so that the Church is a community of all those reconciled with God and with each other because it is a community of those who believe in Jesus Christ and are justified through God's grace. So all ecumenical activity, including an ecumenism of life, is based on something that we share, that is a gift of the spirit, that is the grace of God which enables us to believe in Jesus Christ and thus have a real communion or community with each other.

This ecumenism of life is the way we express in concrete terms the real though as yet imperfect communion that we share — it complements the spiritual ecumenism and the ecumenism of truth that must also pave the path to unity. Ecumenism of life is also enabling us to see more clearly where a sustained or greater sharing can lead towards the *fullness* of communion in truth and in love. As Catholics we do well to remember that the divisions between us also hold *us* back from experiencing the *fullness* of the unity that exists in the Catholic Church. Ecumenism of life is not just *ad extra,* for the 'improvement' of everybody else. It is *ad intra,* for the renewal of the Catholic Church itself. If we share so much, why is it then that we have not progressed as far as we would wish on the ecumenical path? And what are the inhibiting factors that could undermine our ecumenism of life? The three enemies of ecumenism are, suspicion, inertia, and impatience.

Let me begin with 'suspicion'. It has been a fact that for many years, some Catholics and other Christians have felt that the ecumenical movement is a subtle sell-out. Some Catholics fear that ecumenism is a diluting of the truths of faith and traditional devotion. Some non-Catholic Christians feel that ecumenism compromises the principles of the Reformation and that the movement towards Christian unity is blunting their own convictions of the primacy of the Word of God. But suspicion is overcome, first of all when we meet with our fellow-Christians. The heart of ecumenism is prayer, as the Vatican Council says. When we pray together, the gift of the Spirit draws us closer together. I remember the time when Pope John Paul paid a pastoral visit to Great Britain. During that visit he met with fellow-Christians of different denominations and invited a group of them to come back to visit him in Rome. Well do I remember sitting round in a semi-circle with Pope John Paul in his study in the Vatican, talking together about the way forward in ecumenical relations. I could not help feeling then that the importance of our being together lay in the remarkable ease, openness, normality of fellow-Christians praying and talking together and appreciating and understanding each other. So often in my own life, as a priest and bishop, has it been the meeting with fellow-Christians and praying with them and enjoying their company, that we have begun to appreciate each other in a new way. The Vatican Council says, "There can be no ecumenism worthy of the name without interior conversion, for it is from newness or attitudes of mind, from self-denial and unstinted love that desires for unity take their rise and develop in a mature way". We should therefore pray to the Holy Spirit for the grace to be genuinely self-denying, humble, gentle, in the service of others. Change of heart and holiness of life, along with public and private prayer for the unity of Christians, should be regarded as the soul of the ecumenical movement and merits the name, *"spiritual ecumenism"*.

One essential way of walking the ecumenical path, from which there is no exit — there is no going back — is to meet with fellow-Christians on particular occasions, to pray together, to find occasions for worship in a common celebration. I remember in my former diocese of Arundel and Brighton in England, that after a period when Christians of different denominations met in small groups during the Lenten period, all those who had participated were invited to a common celebration at a very large abbey church. It was a wonderful occasion, with all the Christian leaders standing together and all the Christians of different denominations praying, singing and greeting each other in the Name of Christ.

Spiritual ecumenism — coming together in prayer — is the first step in overcoming suspicion and paves the way for dialogue and the ecumenism of truth. It also drives the ecumenism of life that brings Christians together in mission and pastoral outreach. It is important that suspicion is overcome locally, but what happens locally is often powerfully encouraged by what takes place on the world stage. As for example at the opening of the Holy Doors in St Paul's Outside the Walls, when the representative of the Ecumenical Patriarch and the Archbishop of Canterbury together with many other Christian leaders accompanied the Holy Father. First they knelt in prayer and then walked as it were into the Holy Year together. That was much more than an expression of diplomacy or courtesy — it had a most profound ecclesial significance which gave added impetus to our ecumenism of life locally in England and Wales. The second enemy of ecumenism is inertia. Sometimes we pay lip service to ecumenism. We Catholics say that we believe what the Catholic Church teaches in its doctrinal statements from the Vatican Council and in the Catechism but we do not live it out fully in daily life. It seems to me that there should be, in every diocese, in every parish, some aspect of Christian life that can be fully accomplished together with fellow-Christians. What is it Jesus says? — "It is not those who say, Lord, Lord, who will enter the Kingdom of heaven but those who do the will of my Father in heaven".

Did you ever hear the story of the four Polish tailors? They all lived in the same street in a Polish town and times were bad. So one of the tailors put up an advertisement in his window. It read, 'Here is the best tailor in the town'. The second tailor came along, saw the advertisement and put up in his window, 'Here lives the best tailor in all Poland'. The third tailor saw the first two and put up in his window, 'Here is the best tailor in the whole world'. The fourth tailor came along and he looked at the first, and the second, and the third advertisement and put up in his window, 'Here lives the best tailor in the street'. Ecumenism happens where it happens. Our theology of communion emphasises the bonds between the local and the universal Church, and ecumenism of life, if it is to overcome inertia, must be vigorous in both dimensions. Some developments in recent years in Anglican-Catholic relations may serve to illustrate this.

The international dialogue conducted through ARCIC has for many years been complemented by national conversations between Anglicans and Catholics in England, Canada, Australia and elsewhere. Now the International Anglican-Roman Catholic Commission for Unity and Mission (IARCCUM) has the task of fostering the reception of ARCIC's agreements, especially at local level and in particular through the ecumenism of life. IARCCUM itself and the Mississauga meeting between Anglican and Catholic bishops which had led to its establishment were both the outcome of a meeting between the Archbishop of Canterbury and the Holy Father. They had acknowledged new and continuing obstacles to unity but had determined that our dialogue and ecumenical relations needed a fresh impetus.

In England the Archbishop of Canterbury and I have formed a Church Leaders' Covenant with the other two Presidents or our national Council of Churches, known as Churches Together in England. We seek on occasions to respond together to national needs, to contact political leaders on issues of agreed concern, or even to express pastoral concern where it is appropriate. In recent months I have written jointly with Archbishop Rowan Williams to express our views to government on the war in Iraq and on bio-ethical issues. We try to meet regularly and hope to help others overcome the effects of suspicion and inertia. Consequently, when Archbishop Williams came to Rome for his first meeting as leader of the Anglican Communion with the Holy Father there were good ecclesial reasons for involving myself as Archbishop of Westminster. Ecumenism happens where it happens and the ecumenism of life at local and national level should both influence and be influenced by ecumenical relations at the highest level.

In a diocese bordering my own the bishop has worked closely for many years with his Anglican counterpart, encouraged by a Covenant between the two bishops to pray and work together. They have written jointly to the press and local politicians on important issues. They encourage their two cathedrals to work closely together, with joint events and awards for the two cathedral choirs. They have representatives on each other's diocesan bodies and jointly lead the annual pilgrimage to the shrine of their local saint. What happens in your community, in your parish, in your diocese that reflects the wish and will of the Church that we develop what is called 'common witness', the ecumenism of life? In the European context, I should also mention the various Ecumenical Assemblies that have taken place at Basilea and Graz and, of course, the *Charta Oecumenica* which is a document setting out principles for ecumenical dialogue and cooperation for all the countries of Europe — a noble step.

The last enemy of ecumenism is impatience and it is perhaps the most difficult to overcome, since prudent and careful steps forward often seem opposed to the kind of inspiring ecumenical break-through for which so many have longed. There are some people in our churches who feel that we should ignore the real obstacles and difficulties that exist between the different denominations and proceed as if they did not matter. They would brush over the differences and difficulties and celebrate a common Eucharist and imagine that in this way they would present a better common Christian witness to the world. But we have to remember, as Catholic-Christians, that the Church's unity can never be just a kind of federation of Christian denominations. Nor could it be just a gathering of those who personally, or as a community, follow Christ and devote themselves to evangelisation and the service of other people. The Catholic

Church's vision must always be the full visible unity of Christians held together by bonds of faith, sacramental life and pastoral governance. Fostering Christian unity has always a pastoral dimension, shepherding and holding together in one effective movement those made sluggish by inertia and those who would impatiently run ahead. Those moving steadily forward cannot neglect those who might be left behind or become lost in unfamiliar territory.

At the same time, we build up the community together yet recognise that this is also the womb that carries us, the maternal community that begets us to the life of God in Jesus Christ, through the Holy Spirit. It is in this sense that we pray in the Mass, "Look not on our sins but on the faith of your Church". Jesus has not left us orphans and in order to be with us to the end of time has left us his Holy Spirit and His Bride, which is the Church. For us Catholics, a belief in the Church is a fundamental expression of our faith. We have to accept that there are still fundamental disagreements about our Catholic understanding of the Church and other forms of ecclesial community. The ecumenical debate following the publication of *Dominus Iesus* reminds us of our own need to express our ecclesiology with clarity as well as charity. But we can never forget that together with all Christians we are believers who are on a pilgrimage together. We are the faithful people on a journey back to their Father but we are not alone on our journey. We have to live as Catholic-Christians with fellow-Christians in this transitional period where we have a real but not a complete communion together. And in this period we must live out our ecumenism of life. This can take expression in various initiatives which I hope you will be able to take back to your dioceses, to your countries.

a) Find some institutional structures whereby in dioceses and in towns or cities Christians can meet and pray and plan together. In my own country we have local Councils of Churches and the local Church leaders meet together regularly. This is a normal path of Christian cooperation.

b) It seems to me that every parish priest should have someone helping him in his parish who would be an Ecumenical Officer, who would ensure that there is, during each year, at least some events with fellow-Christians that take place together. As I have said before, 'Small aims, well carried out, are better than having grandiose ideas but which never materialise'.

c) Nothing can take the place of personal contact. Your meeting and discussion with fellow-Christians and practical cooperation are obvious means of developing the ecumenical path.

So it seems to me we should go forward on the ecumenical path with hope in our hearts. Pope John Paul II, in his Encyclical, *Ut unum sint,* begs the Church to turn her gaze during this new millennium and to ask the Holy Spirit for the grace to strengthen her own unity and to make it grow towards full communion with other Christians. We should never forget that an aspect of the ecumenical path is conversion and inner reformation of the Catholic community itself, so that we become more conformed in mind and heart and doctrine and life to Christ's will for His Church. But Pope John Paul in his Encyclical letter assures us that the Church will obtain the grace of unity, first of all through prayer. It is prayer that must occupy the first place as we journey together with our fellow-Christians to the unity for which Christ prayed. Pope John Paul then exhorts us to have hope in the Holy Spirit who will banish from us the painful memories of our separation. We can never forget that the work of ecumenism is not only our work, our efforts, our cooperation, our prayer, but it is God's work, it is His grace, it is His Holy Spirit that urges us on. *May they all be one, Father, as You are in Me and I in You so that the world may believe it was You who sent Me* (John 17).

A Spirituality of Unity
Within Diversity[1]

Chiara Lubich

I am gladdened and honoured to be part of this conference dedicated to *Unitatis redintegratio*[2] the document that
in 1964 opened up great horizons for the ecumenical movement, and that we are now celebrating 40 years after its
promulgation. A 40th anniversary offers the opportunity to
reflect upon, to contemplate more deeply, and to consider
further developments. For this reason, I too have been
asked to give a talk on: "A Spirituality of Unity in Diversity."

We are all familiar with the term spirituality. It means
to translate one's faith into daily life. Today, after the experience of the Second Vatican Council, the ecclesiology of
communion is widely held. Thus, John Paul II in *Novo
millennio ineunte* at the beginning of the third millennium
told the whole Catholic Church: "Before making practical
plans, we need to promote a spirituality of communion."[3]

The words 'a spirituality of communion' represent a
new terminology for spirituality: these same words seem to
represent the end–result of the bimillenary journey of the
Christian experience. In order to understand their full
significance, indeed, we would need to review the complete

---

1. Translated from the original Italian text.
2. Chiara Lubich was unable to attend the conference due to ill
   health. Her text was read in an abbreviated form by Dr Gabriella
   Fallacara of the *Centro Uno* for Christian unity of the Focolare
   Movement. We publish the original text prepared by Ms Lubich.
3. *Novo millennio ineunte*, 43.

history of Christian spirituality, together with all of the saints who have borne witness to the Gospel. This history could be summarized in the two great commandments with which Jesus summed up the Law and the Prophets: "The first is this ... You shall love the Lord your God with all your heart, with all your soul, with all your mind, and with all your strength. The second is this: You shall love your neighbor as yourself" (*Mk* 12:29-31).

During the first Christian millennium the search for union with God found particular expression in the monastic lifestyle, concentrating on prayer, penitence, solitude with God in the desert and in the monasteries, to which people were attracted by the spiritual life they radiated. However, while characterized by personal union with God, this first millennium did not neglect the second commandment on love of one's neighbor. We can call to mind the citadel of charity built by Saint Basil which took its name from him: "Basiliade."

All the same, this care for our brother and sister is expressed in new and more intense ways in the second millennium. The Christian mystics experienced that the more they were united to God, the more they felt urged by him to love that which he loved: the whole of creation and every man and woman.

This 'pivotal turn' towards our brothers and sisters was also the result of a new understanding of Jesus' humanity which emerged at the beginning of the second millennium.

While the first two millenniums were particularly characterized by the love of God and of neighbor, the third millennium seems to be characterized instead by another commandment that Jesus called "his" and "new" with respect to the others: "Love one another; even as I have loved you" (*Jn* 13:34). This is not to say that the mutual communion that Jesus taught had never been experienced in the history of Christian spirituality. We can call to mind the community founded by Saint Pachomius, where the monks felt that they were "one heart with their brothers,"[4] and the sisters of Clare of Assisi gathered together to live in "holy unity."[5]

We can say that unity, in all of these experiences, was a privileged moment of the spiritual experience, although it was an intuition that did not develop to the point of conceiving of a spirituality totally centered on communion. The Holy Spirit underscored other characteristics in past centuries, highlighting other evangelical aspects.

Today, there is a growing thrust in the Church to reach union with God, even sanctity, by going through our brother or sister. Not only, where mutual love is lived, this is where one can experience the presence and union with God, where our neighbor is sought out right from the start so as to go to God together.

The Holy Spirit, who brings about different charisms so that God's plan for humanity can be fulfilled, has also given new charisms to the Church today which render a spirituality of communion possible. The charism of unity of the Focolare Movement is among these new movements and its "spirituality of unity" provides a full response to the need for such a new spirituality. It has its own precise characteristic, being both a personal and communitarian spirituality.

The similarity between "the spirituality of communion" proposed by John Paul II and the "spirituality of unity" is evident in his letters written to "Cardinals and Bishops Friends of the Focolare Movement." In them, he writes that

---

4. *Catechesi, 8, Pacomio e i suoi discepoli. Regola e scritti*, Introduzione, traduzione e note a cura di L. Cremaschi (Bose, 1988), p.208.
5. *Regola*, Prologo: FF 2749.

"the spirituality of unity" or "of communion" characterizes "your movement ..."[6] This "spirituality of unity," which strives to contribute to the fulfilment of Jesus' last testament: "May they all be one" (*Jn* 17:21), is based on precepts that emerge from the Gospel, unfolding one after the other according to a divine logic; they are precepts that must be lived authentically and radically.

The first precept calls for a fervent faith in God who is love, in God-Love, to make him the ideal of our lives. The second asks us to respond to his love with our love, by striving to live according to his will rather than our own.

Then we try to discern the will of God, looking to the Gospel and especially putting into practice those words which speak of love of neighbor; with everyone, by being the first to love, in a concrete way, recognizing that in each person there is Jesus to be loved.

We try to live that mutual love of Jesus with our brothers and sisters: "I give you a new commandment ... " (*Jn* 13:34). We strive to do so radically, with Jesus' measure when he said "as": that is, loving one another and being ready — as he did — to die for one another.

In this way, we strive to contribute to bringing about that unity which Jesus prayed for to the Father before dying.

And if a rift should develop in our unity, we could find the key to recompose it in Jesus crucified and forsaken who cried out: "My God, my God, why have you forsaken me?" (*Mt* 27:46). He, who had overcome that immense trial by abandoning himself to the Father: "Into your hands I commend my spirit" (*Lk* 23:46) — thus reuniting all men

---

6. John Paul II, *Message to the Participants at the Spiritual Congress of the Bishops Friends of the Focolare Movement*, 14 February 2001.

and women with God and among themselves – is the model
for anyone who is committed to bringing about unity.

There are some essential aspects to this life: to receive
the Eucharist, to love the Holy Spirit by listening to his
voice in the depth of our heart, that Holy Spirit which
unites the members of the mystical Body of Christ; to see
Mary as our model, Mother of unity; to thus have the possibility of living the Church as communion. And to experience — having encountered these precepts of spirituality —
the presence of Christ among us "for where two or three are
gathered together in my name, there am I in the midst of
them" (*Mt* 18:20).

With regard to the presence of Jesus in the midst of his
disciples, the works of the Fathers of the Church, which we
all have in common, are enlightening. The Fathers delineate
the conditions required so that Jesus may be present in the
midst of his disciples. For John Chrysostom the condition is
to love our neighbor for the sake of Jesus, in the same
measure, for he gave his life for his enemies.

It is especially because of this particular presence of
"Jesus in the midst" of those who are united in his name
that our Movement has had an unexpected ecumenical
development which enables it today to give its specific
contribution towards full communion among the Churches. We understood that Jesus in our midst vivified His
mystical Body. With him in our midst we became "living
cells" of his mystical Body which is the Church.

Owing to our common baptism there was already a
sacramental bond of unity, but, generally speaking, the
implications of this were not lived out among us Christians.
Among his disciples, Jesus had 'activated' that bond, making it function — so to speak — as a new life source.

Even before the Second Vatican Council (which in 1964 spoke of Jesus in the midst of Christians in its Decree on Ecumenism)[7], and many years before John Paul II wrote, "We gather together in the name of Christ who is One. He is our unity,"[8] our Movement was motivated to place Jesus in the midst also among Christians of different Churches (between a Catholic and an Armenian, for example, between Catholics and Lutherans, between Anglicans and Orthodox, and so forth).

And not just when we pray together. And all this has indeed been possible. If they were in the grace of God and were willing to die for us as we were for them (as required by mutual love), Jesus was then present among us.

Over the past forty years of the Movement's ecumenical commitment, Christians of different Churches, fully committed in their own Churches, have striven to revive in this way their own parishes and communities. Groups of Christians united in the name of Jesus were thus formed and continue to be formed while awaiting full and visible communion, "when and however God should wish it."[9]

John Paul II sees great value in the spirituality of unity and its guiding precepts. While addressing some bishops, he stated: "The 'spirituality of communion' is articulated into different elements that are rooted in the Gospel and enriched by the contribution made to the entire Christian community by the Focolare Movement, committed to witnessing to the 'spirituality of unity.' Among other things," the Pope continued, "I would like here to mention unity as the 'testament' that Jesus left to his disciples (cf. *Jn* 17), the mystery of the crucified and abandoned Christ as the 'way' to reach it,

---

7. *Unitatis redintegratio,* 8.
8. *Ut unum sint,* 23.
9. Cf. Paul Couturier.

the celebration of the Eucharist as the bond of communion, the unifying and life-giving action of the Holy Spirit in the mystical Body of Christ and in its members, the presence of the Virgin Mary, Mother of unity, who leads us all to Christ."[10]

Therefore the "spirituality of unity," up to now available to the members of a movement in the Church, is now being offered to the whole Catholic Church with the name "spirituality of communion."

And through the "spirituality of communion" we find the possibility to bring about what the *Novo millennio ineunte* proposes. "To make the Church the home and the school of communion: that is the great challenge facing us in the millennium which is now beginning, if we wish to be faithful to God's plan and respond to the world's deepest yearnings."[11]

This is the "spirituality of communion" which John Paul II affirmed: "gives a renewed thrust to ecumenism".[12] Cardinal Kasper reiterated: "It is especially important for us to develop a 'spirituality of communion' in our own Church and among Churches."[13]

The "spirituality of unity" is also recognised by Christians of other Churches. It is, in fact, called "an ecumenical spirituality."As a consequence, in the Focolare Movement it is lived in various degrees by Christians from more than 350 Churches and Ecclesial Communities. Perhaps this has also been due to the fact that this spirituality has interested and

10. John Paul II, *Speech to Bishop Friends of the Focolare Movement*, published in the *Osservatore Romano* (Weekly Edition in English), 19 February, 2003.
11. *Novo millennio ineunte*, 43.
12. John Paul II, *Speech to Bishop Friends of the Focolare Movement*, op.cit.
13. W. Kasper, "Situazione e visione del movimento ecumenico" in,*"Il Regno – Attualità"* 2002 n.4, p.141.

impressed, for one reason or another, the faithful of a wide range of Churches.

The Evangelical Lutherans, for example, who had been in contact with us Catholics before the Second Vatican Council, were surprised to see that we loved the Gospel and that we lived it with great intensity. So then they wanted to live it with us and they wanted us to bring this life with them into their parishes. The Anglicans, first in England and then in the Anglican Communion, were attracted by the idea and practice of unity. Likewise, the Orthodox were struck by the fact that we highlight life, love and Mary. The members of the Reformed Church, by the presence of "Jesus in the midst" of small groups. The Methodists liked the accent on holiness of this spirituality. The Armenians feel a great affinity with our love for Jesus crucified and risen in the sufferings of life; the Syrian Orthodox, with our desire to live like the first Christian communities. And so forth.

Although we were Christians who belonged to different Churches, we found that this lifestyle, this spirituality had joined us all together as brothers and sisters. Therefore, the "spirituality of unity" proved to be, with time, an ecumenical spirituality and it was confirmed as such by many during the Second European Ecumenical Assembly in Graz, Austria, in June, 1997.

Wherever the spirituality is known, it is accepted by the Churches above all because it is a Gospel that is lived out. The absence of an ecumenical spirituality (that ecumenists today continue to highlight) renders unity among Churches more difficult to achieve.

I remember the first time that I met with a group of Christians from other Churches. It was 1961 and I had been invited to Darmstadt, Germany, to speak to some Evangelical-Lutheran sisters and pastors. They wanted to know about the beginnings of the Focolare Movement, from its birth in 1943 in Italy. I received a very warm welcome from them. I was particularly struck by a comment by one of the German Lutheran pastors when he more or less said: "I had no idea that Catholics are actually living the Gospel in this way!". Since we had already adopted the practice of living the Gospel one phrase at a time with the monthly "Word of Life" (a complete thought from the Gospel accompanied by a commentary), we saw the possibility of living it together with our Evangelical-Lutheran brothers and sisters, sharing our subsequent experiences of life.

This was the catalyst event which opened the door for us to ecumenical dialogue. It was in that moment that we understood how we could speak of a "spirituality of unity in diversity." This was the road that God had indicated to us: to live the Gospel together by focusing on all that already united us.

The contacts between us, Catholics, with our Evangelical-Lutheran friends and their communities became very frequent. A small ecumenical town came to life in Ottmaring, Germany (close to Augsburg), which is now 36 years old and has 140 Evangelical-Lutheran and Catholic citizens. At its inauguration in 1968, Cardinal Augustin Bea, the first President of the Pontifical Council for Promoting Christian Unity, who always encouraged us in this dialogue, said in his message: "The more we understand and live the Gospel, the more we will be united among us, because then we will be more similar to Christ,"[14] which is a concept of *Unitatis redintegratio.*[15]

Our life together has always been blessed and encouraged, besides by the Catholic authorities, also by all the

---

14. Text of the message of Cardinal Bea included by G. Bossi, "Qui vivranno insieme cattolici e luterani" in *"Città Nuova,"* n. 14 (1968), p.35.
15. *Unitatis redintegratio,* 7.

authorities of other Churches where we were seriously working: beginning with Patriarch Athenagoras I and Bartholomew I, Patriarch Theoctist from Romania; Patriarch Ignatius Zakka Iwas; by the last five Archbishops of Canterbury (from Ramsey to Williams), the various leaders of the Reformed Church such as in Switzerland and Hungary and the Lutheran Bishops of Bavaria, Germany: Bishops Dietzfelbinger, Hanselmann and Friedrich. I was also welcomed by the World Council of Churches.

The effects of living this spirituality in the individual Churches are the same: people convert to God, new vocations are born, parishes and communities are renewed, families are reconciled, the gap between generations is overcome, and so forth.

A new phenomenon came about as a result of living the same spirituality among Christians from different Churches. In 1996, during a meeting of the Focolare Movement in London, Great Britain, with about 1200 participants from various Churches, we realized for the first time that we are called to bring a specific contribution to the ecumenical world. I am speaking about the so-called "dialogue of life" or "of the people." Having always placed mutual and constant charity at the base of our life and of all our fraternal meetings, Jesus was so present among us that we felt urged, like Saint Paul, to say: "Who will separate us from the love of Christ?" (*Rom* 8:35). "No one can separate us", because it is Christ who unites us.

Throughout the years, the "spirituality of unity" had brought about something marvellous: even though we were conscious of the road we have to still travel for a full and visible unity among Churches, we all felt — so to say — that we were one Christian people, composed of laity; people of every age, nation and language; monks, religious, priests, deacons, pastors, bishops of various Churches.

We can truly be a portion of Christianity which is alive, one heart and one soul, at least as far as is possible at this time. In fact, with all the brothers and sisters of various Churches who adhere to our Movement, in knowing one another and living together the same spirituality which unites us, bringing among us Jesus and his light, we have given the utmost value to the fact that we are all members of the mystical Body of Christ through our common baptism. We have discovered as our personal and collective patrimony the great riches of the Old and New Testaments, the dogmas of the first Councils which we share, the Creed, (Nicene-Constantinopolitan), the Greek and Latin Church Fathers, the martyrs and other values as well, like the life of grace, faith, hope, charity.

Before, we were not fully aware of these riches or we recognized them only theoretically. Whereas now we lived together all that is shared by the Churches.

I would like to emphasize however that by focusing on what unites us, while still respecting the legitimate differences of expression and of life of the same apostolic faith, does not negate the fact that there are often factors which we still do not agree upon.

Whoever is trained in this "dialogue of life" also has the necessary theological background to face head-on the differences in our faith, thus avoiding the pursuit of false irenics. The "dialogue of life" is the cradle which can give life not only to a theological dialogue. It also serves as the "cradle" for the promotion of an on-going ecumenical formation.

The "dialogue of the people" is not a base or grassroots dialogue that sets itself against or alongside that of the Church leaders or directors, but a dialogue in which all Christians can participate.

This people is like a leaven in the ecumenical movement which enlivens among all the understanding that because we are baptized Christians capable of loving one another, we can all contribute towards realizing the Testament of Jesus.

The Lord really brought about something new through the charism of unity he gave us. Whereas before each one went off on his own, now each one is interested in the others as well. Through our reciprocal love that circulates among us, we come to know more about our different traditions and we appreciate the specific gifts that each one has, as well as those we have in common. This increases among us the dialogue of charity — because we know one another better. Jesus in our midst brought us forward in communion and made us brothers and sisters.

Prayer has had a prominent place in our ecumenical commitment as well because unity is above all a gift from above. It was evident that it would be easier to obtain the grace of unity by asking for it together rather than alone. Jesus said: "Again, I say to you, if two of you *agree* (*consenserint*) on earth about anything for which they are to pray, it shall be granted to them by my heavenly Father" (*Mt* 18:19).

It is not a matter of simply being shoulder to shoulder (as we are in church, at times), but of praying truly united spiritually, with Jesus in the midst of the community.

John Chrysostom says that no one meets together with others to pray "trusting in his own virtue, but rather in the multitude, in agreement, which God holds in the highest consideration and by which he is moved and pleased. 'For where two or three are gathered together in my name,' says Jesus, 'there am I in the midst of them'."[16]

Through this prayer offered to the Father in unity, countless graces have continued to pour over the movement for both spiritual and material needs. For this reason we are confident that the prayer of a Christian people united in the name of Jesus will also have the greatest effect towards attaining full communion among the Churches.

Also the theological dialogue will be able to derive great benefits from the "dialogue of life." If the theologians love one another and thus establish the presence of Jesus in their midst, he who is the one truth toward which everyone is striving, will enlighten their minds and show them the way to follow towards full unity of mind.

Finally, we also hope that the unending problem of "reception," that is, how people perceive the progress made in the official theological dialogues, can be overcome by a people who are ecumenically prepared.

The positive effects of the "dialogue of the people" is beginning to be felt even in the field of evangelisation. We saw this happen last May 8th during the event "Together for Europe" in Stuttgart, Germany, organized by Christians from more than 100 European movements and various Churches, united among themselves by Jesus. Everyone felt called to contribute to bring about — alongside the political and economic Europe (of the Euro) — a "Europe of the spirit." Their various charisms and their typically networked presence in many or all of the European nations

---

16. John Chrysostom, Epist. II ad Thess. Hom. 4.4, in PG 62, 491.

guaranteed this outcome. It was a triumph of the Spirit which will have a follow-up also in other continents.

What shall I say then in conclusion? We need to remember that even though the experiences which I have told you regard a particular Movement in the Church, the "spirituality of unity" or "of communion" which was the catalyst behind them, is a hope and a new road, yet to be discovered in its full potential, but which has opened up before us. If many will put this spirituality into practice, we cannot imagine the ecumenical fruits which it could bring about.

God himself will then give us the gift of unity.

May the Holy Spirit inspire us all.

A Spirituality of Communion: Unity in Diversity[1]

Enzo Bianchi

Please forgive the foolish alacrity with which I responded positively to the invitation to offer a reflection on the theme of the spirituality of communion. I am only a monk, a simple lay person who strives daily to live this spirituality in an ecumenical community: my words will be imbued with simplicity and, I trust, will be obedient to the word of our Lord who desires "all men to be saved" (1 *Tim* 2:4) and all believers to be one, partaking in the communion of the Father, the Son and the Holy Spirit.

The authoritative concluding report of the 1985 Synod of Bishops stated that "the central and fundamental idea of the documents of the Second Vatican Council can be identified in the term *ecclesiology of communion.*" This is now a widely shared view within the Catholic Church, and has formed the basis of many theological studies, the most influential by Jérôme Hamer, Jean–Marie Roger Tillard, Ioannis Zizioulas, Walter Kasper, among others.

However, an authentic theology is capable also of inspiring spirituality or, rather, an authentic theology is always spiritual, pneumatic, capable of making an impact on the interior life and on the experience of the Christian and of the community. Indeed, the word *koinonia* in the New Testament signifies first and foremost the life of the Church born from the descent of the Holy Spirit, that life *"epìtò auto"* (*Acts* 2:44) that is maintained in the apostolic *didaké,*

---

1. Translated from the original Italian text.

in the breaking of bread, in prayer. The word *koinonia* summarises the essential features of the newly created Church and gives these an outward aspect, as the Church is *epiphaneia* of the Trinitarian *koinonia*, a *koinonia* shared in the *dynamis* of the Holy Spirit through the apostolic communion (cf. 1 *Jn* 1:3, 6), a *koinonia* that is the fulfilment of the salvation proclaimed by the Gospel.

When as Christians we speak of communion, we mean the eternal mystery of communion which is the very life of God, but we also mean — given that we are ourselves *"syn–koinonoi"* or partakers (cf. *Phil* 1:7, *Rev* 1:9) — that in this communion we participate in the body of Christ, in the blood of Christ: *koinonia* is therefore of the 'essence' and not simply a 'feature' of the Church. If the life of the Christian and of the Church is life in conformity to the Holy Spirit, originating in the Spirit and life of Christ, then spirituality cannot be anything other than a spirituality of communion. The life of the Christian and of the Church must therefore be shaped by communion, which is neither an optional nor a recent theological discovery, but *forma ecclesiae*. Undoubtedly, communion among Christians and with God in the pilgrimage of the Church towards the Kingdom will always be fragile, continuously challenged and often even contradicted; it will be a communion tending towards fullness, but that will never be such, except in the eternal Kingdom. The communion that every Christian and every Church must live has therefore been wounded and affronted, and this has been so from the time of the New Testament (cf. 1 *Jn* 2:18; 3 *Jn* 9–10 ...), but then as now the Church safeguards and pursues the will of God who makes a claim to the visible communion of the body of Christ, the being one *(hén einai)* just as the Father and Son are one *(Jn* 17:11).

Are Christians aware of this radical need for communion as the structure of their own lives and of their ecclesial life? In this regard, I think it is important that in *Novo millennio ineuente* John Paul II not only identified the force of *koinonia*, but actually called for a spirituality of communion, outlining its concrete forms and attributes, and recapturing the terminology of the medieval Fathers who spoke of the Christian community as a 'home of communion', capable of being a 'school of communion' (*NMI*, 43). While the ecclesiology of communion must clearly take form in a given system and structure, this can only be possible and authentic within the context of a *spiritual journey*, and only if we are able to introduce a spirituality of communion into the daily weave of the Churches.

John Paul II delineates this spirituality of communion above all in the contemplation of the mystery of the Trinity that dwells in us and finds its home in the Christian. This — continues John Paul II — is therefore a question of inculcating and developing the capacity to perceive our brother in faith (also the brother with whom communion is not complete) as a partaker in the body of Christ, my very own brother, towards whom there must be mutual understanding and sharing. Hence, in the Christian landscape, the other is not "hell" (cf. J. P. Sartre), but a "gift of God", who makes up my lack and reveals my insufficiency.

Indeed, it is not possible to be a Christian and not only not want unity, but not do all that is possible for the sake of communion. Whoever advocates and strives for communion with Christ cannot but at the same time advocate and strive for reconciliation and communion with his brother, member of his own body.

To these reflections offered by *Novo millennio ineunte* I would like to add a number of priorities for a spirituality of communion that is truly inspired by the *ecclesiae primitivae forma*.

First and foremost, the priority that communion be manifold. We must not forget that plurality, diversity, is attested to in the writings of the founders of our faith. The one Lord Jesus Christ — "the same yesterday and today and forever" (*Heb* 13:8) — has inspired four Gospels, four different proclamations; indeed, we trace the origin of Christianity not to a single book or writing but to the dynamism of the Holy Spirit. From the very outset, there has been a plurality of scriptural forms, of ecclesiologies, of Christological perspectives, of liturgical practices, of witnesses and forms of *missio*, of spiritual inflections. This plurality — which reflects the polychromy, the multicoloured *Sophia* of God, as well as the inexhaustibility of the mystery of Christ within the widest cultural spectrum — constitutes not only a richness of gifts, but also at the same time the condemnation of any sort of Christian fundamentalism or integralism. Since the very start, the one Jesus Christ makes room for diverse Christianities (Jewish–Christians, ethnic–Christians, and so on), for belief in Christ is enmeshed within a diverse range of communities, which are each open to a different understanding and realisation of the mystery. This diversity is not negated but absorbed in the New Testament scriptures, in the liturgies, in the life of the churches, in the same way that the one truth, who is Jesus Christ, is proclaimed, celebrated and perceived in different ways.

Can there be a limit to diversity, which we can understand as enrichment, but which can also mean a possible tendency towards division and mutual antagonism? This is a sensitive issue — as Metropolitan Zizioulas recognises — that is of principal importance in the ecumenical debate.

And with wisdom he affirms that the most important condition for diversity is that it must not destroy unity. This is
the ecclesial application of the Pauline exhortation regarding the unity of the body, the possibility of scandalising
a member, and the charity that must always prevail.
The relationship between 'one–many' and 'unity–diversity'
must always be lived in the obedience of the one body and
the diversity of gifts of the Holy Spirit. There can be no life
'*en Christo*' without the *koinonia* of the Holy Spirit. In the
words of Saint Maximus Confessor, 'difference' *(diaphoria)*
is positive, but must never become 'division' *(diairesis)*.

Today, thanks also to the philosophical contributions
of Martin Buber and Emmanuel Lévinas, we are culturally
more prepared to embrace the logic of *koinonia*, for otherness is understood by us as essential to existence. It is quite
inconceivable not to think in terms of the other, the other
brother, the other Church, the other theological framework. While belonging to another confession must find its
way to some form of ecclesial *koinonia*, it must also seem to
be legitimate: it cannot be either absolutised or demonised,
for in that case the other would be cast in the role of an
enemy and no longer "the brother for whom Christ died"
(cf. 1 *Cor* 8:11). It is a question of learning that what unites
is far greater than what divides, and that the greater good of
encounter and communion may necessitate relinquishing
non–essential features. In this sense the spirituality of
communion becomes ascetic in nature or, rather, deals with
the capacity to discern and select only the essential.

Thus, the spirituality of communion means practising
the art of listening: not to seek in the other, the other
Church, that which is most similar, but in order to bear this
otherness without obliterating it. In the ecumenical encounter, listening tends above all towards sharing life and

spiritual treasures, mutual acquaintance in order to learn each other's ways, and learning to be sensitive to what may wound the other or may make it difficult for the other to be receptive. In this way, prejudices crumble, and the fear of the other and the temptation to perceive difference and division are overcome: there emerges the possibility to think with the other about faith, its future, its transmission, and evangelisation in the world that God so loved as to give it His only Son (cf. *Jn* 3:16).

Yet, this capacity to bear diversity and otherness does not inevitably open the way for relativism if we accept that in every comparative encounter there is a salvific third party, Jesus Christ, the *Kyrios*. It is He, the *Kyrios*, who merges yet distinguishes, who unites yet individualises, who guides all to the coming Kingdom. In this spirituality of communion, the acknowledgement of the *Kyrios* reminds and assures us that the diversity of gifts is fostered also through prayer: prayer for one another and common prayer, which is the true *epiclesis* of the one Eucharist. It is in prayer that we bring all that we are and all that we are not yet, but that we must become according to the will and calling of the Lord.

Our insistent prayer could evoke the words of Anselm of Havelberg, that the Lord may grant that we may live:

Unum corpus Ecclesiae,
quod Spiritu sancto vivificatur, regitur et gubernatur ...
unum corpus Ecclesiae uno Spiritu sancto vivificari ...
semper unum una fide sed multiformiter distinctum
multiplici vivendi varietate.
(Dialogi I, PL 188, 1144).

In history, we already participate in the eschatological encounter of the dispersed children of God, and in the Christ event we witness the fall of the divisive walls of enmity and are called to share his peace (cf. *Eph* 2:18). If we are authentic disciples of Jesus Christ, we must do all we can in view of communion with him, who gathers all into himself, so that God may be everything to every one (cf. 1 *Cor* 15:28).

Indeed, every Christian spirituality can only ever and always be a spirituality of communion: the spiritual battle against Babel, the *epiclesis* of a renewed Pentecost! Thank you for your attention.

Concluding Observations

Cardinal Walter Kasper

It is not easy to make a summary of our meeting. Without assuming to be exhaustive, I would raise three essential points.

1. The ecumenical direction of *Unitatis redintegratio* forty years ago is irreversible and its validity is permanent, both for today and for the future:
    - it is in conformity with the will of Jesus Christ;
    - it is the will of a universal Council approved by Popes John XXIII, Paul VI and John Paul II;
    - it corresponds to the signs of the times, to the need for evangelisation and for the new evangelisation to which we are called;
    - it has already borne many positive results in the life of the Church, fruits that are a gift of the Spirit of the Lord, for which we must be grateful. These very fruits oblige and constrain us to move onwards and to maintain our ecumenical commitment.

2. In the past forty years the ecumenical situation has undergone great change, with many lights and shadows:

2.1 The lights
- We have reached an intermediary stage in which reception and ecumenical understanding in the Church has grown; at the same time, we experience a growth also in expectations and impatience. Moreover, Pope John Paul II, from the very first day of his long pontificate, made the ecumenical commitment

his own and promoted it with encouraging words
and compelling actions.

- Through dialogue at both the international and
regional/local levels, we have overcome misunderstandings and prejudices, as well as past differences,
and we have deepened and strengthened our agreement in faith, and have formed closer friendships.
- In the majority of cases ecumenical contacts and
collaboration are part of the daily life of the parishes
and dioceses; ecumenism is an integral and normal
part of the life of the Church.
- We are above all grateful for ecumenical prayer
groups and spiritual networks among monasteries,
convents, communities and movements. With
God's help, spiritual ecumenism is growing. There is
no question of an ecumenical 'ice age'.

2.2   The shadows

- Old prejudices sometimes persist; the memory of
the past may weigh heavily on the present and
obstruct a common future. Inactivity and
narrow–mindedness may also surface, as well as a
withdrawal of the Churches and Ecclesial Communities into themselves. On the opposite end, ecumenism can sometimes become prey to a superficial
activism or become a question of purely formal relations based on courtesy, diplomacy or even bureau-
cracy.
- The image of ecumenism as it is understood by the
Church is sometimes distorted by misunderstanding
or abuse, which not only do not help but even
provoke opposing reactions that are counterproduc-

tive. Only ecumenism based on the doctrine and discipline of the Church has a future.

- Today we are faced with new challenges: on the one hand, we find ourselves before a qualitative post–modern relativism and pluralism that no longer raises the question of truth; and on the other hand, we also see an aggressive form of fundamentalism on the part of old and new sects, with which more often than not it is impossible to establish a dialogue based on respect.

- In some Ecclesial Communities we find a sort of doctrinal and especially ethical liberalism that has created new differences within the Communities themselves, as well as between them and the Catholic Church. These so–called progressive developments undermine ecumenical progress. True ecumenism is the ecumenism of charity and truth.

3.   The good fruits produced so far and the new challenges require a clear and shared concept of the future of the ecumenical movement.

- There is a need for a deeper and shared reflection on the foundations of ecumenism: common baptism and baptismal faith: the profession of the trinitarian God and of Jesus Christ as the only Saviour and Redeemer, together with the commitment to live according to the commandments of God and the spirit of the Gospel. A vague family feeling is not enough. We must promote ecumenical formation regarding what unites us and what still divides us. Ignorance and indifference to one's own faith and the faith of others are obstacles to true ecumenism.

• We must clarify the aim of ecumenical activities, i.e., communion in faith, sacraments and apostolic ministry. This communion must not be confused with uniformity; it makes room for a legitimate diversity of expression, spirituality, rites, theology, inculturation, etc. In the meantime, ecumenism moves ahead thanks to the exchange of gifts, entailing not an impoverishment but an enrichment. In this way, the ecumenical movement contributes to achieving the concrete and full realisation of catholicity.

• Ecumenism is not an end in itself, as it is related to evangelisation. The missionary and ecumenical movements have been twins from the very beginning and together they represent the historical dynamism of the Church, through which God — in line with His salvific design — gathers His people from all parts of the earth. The ecumenical journey falls within this eschatological dynamic and lives in the light of a hope that cannot disappoint.

• In the final analysis, the ecumenical journey is an adventure of the Holy Spirit and a spiritual process. Thus, spiritual ecumenism is the very heart of ecumenism, that is, conversion and renewal, sanctity and a life inspired by the Gospel, private and common prayer. It is for this reason that we are grateful to those who pray privately for unity, to the prayer groups, and to the spiritual networks among monasteries, convents, communities and spiritual movements. We are determined to promote this spiritual ecumenism. The Pontifical Council for Promoting Christian Unity intends to publish a *Vademecum* on spiritual ecumenism, which will take into account the diversity of situations in the Church.

The modern Church comprises a wide range of situations, and not only from the ecumenical point of view. A single programme would not be possible nor would it either be necessary or desirable. Meetings such as the one held in these days enable us to strengthen our common desire to undertake the ecumenical journey; they deepen our common ecumenical understanding and vision; and they offer a common direction for the future. Drawing to the close of our meeting and preparing to take leave of one another, our conviction remains steadfast that ecumenism together with evangelisation are the path of the Church towards the future. Each is the will of the Lord and a gift of the Spirit.

Appendix

Unitatis redintegratio
[Text of the Conciliar document]

Introduction

1. The restoration of unity among all Christians is one of the principal concerns of the Second Vatican Council. Christ the Lord founded one Church and one Church only. However, many Christian communions present themselves to men as the true inheritors of Jesus Christ; all indeed profess to be followers of the Lord but differ in mind and go their different ways, as if Christ Himself were divided.[1] Such division openly contradicts the will of Christ, scandalizes the world, and damages the holy cause of preaching the Gospel to every creature.

But the Lord of Ages wisely and patiently follows out the plan of grace on our behalf, sinners that we are. In recent times more than ever before, He has been rousing divided Christians to remorse over their divisions and to a longing for unity. Everywhere large numbers have felt the impulse of this grace, and among our separated brethren also there increases from day to day the movement, fostered by the grace of the Holy Spirit, for the restoration of unity among all Christians. This movement toward unity is called "ecumenical." Those belong to it who invoke the Triune God and confess Jesus as Lord and Savior, doing this not merely as individuals but also as corporate bodies. For almost everyone regards the body in which he has heard the Gospel as his Church and indeed, God's Church. All however, though in different ways, long for the one visible Church of God, a Church truly universal and set forth into the world that the world may be converted to the Gospel and so be saved, to the glory of God.

The Sacred Council gladly notes all this. It has already declared its teaching on the Church, and now, moved by a desire for the restoration of unity among all the followers of Christ, it wishes to set before all Catholics the ways and means by which they too can respond to this grace and to this divine call.

Chapter 1

Catholic Principles on Ecumenism

2. What has revealed the love of God among us is that the Father has sent into the world His only-begotten Son, so that, being made man, He might by His redemption give new life to the entire human race and unify it.[2] Before offering Himself up as a spotless victim upon the altar, Christ prayed to His Father for all who believe in Him: "that they all may be one; even as thou, Father, art in me, and I in thee, that they also may be one in us, so that the world may believe that thou has sent me."[3] In His Church He instituted the wonderful sacrament of the Eucharist by which the unity of His Church is both signified and made a reality. He gave His followers a new commandment to love one another,[4] and promised the Spirit, their Advocate,[5] who, as Lord and life-giver, should remain with them forever.

After being lifted up on the cross and glorified, the Lord Jesus poured forth His Spirit as He had promised, and through the Spirit He has called and gathered together the people of the New Covenant, who are the Church, into a unity of faith, hope and charity, as the Apostle teaches us: "There is one body and one Spirit, just as you were called to the one hope of your calling; one Lord, one faith, one Baptism".[6] For "all you who have been baptized into Christ have put on Christ ... for you are all one in Christ Jesus."[7] It is the Holy Spirit, dwelling in those who believe and pervading and ruling over the Church as a whole, who brings about that wonderful communion of the faithful. He brings them into intimate union with Christ, so that He is the principle of the Church's unity. The distribution of graces and offices is His work too,[8] enriching the Church of Jesus Christ with different functions "in order to equip the saints for the work of service, so as to build up the body of Christ".[9]

In order to establish this His holy Church everywhere in the world till the end of time, Christ entrusted to the College of the Twelve the task of teaching, ruling and sanctifying.[10] Among their number He selected Peter, and after his confession of faith determined that on him He would build His Church. Also to Peter He promised the keys of the kingdom of heaven,[11] and after His profession of love, entrusted all His sheep to him to be confirmed in faith[12] and shepherded in perfect unity.[13] Christ Jesus Himself was forever to remain the chief cornerstone[14] and shepherd of our souls.[15]

Jesus Christ, then, willed that the apostles and their successors — the bishops with Peter's successor at their head — should preach the Gospel faithfully, administer the sacraments, and rule the Church in love. It is thus, under the action of the Holy Spirit, that Christ wills His people to increase, and He perfects His people's fellowship in unity:

in their confessing the one faith, celebrating divine worship in common, and keeping the fraternal harmony of the family of God.

The Church, then, is God's only flock; it is like a standard lifted high for the nations to see it:[16] for it serves all mankind through the Gospel of peace[17] as it makes its pilgrim way in hope toward the goal of the fatherland above.[18]

This is the sacred mystery of the unity of the Church, in Christ and through Christ, the Holy Spirit energizing its various functions. It is a mystery that finds its highest exemplar and source in the unity of the Persons of the Trinity: the Father and the Son in the Holy Spirit, one God.

3. Even in the beginnings of this one and only Church of God there arose certain rifts,[19] which the Apostle strongly condemned.[20] But in subsequent centuries much more serious dissensions made their appearance and quite large communities came to be separated from full communion with the Catholic Church — for which, often enough, men of both sides were to blame. The children who are born into these Communities and who grow up believing in Christ cannot be accused of the sin involved in the separation, and the Catholic Church embraces upon them as brothers, with respect and affection. For men who believe in Christ and have been truly baptized are in communion with the Catholic Church even though this communion is imperfect. The differences that exist in varying degrees between them and the Catholic Church — whether in doctrine and sometimes in discipline, or concerning the structure of the Church — do indeed create many obstacles, sometimes serious ones, to full ecclesiastical communion. The ecumenical movement is striving to overcome these obstacles. But even in spite of them it remains true that all who have been justified

by faith in Baptism are members of Christ's body,[21] and have a right to be called Christian, and so are correctly accepted as brothers by the children of the Catholic Church.[22]

Moreover, some and even very many of the significant elements and endowments which together go to build up and give life to the Church itself, can exist outside the visible boundaries of the Catholic Church: the written word of God; the life of grace; faith, hope and charity, with the other interior gifts of the Holy Spirit, and visible elements too. All of these, which come from Christ and lead back to Christ, belong by right to the one Church of Christ.

The brethren divided from us also use many liturgical actions of the Christian religion. These most certainly can truly engender a life of grace in ways that vary according to the condition of each Church or Community. These liturgical actions must be regarded as capable of giving access to the community of salvation.

It follows that the separated Churches[23] and Communities as such, though we believe them to be deficient in some respects, have been by no means deprived of significance and importance in the mystery of salvation. For the Spirit of Christ has not refrained from using them as means of salvation which derive their efficacy from the very fullness of grace and truth entrusted to the Church.

Nevertheless, our separated brethren, whether considered as individuals or as Communities and Churches, are not blessed with that unity which Jesus Christ wished to bestow on all those who through Him were born again into one body, and with Him quickened to newness of life — that unity which the Holy Scriptures and the ancient Tradition of the Church proclaim. For it is only through Christ's Catholic Church, which is "the all-embracing means of salvation," that they can benefit fully from the means of salvation. We believe that Our Lord entrusted all the blessings of the New Covenant to the apostolic college alone, of which Peter is the head, in order to establish the one Body of Christ on earth to which all should be fully incorporated who belong in any way to the people of God. This people of God, though still in its members liable to sin, is ever growing in Christ during its pilgrimage on earth, and is guided by God's gentle wisdom, according to His hidden designs, until it shall happily arrive at the fullness of eternal glory in the heavenly Jerusalem.

4. Today, in many parts of the world, under the inspiring grace of the Holy Spirit, many efforts are being made in prayer, word and action to attain that fullness of unity which Jesus Christ desires. The Sacred Council exhorts all the Catholic faithful to recognize the signs of the times and to take an active and intelligent part in the work of ecumenism.

The term "ecumenical movement" indicates the initiatives and activities planned and undertaken, according to the various needs of the Church and as opportunities offer, to promote Christian unity. These are: first, every effort to avoid expressions, judgments and actions which do not represent the condition of our separated brethren with truth and fairness and so make mutual relations with them more difficult; then, "dialogue" between competent experts from different Churches and Communities. At these meetings, which are organized in a religious spirit, each explains the teaching of his Communion in greater depth and brings out clearly its distinctive features. In such dialogue, everyone gains a truer knowledge and more just appreciation of the teaching and religious life of both Communions. In addition, the way is prepared for cooperation between them in the duties for the common good of humanity which are demanded by every Christian conscience; and, wherever this is allowed, there is prayer in common. Finally, all are led to examine their own faithfulness to Christ's will for the Church and accordingly to undertake with vigor the task of renewal and reform.

When such actions are undertaken prudently and patiently by the Catholic faithful, with the attentive guidance of their bishops, they promote justice and truth, concord and collaboration, as well as the spirit of brotherly love and unity. This is the way that, when the obstacles to perfect ecclesiastical communion have been gradually overcome, all Christians will at last, in a common celebration of the Eucharist, be gathered into the one and only Church in that unity which Christ bestowed on His Church from the beginning. We believe that this unity subsists in the Catholic Church as something she can never lose, and we hope that it will continue to increase until the end of time.

However, it is evident that, when individuals wish for full Catholic communion, their preparation and reconciliation is an undertaking which of its nature is distinct from ecumenical action. But there is no opposition between the two, since both proceed from the marvelous ways of God.

Catholics, in their ecumenical work, must assuredly be concerned for their separated brethren, praying for them, keeping them informed about the Church, making the first approaches toward them. But their primary duty is to make a careful and honest appraisal of whatever needs to be done or renewed in the Catholic household itself, in order that its life may bear witness more clearly and faithfully to the teachings and institutions which have come to it from Christ through the Apostles.

For although the Catholic Church has been endowed with all divinely revealed truth and with all means of grace, yet its members fail to live by them with all the fervor that they should, so that the radiance of the Church's image is less clear in the eyes of our separated brethren and of the world at large, and the growth of God's kingdom is delayed. All Catholics must therefore aim at Christian perfection[24] and, each according to his station, play his part that the Church may daily be more purified and renewed. For the Church must bear in her own body the humility and dying of Jesus,[25] against the day when Christ will present her to Himself in all her glory without spot or wrinkle.[26]

All in the Church must preserve unity in essentials. But let all, according to the gifts they have received enjoy a proper freedom, in their various forms of spiritual life and discipline, in their different liturgical rites, and even in their theological elaborations of revealed truth. In all things let charity prevail. If they are true to this course of action, they will be giving ever better expression to the authentic catholicity and apostolicity of the Church.

On the other hand, Catholics must gladly acknowledge and esteem the truly Christian endowments from our common heritage which are to be found among our separated brethren. It is right and salutary to recognize the riches of Christ and virtuous works in the lives of others who are bearing witness to Christ, sometimes even to the shedding of their blood. For God is always wonderful in His works and worthy of all praise.

Nor should we forget that anything wrought by the grace of the Holy Spirit in the hearts of our separated brethren can be a help to our own edification. Whatever is truly Christian is never contrary to what genuinely belongs to the faith;

indeed, it can always bring a deeper realization of the mystery of Christ and the Church.

Nevertheless, the divisions among Christians prevent the Church from attaining the fullness of catholicity proper to her, in those of her sons who, though attached to her by Baptism, are yet separated from full communion with her. Furthermore, the Church herself finds it more difficult to express in actual life her full catholicity in all her bearings.

This Sacred Council is gratified to note that the participation by the Catholic faithful in ecumenical work is growing daily. It commends this work to the bishops everywhere in the world to be vigorously stimulated by them and guided with prudence.

Chapter II

The Practice of Ecumenism

5. The attainment of union is the concern of the whole Church, faithful and shepherds alike. This concern extends to everyone, according to his talent, whether it be exercised in his daily Christian life or in his theological and historical research. This concern itself reveals already to some extent the bond of brotherhood between all Christians and it helps toward that full and perfect unity which God in His kindness wills.

6. Every renewal of the Church[27] is essentially grounded in an increase of fidelity to her own calling. Undoubtedly this is the basis of the movement toward unity.

Christ summons the Church to continual reformation as she sojourns here on earth. The Church is always in need of this, in so far as she is an institution of men here on earth.

Thus if, in various times and circumstances, there have been deficiencies in moral conduct or in church discipline, or even in the way that church teaching has been formulated — to be carefully distinguished from the deposit of faith itself — these can and should be set right at the opportune moment.

Church renewal has therefore notable ecumenical importance. Already in various spheres of the Church's life, this renewal is taking place. The Biblical and liturgical movements, the preaching of the word of God and catechetics, the apostolate of the laity, new forms of religious life and the spirituality of married life, and the Church's social teaching and activity — all these should be considered as pledges and signs of the future progress of ecumenism.

7. There can be no ecumenism worthy of the name without a change of heart. For it is from renewal of the inner life of our minds,[28] from self-denial and an unstinted love that desires of unity take their rise and develop in a mature way. We should therefore pray to the Holy Spirit for the grace to be genuinely self-denying, humble. gentle in the service of others, and to have an attitude of brotherly generosity towards them. St. Paul says: "I, therefore, a prisoner for the Lord, beg you to lead a life worthy of the calling to which you have been called, with all humility and meekness, with patience, forbearing one another in love, eager to maintain the unity of the spirit in the bond of peace".[29] This exhortation is directed especially to those raised to sacred Orders precisely that the work of Christ may be continued. He came among us "not to be served but to serve".[30]

The words of St. John hold good about sins against unity: "If we say we have not sinned, we make him a liar, and his word is not in us".[31] So we humbly beg pardon of

God and of our separated brethren, just as we forgive them that trespass against us.

All the faithful should remember that the more effort they make to live holier lives according to the Gospel, the better will they further Christian unity and put it into practice. For the closer their union with the Father, the Word, and the Spirit, the more deeply and easily will they be able to grow in mutual brotherly love.

8. This change of heart and holiness of life, along with public and private prayer for the unity of Christians, should be regarded as the soul of the whole ecumenical movement, and merits the name, "spiritual ecumenism."

It is a recognized custom for Catholics to have frequent recourse to that prayer for the unity of the Church which the Saviour Himself on the eve of His death so fervently appealed to His Father: "That they may all be one".[32]

In certain special circumstances, such as the prescribed prayers "for unity," and during ecumenical gatherings, it is allowable, indeed desirable that Catholics should join in prayer with their separated brethren. Such prayers in common are certainly an effective means of obtaining the grace of unity, and they are a true expression of the ties which still bind Catholics to their separated brethren. "For where two or three are gathered together in my name, there am I in the midst of them".[33]

Yet worship in common (communicatio in sacris) is not to be considered as a means to be used indiscriminately for the restoration of Christian unity. There are two main principles governing the practice of such common worship: first, the bearing witness to the unity of the Church, and second, the sharing in the means of grace. Witness to the unity of the Church very generally forbids common worship to Christians, but the grace to be had from it sometimes commends this practice. The course to be adopted, with due regard to all the circumstances of time, place, and persons, is to be decided by local episcopal authority, unless otherwise provided for by the Bishops' Conference according to its statutes, or by the Holy See.

9. We must get to know the outlook of our separated brethren. To achieve this purpose, study is of necessity required, and this must be pursued with a sense of realism and good will. Catholics, who already have a proper grounding, need to acquire a more adequate understanding of the respective doctrines of our separated brethren, their history, their spiritual and liturgical life, their religious psychology and general background. Most valuable for this purpose are meetings of the two sides — especially for discussion of theological problems — where each can treat with the other on an equal footing — provided that those who take part in them are truly competent and have the approval of the bishops. From such dialogue will emerge still more clearly what the situation of the Catholic Church really is. In this way too the outlook of our separated brethren will be better understood, and our own belief more aptly explained.

10. Sacred theology and other branches of knowledge, especially of an historical nature, must be taught with due regard for the ecumenical point of view, so that they may correspond more exactly with the facts.

It is most important that future shepherds and priests should have mastered a theology that has been carefully worked out in this way and not polemically, especially with regard to those aspects which concern the relations of separated brethren with the Catholic Church.

This importance is the greater because the instruction and spiritual formation of the faithful and of religious depends so largely on the formation which their priests have received.

Moreover, Catholics engaged in missionary work in the same territories as other Christians ought to know, particularly in these times, the problems and the benefits in their apostolate which derive from the ecumenical movement.

11. The way and method in which the Catholic faith is expressed should never become an obstacle to dialogue with our brethren. It is, of course, essential that the doctrine should be clearly presented in its entirety. Nothing is so foreign to the spirit of ecumenism as a false irenicism, in which the purity of Catholic doctrine suffers loss and its genuine and certain meaning is clouded.

At the same time, the Catholic faith must be explained more profoundly and precisely, in such a way and in such terms as our separated brethren can also really understand.

Moreover, in ecumenical dialogue, Catholic theologians standing fast by the teaching of the Church and investigating the divine mysteries with the separated brethren must proceed with love for the truth, with charity, and with humility. When comparing doctrines with one another, they should remember that in Catholic doctrine there exists a "hierarchy" of truths, since they vary in their relation to the fundamental Christian faith. Thus the way will be opened by which through fraternal rivalry all will be stirred to a deeper understanding and a clearer presentation of the unfathomable riches of Christ.[34]

12. Before the whole world let all Christians confess their faith in the triune God, one and three in the incarnate Son of God, our Redeemer and Lord. United in their efforts, and with mutual respect, let them bear witness to our common hope which does not play us false. In these days when cooperation in social matters is so widespread, all men without

exception are called to work together, with much greater reason all those who believe in God, but most of all, all Christians in that they bear the name of Christ. Cooperation among Christians vividly expresses the relationship which in fact already unites them, and it sets in clearer relief the features of Christ the Servant. This cooperation, which has already begun in many countries, should be developed more and more, particularly in regions where a social and technical evolution is taking place be it in a just evaluation of the dignity of the human person, the establishment of the blessings of peace, the application of Gospel principles to social life, the advancement of the arts and sciences in a truly Christian spirit, or also in the use of various remedies to relieve the afflictions of our times such as famine and natural disasters, illiteracy and poverty, housing shortage and the unequal distribution of wealth. All believers in Christ can, through this cooperation, be led to acquire a better knowledge and appreciation of one another, and so pave the way to Christian unity.

Chapter III

Churches and Ecclesial Communities separated
from the Roman Apostolic See

13. We now turn our attention to the two chief types of division as they affect the seamless robe of Christ.

The first divisions occurred in the East, when the dogmatic formulae of the Councils of Ephesus and Chalcedon were challenged, and later when ecclesiastical communion between the Eastern Patriarchates and the Roman See was dissolved.

Other divisions arose more than four centuries later in the West, stemming from the events which are usually referred to as "The Reformation." As a result, many Communions, national or confessional, were separated from the Roman See. Among those in which Catholic traditions and institutions in part continue to exist, the Anglican Communion occupies a special place.

These various divisions differ greatly from one another not only by reason of their origin, place and time, but especially in the nature and seriousness of questions bearing on faith and the structure of the Church. Therefore, without minimizing the differences between the various Christian bodies, and without overlooking the bonds between them which exist in spite of divisions, this holy Council decides to propose the following considerations for prudent ecumenical action.

The Special Consideration of the Eastern Churches

14. For many centuries the Church of the East and that of the West each followed their separate ways though linked in a brotherly union of faith and sacramental life; the Roman See by common consent acted as guide when disagreements arose between them over matters of faith or discipline. Among other matters of great importance, it is a pleasure for this Council to remind everyone that there flourish in the East many particular or local Churches, among which the Patriarchal Churches hold first place, and of these not a few pride themselves in tracing their origins back to the apostles themselves. Hence a matter of primary concern and care among the Easterns, in their local churches, has been, and still is, to preserve the family ties of common faith and charity which ought to exist between sister Churches.

Similarly it must not be forgotten that from the beginning the Churches of the East have had a treasury from which the Western Church has drawn extensively — in liturgical practice, spiritual tradition, and law. Nor must we undervalue the fact that it was the ecumenical councils held in the East that defined the basic dogmas of the Christian faith, on the Trinity, on the Word of God Who took flesh of the Virgin Mary. To preserve this faith these Churches have suffered and still suffer much.

However, the heritage handed down by the apostles was received with differences of form and manner, so that from the earliest times of the Church it was explained variously in different places, owing to diversities of genius and conditions of life. All this, quite apart from external causes, prepared the way for decisions arising also from a lack of charity and mutual understanding.

For this reason the Holy Council urges all, but especially those who intend to devote themselves to the restoration of full communion hoped for between the Churches of the East and the Catholic Church, to give due consideration to this special feature of the origin and growth of the Eastern Churches, and to the character of the relations which obtained between them and the Roman See before separation. They must take full account of all these factors and, where this is done, it will greatly contribute to the dialogue that is looked for.

15. Everyone also knows with what great love the Christians of the East celebrate the sacred liturgy, especially the eucharistic celebration, source of the Church's life and pledge of future glory, in which the faithful, united with their bishop, have access to God the Father through the Son, the Word made flesh, Who suffered and has been glorified, and so, in the outpouring of the Holy Spirit, they enter into communion with the most holy Trinity, being made "sharers of the divine nature".[35] Hence, through the celebration of the Holy

Eucharist in each of these churches, the Church of God is built up and grows in stature[36] and through concelebration, their communion with one another is made manifest.

In this liturgical worship, the Christians of the East pay high tribute, in beautiful hymns of praise, to Mary ever Virgin, whom the ecumenical Council of Ephesus solemnly proclaimed to be the holy Mother of God, so that Christ might be acknowledged as being truly Son of God and Son of Man, according to the Scriptures. Many also are the saints whose praise they sing, among them the Fathers of the universal Church.

These Churches, although separated from us, yet possess true sacraments and above all, by apostolic succession, the priesthood and the Eucharist, whereby they are linked with us in closest intimacy. Therefore some worship in common (communicatio in sacris), given suitable circumstances and the approval of Church authority, is not only possible but to be encouraged.

Moreover, in the East are found the riches of those spiritual traditions which are given expression especially in monastic life. There from the glorious times of the holy Fathers, monastic spirituality flourished which, then later flowed over into the Western world, and there provided the source from which Latin monastic life took its rise and has drawn fresh vigor ever since. Catholics therefore are earnestly recommended to avail themselves of the spiritual riches of the Eastern Fathers which lift up the whole man to the contemplation of the divine.

The very rich liturgical and spiritual heritage of the Eastern Churches should be known, venerated, preserved and cherished by all. They must recognize that this is of supreme importance for the faithful preservation of the fullness of

Christian tradition, and for bringing about reconciliation between Eastern and Western Christians.

16. Already from the earliest times the Eastern Churches followed their own forms of ecclesiastical law and custom, which were sanctioned by the approval of the Fathers of the Church, of synods, and even of ecumenical councils. Far from being an obstacle to the Church's unity, a certain diversity of customs and observances only adds to her splendor, and is of great help in carrying out her mission, as has already been stated. To remove, then, all shadow of doubt, this holy Council solemnly declares that the Churches of the East, while remembering the necessary unity of the whole Church, have the power to govern themselves according to the disciplines proper to them, since these are better suited to the character of their faithful, and more for the good of their souls. The perfect observance of this traditional principle not always indeed carried out in practice, is one of the essential prerequisites for any restoration of unity.

17. What has just been said about the lawful variety that can exist in the Church must also be taken to apply to the differences in theological expression of doctrine. In the study of revelation East and West have followed different methods, and have developed differently their understanding and confession of God's truth. It is hardly surprising, then, if from time to time one tradition has come nearer to a full appreciation of some aspects of a mystery of revelation than the other, or has expressed it to better advantage. In such cases, these various theological expressions are to be considered often as mutually complementary rather than conflicting. Where the authentic theological traditions of the Eastern Church are concerned, we must recognize the admirable way in which they have their roots in Holy Scripture, and how they are nurtured and given expression in the

life of the liturgy. They derive their strength too from the living tradition of the apostles and from the works of the Fathers and spiritual writers of the Eastern Churches. Thus they promote the right ordering of Christian life and, indeed, pave the way to a full vision of Christian truth.

All this heritage of spirituality and liturgy, of discipline and theology, in its various traditions, this holy synod declares to belong to the full Catholic and apostolic character of the Church. We thank God that many Eastern children of the Catholic Church, who preserve this heritage, and wish to express it more faithfully and completely in their lives, are already living in full communion with their brethren who follow the tradition of the West.

18. After taking all these factors into consideration, this Sacred Council solemnly repeats the declaration of previous Councils and Roman Pontiffs, that for the restoration or the maintenance of unity and communion it is necessary "to impose no burden beyond what is essential".[37] It is the Council's urgent desire that, in the various organizations and living activities of the Church, every effort should be made toward the gradual realization of this unity, especially by prayer, and by fraternal dialogue on points of doctrine and the more pressing pastoral problems of our time. Similarly, the Council commends to the shepherds and faithful of the Catholic Church to develop closer relations with those who are no longer living in the East but are far from home, so that friendly collaboration with them may increase, in the spirit of love, to the exclusion of all feeling of rivalry or strife. If this cause is wholeheartedly promoted, the Council hopes that the barrier dividing the Eastern Church and Western Church will be removed, and that at last there may be but the one dwelling, firmly established on Christ Jesus, the cornerstone, who will make both one.[38]

Separated Churches and Ecclesial
Communities in the West

19. In the great upheaval which began in the West toward the end of the Middle Ages, and in later times too, Churches and ecclesial Communities came to be separated from the Apostolic See of Rome. Yet they have retained a particularly close affinity with the Catholic Church as a result of the long centuries in which all Christendom lived together in ecclesiastical communion.

However, since these Churches and ecclesial Communities, on account of their different origins, and different teachings in matters of doctrine on the spiritual life, vary considerably not only with us, but also among themselves, the task of describing them at all adequately is extremely difficult; and we have no intention of making such an attempt here.

Although the ecumenical movement and the desire for peace with the Catholic Church have not yet taken hold everywhere, it is our hope that ecumenical feeling and mutual esteem may gradually increase among all men.

It must however be admitted that in these Churches and ecclesial Communities there exist important differences from the Catholic Church, not only of an historical, sociological, psychological and cultural character, but especially in the interpretation of revealed truth. To make easier the ecumenical dialogue in spite of these differences, we wish to set down some considerations which can, and indeed should, serve as a basis and encouragement for such dialogue.

20. Our thoughts turn first to those Christians who make open confession of Jesus Christ as God and Lord and as the sole Mediator between God and men, to the glory of the one God, Father, Son and Holy Spirit. We are aware indeed that

there exist considerable divergences from the doctrine of the Catholic Church concerning Christ Himself, the Word of God made flesh, the work of redemption, and consequently, concerning the mystery and ministry of the Church, and the role of Mary in the plan of salvation. But we rejoice to see that our separated brethren look to Christ as the source and center of Church unity. Their longing for union with Christ inspires them to seek an ever closer unity, and also to bear witness to their faith among the peoples of the earth.

21. A love and reverence of Sacred Scripture which might be described as devotion, leads our brethren to a constant meditative study of the sacred text. For the Gospel "is the power of God for salvation to every one who has faith, to the Jew first and then to the Greek".[39]

While invoking the Holy Spirit, they seek in these very Scriptures God as it were speaking to them in Christ, Whom the prophets foretold, Who is the Word of God made flesh for us. They contemplate in the Scriptures the life of Christ and what the Divine Master taught and did for our salvation, especially the mysteries of His death and resurrection.

But while the Christians who are separated from us hold the divine authority of the Sacred Books, they differ from ours — some in one way, some in another — regarding the relationship between Scripture and the Church. For, according to Catholic belief, the authentic teaching authority of the Church has a special place in the interpretation and preaching of the written word of God.

But Sacred Scriptures provide for the work of dialogue an instrument of the highest value in the mighty hand of God for the attainment of that unity which the Saviour holds out to all.

22. Whenever the Sacrament of Baptism is duly administered as Our Lord instituted it, and is received with the right dispositions, a person is truly incorporated into the crucified and glorified Christ, and reborn to a sharing of the divine life, as the Apostle says: "You were buried together with Him in Baptism, and in Him also rose again-through faith in the working of God, who raised Him from the dead".[40]

Baptism therefore establishes a sacramental bond of unity which links all who have been reborn by it. But of itself Baptism is only a beginning, an inauguration wholly directed toward the fullness of life in Christ. Baptism, therefore, envisages a complete profession of faith, complete incorporation in the system of salvation such as Christ willed it to be, and finally complete ingrafting in eucharistic communion.

Though the ecclesial Communities which are separated from us lack the fullness of unity with us flowing from Baptism, and though we believe they have not retained the proper reality of the eucharistic mystery in its fullness, especially because of the absence of the sacrament of Orders, nevertheless when they commemorate His death and resurrection in the Lord's Supper, they profess that it signifies life in communion with Christ and look forward to His coming in glory. Therefore the teaching concerning the Lord's Supper, the other sacraments, worship, the ministry of the Church, must be the subject of the dialogue.

23. The daily Christian life of these brethren is nourished by their faith in Christ and strengthened by the grace of Baptism and by hearing the word of God. This shows itself in their private prayer, their meditation on the Bible, in their Christian family life, and in the worship of a community gathered together to praise God. Moreover,

their form of worship sometimes displays notable features of the liturgy which they shared with us of old.

Their faith in Christ bears fruit in praise and thanksgiving for the blessings received from the hands of God. Among them, too, is a strong sense of justice and a true charity toward their neighbor. This active faith has been responsible for many organizations for the relief of spiritual and material distress, the furtherance of the education of youth, the improvement of the social conditions of life, and the promotion of peace throughout the world.

While it is true that many Christians understand the moral teaching of the Gospel differently from Catholics, and do not accept the same solutions to the more difficult problems of modern society, nevertheless they share our desire to stand by the words of Christ as the source of Christian virtue, and to obey the command of the Apostle: "And whatever you do, in word or in work, do all in the name of the Lord Jesus Christ, giving thanks to God the Father through Him".[41] For that reason an ecumenical dialogue might start with discussion of the application of the Gospel to moral conduct.

24. Now that we have briefly set out the conditions for ecumenical action and the principles by which it is to be directed, we look with confidence to the future. This Sacred Council exhorts the faithful to refrain from superficiality and imprudent zeal, which can hinder real progress toward unity. Their ecumenical action must be fully and sincerely Catholic, that is to say, faithful to the truth which we have received from the apostles and Fathers of the Church, in harmony with the faith which the Catholic Church has always professed, and at the same time directed toward that fullness to which Our Lord wills His Body to grow in the course of time.

It is the urgent wish of this Holy Council that the measures undertaken by the sons of the Catholic Church should develop in conjunction with those of our separated brethren so that no obstacle be put in the ways of divine Providence and no preconceived judgments impair the future inspirations of the Holy Spirit. The Council moreover professes its awareness that human powers and capacities cannot achieve this holy objective — the reconciling of all Christians in the unity of the one and only Church of Christ. It is because of this that the Council rests all its hope on the prayer of Christ for the Church, on our Father's love for us, and on the power of the Holy Spirit. "And hope does not disappoint, because God's love has been poured into our hearts through the Holy Spirit, who has been given to us".[42]

Each and all these matters which are set forth in this Decree have been favorably voted on by the Fathers of the Council. And We, by the apostolic authority given Us by Christ and in union with the Fathers, approve, decree and establish them in the Holy Spirit and command that they be promulgated for the glory of God.

Given in Rome at St. Peter's, November 21, 1964

Notes

[1] Cf. 1 Cor. 1, 13.

[2] Cf. 1 Jn. 4, 9; Col. 1, 18-20; Jn. 11, 52.

[3] Jn. 17, 21.

[4] Cf. Jn. 13, 34.

[5] Cf. Jn. 16, 7.

[6] Eph. 4, 4-5.

[7] Gal. 3, 27-28.

[8] Cf. 1 Cor. 12, 4-11.

[9] Eph. 4, 12.

[10] Cf. Mt. 28, 18-20, collato Jn. 20 21-23.

[11] Cf. Mt. 16, 18, collato Mt. 18, 18.

[12] Cf. Lc. 22, 32.

[13] Cf. Jn. 21, 15-18.

[14] Cf. Eph. 2, 20.

[15] Cf. 1 Petr. 2, 2S; CONC. VATICANUM 1, Sess. IV (1870), Constitutio Pastor Aeternus: Collac 7, 482 a.

[16] Cf. Is. 11, 10-12.

[17] Cf. Eph. 2, 17-18, collato Mc. 16, 15.

[18] Cf. 1 Petr. 1, 3-9.

[19] Cf. 1 Cor. 11, 18-19; Gal. 1, 6-9; 1 Jn. 2, 18-19.

[20] Cf. 1 Cor. 1, 11 sqq; 11, 22.

[21] Cf. CONC. FLORENTINUM, Sess. VIII (1439), Decretum Exultate Deo: Mansi 31, 1055 A.

[22] Cf. S. AUGUSTINUS, In Ps. 32, Enarr. 11, 29: PL 36, 299.

[23] Cf. CONC. LATERANENSE IV (1215) Constitutio IV: Mansi 22. 990; CONC. LUGDUNENSE II (1274), Professio fidei MichaelisPalaeologi: Mansi 24, 71 E; CONC. FLORENTINUM, Sess. VI (1439), Definitio Laetentur caeli: Mansi 31, 1026 E.

[24] Cf. Iac. 1, 4; Rom. 12, 1-2.

[25] Cf. 2 Cor. 4, 10, Phil. 2, 5-8.

[26] Cf. Eph. 5, 27.

[27] Cf. CONC. LATERANSE V, Sess. XII (1517), Constitutio Constituti: Mansi 32, 988 B-C.

[28] Cf. Eph. 4, 24.

[29] Eph. 4, 1-3.
[30] Mt. 20, 28.
[31] 1 Jn. 1, 10.
[32] Jn. 17, 21.
[33] Mt. 18, 20.
[34] Cf. Eph. 3, 8.
[35] 2 Petr. 1, 4.
[36] Cf. S. IOANNES CHRYSOSTOMOS, In Ioannem Homelia XLVI, PG 59, 260-262.
[37] Acts 15, 28.
[38] Cf. CONC. FLORENTINUM, Sess. VI (1439), Definitio Laetentur caeli: Mansi 31 1026 E.
[39] Rom. 1, 16.
[40] Col. 2, 12; cf. Rom. 6, 4.
[41] Col. 3, 17.
[42] Rom 5, 5.

Directory for the Application of Principles and Norms on Ecumenism

Preface

1. The search for Christian Unity was one of the principal concerns of the Second Vatican Council. The Ecumenical Directory, called for during the Council and published in two parts, one in 1967 and the other in 1970,[1] has given a most valuable service in directing, coordinating and developing the ecumenical effort".[2]

Reasons for this Revision

2. Besides the publication of the Directory, numerous other documents that have a bearing on ecumenism have been published by competent authorities.[3]

The promulgation of the new *Code of Canon Law* for the Latin Church (1983) and of the *Code of Canons of the Eastern Churches* (1990) has created in ecumenical matters a disciplinary situation for the faithful of the Catholic Church which is partly new.

In the same way, "The Catechism of the Catholic Church" recently published (1992), includes the ecumenical dimension as part of the basic teaching for all the faithful of the Church.

3. Furthermore, from the time of the Council onwards fraternal relations with Churches and ecclesial Communities which are not in full communion with the Catholic Church have intensified; theological dialogues have been set up and have increased in number. In his discourse to the plenary session of the Secretariat (1988), which was dedicated to the revision of the Directory, the Holy Father noted that "the

breadth of the ecumenical movement, the multiplication of dialogue statements, the urgent need that is felt for a greater participation by the whole People of God in this movement, and the consequent necessity of accurate doctrinal information, in view of a proper commitment, all of this requires that up-to-date directives be given without delay".[4] It is in this spirit and in the light of these developments that the revision of this Directory has been made.

To Whom is the Directory Addressed

4. The Directory is addressed to the Pastors of the Catholic Church, but it also concerns all the faithful, who are called to pray and work for the unity of Christians, under the direction of their Bishops. The Bishops, individually for their own dioceses, and collegially for the whole Church, are, under the authority of the Holy See, responsible for ecumenical policy and practice.[5]

5. At the same time it is hoped that the Directory will also be useful to members of Churches and ecclesial Communities that are not in full communion with the Catholic Church. They share with Catholics a concern for the quality of ecumenical activity. It will be an advantage for them to know the direction those guiding the ecumenical movement in the Catholic Church wish to give to ecumenical action, and the criteria that are officially approved in the Church. It will help them to evaluate the initiatives that come from Catholics, so as to respond to them adequately, and will also help them better to understand the Catholic responses to their initiatives. It should be kept in mind that the Directory does not intend to deal with the relations of the Catholic Church with sects or with new religious movements.[6]

Aim of the Directory

6. The new edition of the Directory is meant to be an instrument at the service of the whole Church and especially of those who are directly engaged in ecumenical activity in the Catholic Church. The Directory intends to motivate, enlighten and guide this activity, and in some particular cases also to give binding directives in accordance with the proper competence of the Pontifical Council for Promoting Christian Unity.[7] In the light of the experience of the Church in the years since the Council and taking account of the present ecumenical situation, the Directory brings together all the norms already established for implementing and developing the decisions of the Council given up to the present and brings them up to date when necessary. It strengthens the structures that have been developed for the support and guidance of ecumenical activity at every level of the Church. While fully respecting the competence of authorities at different levels, the Directory gives orientations and norms of universal application to guide Catholic participation in ecumenical activity. Their application will provide consistency and coordination to the various practices of ecumenism by which particular Churches[8] and groups of particular Churches respond to their different local situations. It will guarantee that ecumenical activity throughout the Catholic Church is in accordance with the unity of faith and with the discipline that binds Catholics together.

In our day there exists here and there a certain tendency to doctrinal confusion. Also it is very important in the ecumenical sphere, as in other spheres, to avoid abuses which could either contribute to or entail doctrinal indifferentism. The non-observance of the Church's directives on this matter creates an obstacle to progress in the authentic search for full unity among Christians. It is the task of the local Ordinary and of the Episcopal Conferences and Synods of Eastern Catholic Churches to see to it that the principles and norms contained in the Ecumenical Directory are faithfully applied, and with pastoral concern to take care that all possible deviations from them are avoided.

Outline of the Directory

7. The Directory begins with a declaration of the commitment of the Catholic Church to ecumenism (Chapter I). This is followed by an account of the steps taken by the Catholic Church to put this commitment into practice. It does this through the organization and formation of its own members (Chapters II and III). It is to them thus organized and formed, that the provisions of Chapters IV and V on ecumenical activity are addressed.

I. *The Search for Christian Unity*

The ecumenical commitment of the Catholic Church based on the doctrinal principles of the Second Vatican Council.

II. *Organization in the Catholic Church at the Service of Christian Unity*

Persons and structures involved in promoting ecumenism at all levels, and the norms that direct their activity.

III. *Ecumenical Formation in the Catholic Church*

Categories of people to be formed, those responsible for formation; the aim and methods of formation; its doctrinal and practical aspects.

IV. *Communion in Life and Spiritual Activity Among the Baptized*

The communion that exists with other Christians on the basis of the sacramental bond of Baptism, and the norms for sharing in prayer and other spiritual activities, including in particular cases sacramental sharing.

V. *Ecumenical Cooperation, Dialogue and Common Witness*

Principles, different forms and norms for cooperation between Christians with a view to dialogue and common witness in the world.

8. Thus, in a time of increasingly marked secularization, which calls Christians to common action in their hope for the Kingdom of God, the norms that regulate relations between Catholics and other Christians and the different forms of collaboration they practice are laid down, so that the promotion of the unity desired by Christ may be sought in a balanced and consistent way, in the line of, and according to the principles established by the Second Vatican Council.

I. The Search for Christian Unity

9. The ecumenical movement seeks to be a response to the gift of God's grace which calls all Christians to faith in the mystery of the Church according to the design of God who wishes to bring humanity to salvation and unity in Christ through the Holy Spirit. This movement calls them to the hope that the prayer of Jesus "that they all may be one" will be fully realized.[9] It calls them to that charity which is the new commandment of Christ and the gift by which the Holy Spirit unites all believers. The Second Vatican Council clearly asked Catholics to reach out in love to all other Christians with a charity that desires and works actively to overcome in truth whatever divides them from one another. For the Council, Catholics are to act in hope and in prayer to promote Christian unity. They will be

prompted and instructed by their faith in the mystery of the Church, and their ecumenical activity will be inspired and guided by a true understanding of the Church as "a sacrament or instrumental sign of intimate union with God, and of unity of the whole human race".[10]

10. The teaching of the Church on ecumenism, as well as the encouragement to hope and the invitation to love find their official expression in the documents of the Second Vatican Council and especially in *Lumen gentium* and *Unitatis redintegratio*. Subsequent documents about ecumenical activity in the Church, including the Ecumenical Directory (1967-1970) build on the theological, spiritual and pastoral principles stated in the conciliar documents. They have explored more fully some topics indicated in the conciliar documents, developed theological terminology and provided more detailed norms of action, all based, however, on the teaching of the Council itself. All of this furnishes a body of teachings which will be presented in outline in this chapter. These teachings constitute the base of this Directory.

The Church and its Unity in the Plan of God

11. The Council situates the mystery of the Church within the mystery of God's wisdom and goodness which draws the whole human family and indeed the whole of creation into unity with himself.[11] To this end, God sent into the world His only Son, who was raised up on the cross, entered into glory and poured out the Holy Spirit through whom he calls and draws into unity of faith, hope and charity the people of the New Covenant which is the Church. In order to establish this holy Church in every place until the end of the ages, Christ entrusted to the college of

the Twelve to which he chose Peter as head, the office of teaching, ruling and sanctifying. It is the will of Jesus Christ, that through the faithful preaching of the Gospel, the administration of the sacraments, and through government in love exercised by the apostles and their successors under the action of the Holy Spirit, this people should grow and its communion be made ever more perfect.[12] The Council presents the Church as the New People of God, uniting within itself, in all the richness of their diversity, men and women from all nations, all cultures, endowed with manifold gifts of nature and grace, ministering to one another and recognizing that they are sent into the world for its salvation.[13] They accept the Word of God in faith, are baptized into Christ and confirmed in his pentecostal Spirit, and together they celebrate the sacrament of his body and blood in the Eucharist:

"It is the Holy Spirit, dwelling in those who believe and pervading and ruling over the entire Church, who brings about that wonderful communion of the faithful and joins them together so intimately in Christ that he is the principle of the Church's unity. By distributing various kinds of spiritual gifts and ministeries, he enriches the Church of Jesus Christ with different functions, 'in order to equip the saints for the work of service, so as to build up the Body of Christ' ".[14]

12. The People of God in its common life of faith and sacraments is served by ordained ministers: bishops, priests and deacons.[15] Thus united in the three-fold bond of faith, sacramental life and hierarchical ministry, the whole People of God comes to be what the tradition of faith from the New Testament[16] onwards has always called koinonia/communion. This is a key concept which inspired the ecclesiology

of the Second Vatican Council,[17] and to which recent teaching of the magisterium has given great importance.

The Church as Communion

13. The communion in which Christians believe and for which they hope is, in its deepest reality, their unity with the Father through Christ in the Spirit. Since Pentecost, it has been given and received in the Church, the communion of saints. It is accomplished fully in the glory of heaven, but is already realized in the Church on earth as it journeys towards that fullness. Those who live united in faith, hope and love, in mutual service, in common teaching and sacraments, under the guidance of their pastors [18] are part of that communion which constitutes the Church of God. This communion is realized concretely in the particular Churches, each of which is gathered together around its Bishop. In each of these "the one, holy, catholic and apostolic Church of Christ is truly present and alive".[19] This communion is, by its very nature, universal.

14. Communion between the Churches is maintained and manifested in a special way in the communion between their Bishops. Together they form a college which succeeds the apostolic college. This college has as its head the Bishop of Rome as successor of Peter.[20] Thus the Bishops guarantee that the Churches of which they are the ministers continue the one Church of Christ founded on the faith and ministry of the apostles. They coordinate the spiritual energies and the gifts of the faithful and their associations, towards the building up of the Church and of the full exercise of its mission.

15. Each particular Church, united within itself and in the communion of the one, holy catholic and apostolic Church, is sent forth in the name of Christ and in the power

of the Spirit to bring the Gospel of the Kingdom to more and more people, offering to them this communion with God. In accepting it, these persons also enter into communion with all those who have already received it and are constituted with them in an authentic family of God. Through its unity this family bears witness to this communion with God. It is in this mission of the Church that the prayer of Jesus is being fulfilled, for he prayed "May they all be one, Father, may they be one in us, as you are in me and I in you, so that the world may believe it was you who sent me".[21]

16. Communion within the particular Churches and between them is a gift of God. It must be received with joyful thanks and cultivated with care. It is fostered in a special way by those who are called to minister in the Church as pastors. The unity of the Church is realized in the midst of a rich diversity. This diversity in the Church is a dimension of its catholicity. At times the very richness of this diversity can engender tensions within the communion. Yet, despite such tensions, the Spirit continues to work in the Church calling Christians in their diversity to ever deeper unity.

17. Catholics hold the firm conviction that the one Church of Christ subsists in the Catholic Church "which is governed by the successor of Peter and by the Bishops in communion with him".[22] They confess that the entirety of revealed truth, of sacraments, and of ministry that Christ gave for the building up of his Church and the carrying out of its mission is found within the Catholic communion of the Church. Certainly Catholics know that personally they have not made full use of and do not make full use of the means of grace with which the Church is endowed. For all that, Catholics never lose confidence in the Church. Their

faith assures them that it remains "the worthy bride of the Lord, ceaselessly renewing herself through the action of the Holy Spirit until, through the cross, she may attain to that light which knows no setting".[23] Therefore, when Catholics use the words *"Churches"*, *"other Churches"*, *"other Churches and ecclesial Communities"* etc., to refer to those who are not in full communion with the Catholic Church, this firm conviction and confession of faith must always be kept in mind.

Divisions among Christians and the Re-establishing of Unity

18. Human folly and human sinfulness however have at times opposed the unifying purpose of the Holy Spirit and weakened that power of love which overcomes the inherent tensions in ecclesial life. From the beginning of the Church certain rifts came into being. Then more serious dissensions appeared and the Churches in the East found themselves no longer in full communion with the See of Rome or with the Church of the West.[24]

Later in the West more profound divisions caused other ecclesial Communities to come into being. These ruptures had to do with doctrinal or disciplinary questions and even with the nature of the Church.[25] The Decree on Ecumenism of the Second Vatican Council recognizes that some dissensions have come about "for which often enough men of both sides were to blame".[26] Yet however much human culpability has damaged communion, it has never destroyed it. In fact, the fullness of the unity of the Church of Christ has been maintained within the Catholic Church while other Churches and ecclesial Communities, though not in full communion with the Catholic Church, retain in reality a certain communion with it. The Council affirms: "This unity, we believe, subsists in the Catholic Church as something she can never lose, and we hope that it will continue to increase until the end of time".[27] The Council documents refer to those elements that are shared by the Catholic Church and the Eastern Churches [28] on the one hand, and the Catholic Church and other Churches and ecclesial Communities on the other:[29] "The Spirit of Christ has not refrained from using them as means of salvation".[30]

19. No Christian, however, should be satisfied with these forms of communion. They do not correspond to the will of Christ, and weaken his Church in the exercise of its mission. The grace of God has impelled members of many Churches and ecclesial Communities, especially in the course of this present century, to strive to overcome the divisions inherited from the past and to build anew a communion of love by prayer, by repentance and by asking pardon of each other for sins of disunity past and present, by meeting in practical forms of cooperation and in theological dialogue. These are the aims and activities of what has come to be called the ecumenical movement.[31]

20. The Catholic Church solemnly pledged itself to work for Christian unity at the Second Vatican Council. The Decree *Unitatis redintegratio* explains how the unity that Christ wishes for his Church is brought about "through the faithful preaching of the Gospel by the Apostles and their successors — the Bishops with Peter's successor at their head — through their administering the sacraments, and through their governing in love", and defines this unity as consisting of the "confession of one faith, . . . the common celebration of divine worship, ... the fraternal harmony of the family of God".[32] This unity which of its very nature requires full visible communion of all Christians is the ultimate goal of the ecumenical movement. The Council

affirms that this unity by no means requires the sacrifice of the rich diversity of spirituality, discipline, liturgical rites and elaborations of revealed truth that has grown up among Christians in the measure that this diversity remains faithful to the apostolic Tradition.[33]

21. Since the time of the Second Vatican Council ecumenical activity in the entire Catholic Church has been inspired and guided by various documents and initiatives of the Holy See and, in particular Churches, by documents and initiatives of Bishops, Synods of Eastern Catholic Churches and Episcopal Conferences. Also to be noted is the progress made in different kinds of ecumenical dialogue and in the manifold forms of ecumenical collaboration undertaken. Ecumenism has, in the words of the Synod of Bishops of 1985, "inscribed itself deeply and indelibly in the consciousness of the Church".[34]

Ecumenism in the Life of Christians

22. The ecumenical movement is a grace of God, given by the Father in answer to the prayer of Jesus [35] and the supplication of the Church inspired by the Holy Spirit.[36] While it is carried out within the general mission of the Church to unite humanity in Christ, its own specific field is the restoration of unity among Christians.[37] Those who are baptized in the name of Christ are, by that very fact, called to commit themselves to the search for unity.[38] Baptismal communion tends towards full ecclesial communion. To live our Baptism is to be caught up in Christ's mission of making all things one.

23. Catholics are invited to respond according to the directives of their pastors, in solidarity and gratitude with the efforts that are being made in many Churches and ecclesial Communities, and in the various organizations in

which they cooperate, to reestablish the unity of Christians. Where ecumenical work is not being done, or not being done effectively, Catholics will seek to promote it. Where it is being opposed or hampered by sectarian attitudes and activities that lead to even greater divisions among those who confess the name of Christ, they should be patient and persevering. At times, local Ordinaries,[39] Synods of Eastern Catholic Churches [40] and Episcopal Conferences may find it necessary to take special measures to overcome the dangers of *indifferentism* or *proselytism*.[41] This may especially be needed in the case of young Churches. In all their contacts with members of other Churches and ecclesial Communities, Catholics will act with honesty, prudence and knowledge of the issues. This readiness to proceed gradually and with care, not glossing over difficulties, is also a safeguard against succumbing to the temptations of indifferentism and proselytism, which would be a failure of the true ecumenical spirit.

24. Whatever the local situation, if they are to be able to carry out their ecumenical responsibilities, Catholics need to act together and in agreement with their Bishops. Above all they should know their own Church and be able to give an account of its teaching, its discipline and its principles of ecumenism. The more they know these, the better they can present them in discussions with other Christians and give sufficient reason for them. They should also have accurate knowledge of the other Churches and ecclesial Communities with whom they are in contact. Careful note must be taken of the various prerequisites for ecumenical engagement that are set out in the Decree on Ecumenism of the Second Vatican Council.[42]

25. Because ecumenism with all its human and moral requirements is rooted so profoundly in the mysterious

working out of the providence of the Father, through the Son and in the Spirit, it reaches into the depths of Christian spirituality. It calls for that "change of heart and holiness of life, along with public and private prayer for the unity of Christians", that the Decree on Ecumenism of the Second Vatican Council calls "spiritual ecumenism", and regards as "the soul of the ecumenical movement".[43] Those who identify deeply with Christ must identify with his prayer, and especially with his prayer for unity; those who live in the Spirit must let themselves be transformed by the love that, for the sake of unity, "bears all things, believes all things, hopes all things, endures all things"; [44] those whose lives are marked by repentance will be especially sensitive to the sinfulness of divisions and will pray for forgiveness and conversion. Those who seek holiness will be able to recognize its fruits also outside the visible boundaries of their own Church.[45]

They will be led to know, truly, God as the one who alone is able to gather all into unity because he is the Father of all.

The Different Levels of Ecumenical Activity

26. The opportunities and requirements of ecumenical activity do not present themselves in the same way within the parish, in the diocese, within the ambit of a regional or national organization of dioceses, or at the level of the universal Church. Ecumenism requires the involvement of the People of God within the ecclesial structures and the discipline appropriate to each of these levels.

27. In the diocese, gathered around the Bishop, in the parishes and in the various groups and communities, the unity of Christians is being constructed and shown forth day by day: [46] men and women hear the Word of God in

faith, pray, celebrate the sacraments, serve one another, and show forth the Gospel of salvation to those who do not yet believe.

However, when members of the same family belong to different Churches and ecclesial Communities, when Christians cannot receive Communion with their spouse or children, or their friends, the pain of division makes itself felt acutely and the impulse to prayer and ecumenical activity should grow.

28. The fact of bringing together particular Churches, belonging to the Catholic communion, to form part of bodies such as Synods of Eastern Catholic Churches and Episcopal Conferences, manifests the communion that exists between those Churches. These assemblies can greatly facilitate the development of effective ecumenical relations with the Churches and ecclesial Communities in the same area that are not in full communion with us. As well as a common cultural and civic tradition, they share a common ecclesial heritage dating from the time before the divisions occurred. Synods of Eastern Catholic Churches and Episcopal Conferences can deal more representatively with these regional or national factors in ecumenism than may be possible for a particular Church, and so may they be able to establish organizations for building up and coordinating ecumenical resources and efforts within the territory, in such a way as to support the activities of particular Churches and help them to follow a coherent Catholic direction in their ecumenical activities.

29. It belongs to the College of Bishops and to the Apostolic See to judge in the final instance about the manner of responding to the requirements of full communion.[47] It is at this level that the ecumenical experience of all the particular Churches is gathered and evaluated; necessary resources

can be coordinated for the service of communion at the universal level and among all the particular Churches that belong to this communion and work for it; directives are given which serve to guide and regulate ecumenical activities throughout the Church. It is often to this level of the Church that other Churches and ecclesial Communities address themselves when they wish to be in ecumenical relation with the Catholic Church. And it is at this level that ultimate decisions about the restoration of communion must be taken.

Complexity and Diversity of the Ecumenical Situation

30. The ecumenical movement seeks to be obedient to the Word of God, to the promptings of the Holy Spirit and to the authority of those whose ministry it is to ensure that the Church remains faithful to that apostolic Tradition in which the Word of God and the gifts of the Spirit are received. What is being sought is the communion that is at the heart of the mystery of the Church, and for this reason there is a particular need for the apostolic ministry of Bishops in the area of ecumenical activity. The situations being dealt with in ecumenism are often unprecedented, and vary from place to place and time to time. The initiatives of the faithful in the ecumenical domain are to be encouraged. But there is need for constant and careful discernment by those who have ultimate responsibility for the doctrine and the discipline of the Church.[48] It belongs to them to encourage responsible initiatives and to ensure that they are carried out according to Catholic principles of ecumenism. They must reassure those who may be discouraged by difficulties and moderate the imprudent generosity of those who do not give sufficiently serious consideration to the real difficulties in the way of reunion. The Pontifical

Council for Promoting Christian Unity, whose role and responsibility it is to provide direction and advice on ecumenical activity, offers the same service to the whole Church.

31. The nature of the ecumenical activity undertaken in a particular region will always be influenced by the particular character of the local ecumenical situation. The choice of appropriate ecumenical involvement pertains especially to the Bishop who must take account of the specific responsibilities and challenges that are characteristic for his diocese. It is not possible to review here the variety of situations but a few rather general comments can be made.

32. In a predominantly Catholic country the ecumenical task will emerge differently from that arising in one which has a high proportion or a majority who are Eastern Christians or Anglicans or Protestants. The task is different again in countries where the majority is non-Christian. The participation in the ecumenical movement by the Catholic Church in countries with a large Catholic majority is crucial if ecumenism is to be a movement that involves the whole Church.

33. Likewise the ecumenical task will greatly vary depending on whether our Christian partners belong mostly to one or more of the Eastern Churches rather than to the Communities of the Reformation. Each has its own dynamic and its own particular possibilities. There are many other factors, political, social, cultural, geographical and ethnic, which can give distinct shape to the ecumenical task.

34. The particular local context will always furnish the different characteristics of the ecumenical task. What is important is that, in this common effort, Catholics throughout the world support one another with prayer and

mutual encouragement so that the quest for Christian unity may be pursued in its many facets in obedience to the command of Our Lord.

Sects and New Religious Movements

35. The religious landscape of our world has evolved considerably in recent decades and in some parts of the world the most noticeable development has been the growth of sects and new religious movements whose desire for peaceful relations with the Catholic Church may be weak or non-existent. In 1986, a report[49] was published jointly by four dicasteries of the Roman Curia which draws attention to the vital distinction that must be made between sects and new religious movements on the one hand and Churches and ecclesial Communities on the other. Further studies are in progress on this question.

36. The situation in regard to sects and new religious movements is highly complex and differs from one cultural context to another. In some countries sects are growing in a cultural climate that is basically religious. In other places they are flourishing in societies that are increasingly secularized but at the same time credulous and superstitious. Some sects are non-Christian in origin and in self-understanding; others are eclectic; others again identify themselves as Christian and may have broken away from Christian Communities or else have links with Christianity. Clearly it is especially up to the Bishop, the Synod of Eastern Catholic Churches or the Episcopal Conference to discern how best to respond to the challenge posed by sects in a given area. But it must be stressed that the principles for spiritual sharing or practical cooperation outlined in this Directory only apply to the Churches and ecclesial

Communities with which the Catholic Church has established ecumenical relations. As will be clear to the reader of this Directory, the only basis for such sharing and cooperation is the recognition on both sides of a certain, though imperfect, communion already existing. Openness and mutual respect are the logical consequences of such recognition.

II. The Organization in the Catholic Church of the Service of Christian Unity

Introduction

37. Through its particular Churches, the Catholic Church is present in many localities and regions in which it lives together with other Churches and ecclesial Communities. Such regions have their distinctive spiritual, ethnic, political and cultural characteristics. In many cases one finds in these regions the highest religious authority of other Churches and ecclesial Communities: these regions often correspond to the territory of a Synod of Eastern Catholic Churches or of an Episcopal Conference.

38. Therefore, a Catholic particular Church, or several particular Churches, acting closely together may find themselves in a very favourable position to make contact with other Churches and ecclesial Communities at this level. They may be able to establish with them fruitful ecumenical relations which contribute to the wider ecumenical movement.[50]

39. The Second Vatican Council specifically entrusted the ecumenical task "to the Bishops everywhere in the world for their diligent promotion and prudent guidance".[51] This directive, which has already been acted upon often by indi-

vidual Bishops, Synods of Eastern Catholic Churches and Episcopal Conferences, has been incorporated into the Canon Law of the Latin Church, canon 755, which states:

§ 1. It is within the special competence of the entire college of Bishops and of the Apostolic See to promote and direct the participation of Catholics in the ecumenical movement, whose purpose is the restoration of unity among all Christians, which the Church is bound by the will of Christ to promote.

§ 2. It is likewise within the competence of Bishops and, in accord with the norms of law, of Conferences of Bishops to promote the same unity and to issue practical norms for the needs and opportunities presented by diverse circumstances in light of the prescriptions of the supreme Church authority.

For the Eastern Catholic Churches the *CCEO*, cann. 902-904, § 1 affirms:

Can. 902: Since concern for the restoration of the unity of all Christians belongs to the entire Church, all Christian faithful, especially pastors of the Church, shall pray for that fullness of unity desired by the Lord and work zealously participating in the ecumenical work brought about by grace of the Holy Spirit.

Can. 903: The Eastern Catholic Churches have a special duty of fostering unity among all Eastern Churches, first of all through prayers, by the example of life, by the religious fidelity to the ancient traditions of the Eastern Churches, by better knowledge of each other, and by collaboration and brotherly respect in practice and spirit.

Can. 904: 1. The undertakings of the ecumenical movement in every Church *sui iuris* are to be diligently encouraged by special norms of particular law, while the Apostolic Roman See directs the movement for the universal Church.

40. In the light of this special competence for promoting and guiding ecumenical work, it is the responsibility of the individual diocesan Bishop, or of Synods of Eastern Catholic Churches or of Episcopal Conferences to establish norms according to which the persons or commissions described below are to carry out the activities ascribed to them and to oversee the implementation of these norms. Furthermore, care should be taken that those to whom these ecumenical responsibilities are to be assigned have a proper knowledge of the Catholic principles of ecumenism and are seriously prepared for their task.

The Diocesan Ecumenical Officer

41. In the dioceses, the Bishop should appoint a competent person as diocesan officer for ecumenical questions. He/she will serve as the animator of the diocesan ecumenical Commission and coordinate the Commission's activities as indicated below in n. 44 (or carry them out if such a Commission does not exist). As a close collaborator of the Bishop and with suitable assistance, this person will encourage various initiatives in the diocese for prayer for Christian unity, will work to see that ecumenical attitudes influence the activities of the diocese, identify special needs and keep the diocese informed about these. This officer is also responsible for representing the Catholic community in its relations with the other Churches and ecclesial Communities and their leaders and will facilitate contacts between the latter and the local Bishop, clergy and laity on various levels. He/she will serve as counselor on ecumenical issues for the Bishop and other offices of the diocese and will facilitate the sharing of ecumenical experiences and initiatives with pastors and diocesan organizations. This officer will see to the maintenance of contacts with officers

or commissions of other dioceses. Even in areas where Catholics are in majority, or in those dioceses with limited personnel or resources, it is recommended that such a diocesan officer be appointed to carry out the activities mentioned above in so far as these are possible or appropriate.

The Diocesan Ecumenical Commission or Secretariat

42. In addition to the diocesan officer for ecumenical questions, the diocesan Bishop should set up a council, commission or secretariat charged with putting into practice any directives or orientations he may give and, in general, with promoting ecumenical activity in the diocese.[52] Where circumstances call for it, several dioceses grouped together may form such a commission or secretariat.

43. The commission or secretariat should reflect the totality of the diocese and generally include among its members clergy, religious men and women and lay people of various competencies, and especially those with particular ecumenical expertise. It is desirable that representatives of the presbyterial council, the pastoral council, diocesan and regional seminaries be included among the members of the commission or secretariat.

This commission should cooperate with such institutions or ecumenical initiatives as already exist, or are to be set up, making use of their help where the occasion presents itself. It should be ready to support the ecumenical officer and to be available to other diocesan work and individual initiatives for mutual exchange of information and ideas. Of particular concern should be contacts with parishes and parish organizations, with the apostolic initiatives being conducted by members of institutes of consecrated life and societies of apostolic life, and with movements and associations of lay people.

44. Besides the other functions already assigned to it, the commission should:

a) put into practice the decisions of the diocesan Bishop for implementing the teaching and directives of the Second Vatican Council on ecumenism, as well as those of the post-conciliar documents emanating from the Holy See, Synods of Eastern Catholic Churches and Episcopal Conferences;

b) maintain relations with the territorial ecumenical commission (cf. below), adapting the latter's recommendations and advice to local conditions. When circumstances suggest, information about experiences and their results as well as other useful information should be sent to the Pontifical Council for Promoting Christian Unity;

c) foster spiritual ecumenism according to the principles given in the conciliar Decree on Ecumenism and in other sections of this Directory about public and private prayer for the unity of Christians;

d) offer help and encouragement by such means as workshops and seminars for the ecumenical formation of both clergy and laity, for the appropriate realization of an ecumenical dimension to all aspects of life, and giving special attention as to how seminary students are prepared for the ecumenical dimension of preaching, catechetics and other forms of teaching, and pastoral activity (e.g., pastoral care in mixed marriages) etc.;

e) promote friendliness and charity between Catholics and other Christians with whom full ecclesial communion does not yet exist according to the suggestions and guidelines given below (especially nn. 205-218);

f) initiate and guide conversations and consultations with them, bearing in mind the adaptation to be observed in accordance with the diversity of the participants and subjects of dialogue; [53]

g) propose experts to undertake dialogue on the diocesan level with other Churches and ecclesial Communities;

h) promote, in collaboration with other diocesan bodies and with other Christians joint witness to Christian faith, to the extent that this is possible, as well as cooperation in such areas as education, public and private morality, social justice, matters connected with culture, learning and the arts; [54]

i) propose to the Bishops the exchange of observers and guests on the occasion of important conferences, synods, installation of religious leaders and other similar occasions.

45. Within the dioceses, parishes should be encouraged to participate in ecumenical initiatives on their own level and, where possible to set up groups which are responsible to carry out these activities (cf. below, n. 67); they should remain in close contact with the diocesan authorities, exchanging information and experience with them and with other parishes and other groups.

The Ecumenical Commission of Synods of Eastern Catholic Churches and Episcopal Conferences

46. Each Synod of the Eastern Catholic Churches and each Episcopal Conference, in accordance with its own procedures, should establish an episcopal commission for ecumenism, assisted by experts, both men and women, chosen from among the clergy, religious and laity. If possible, the commission should be assisted by a permanent secretariat. This commission, whose method of work will be determined by the statutes of the synod or conference,

should have a mandate to give guidance in ecumenical affairs and determine concrete ways of acting in accordance with existing church legislation, directives and legitimate customs and the concrete possibilities of a given region. It should take into account the circumstances of place and persons of the territory with whom they are concerned, as well as the concerns of the universal Church. Where the size of an Episcopal Conference does not permit the establishment of a commission of Bishops, at least one Bishop should be named to assume responsibility for the ecumenical tasks indicated in n. 47.

47. The functions of this commission will include those listed under n. 44 above, insofar as they enter into the competence of the Synods of Eastern Catholic Churches or Episcopal Conferences. In addition, it should carry out other tasks, of which some examples are given here:

a) putting into practice the norms and instructions issued by the Holy See in these matters;

b) giving advice and assistance to Bishops who are setting up an ecumenical commission in their dioceses, and encouraging cooperation among the diocesan ecumenical officers and commissions themselves by sponsoring, for example, periodic gatherings of officers and representatives from diocesan commissions;

c) encouraging and, where indicated, assisting the other commissions of the Episcopal Conferences and Synods of Eastern Catholic Churches in taking account of the ecumenical dimension of the latter's work, public statements, etc.;

d) promoting cooperation among Christians, for example by giving spiritual and material help, where possible, to both existing ecumenical institutions and to ecumenical initiatives to be fostered in the field of instruction and research or in that of pastoral care and the deepening of Christian life according to the principles set out in the conciliar Decree on Ecumenism, nn. 9-12;

e) establishing consultations and dialogue with the church leaders and with Councils of Churches which exist on a national or territorial (as distinct from the diocesan) level and providing adequate structures for these dialogues;

f) appointing those experts who, by an official mandate of the Church, will participate in the consultations and dialogues with experts of the various Churches and ecclesial Communities, and with the organizations mentioned above;

g) maintaining relations and active cooperation with the ecumenical structures established by institutes of consecrated life and societies of apostolic life and with those of other Catholic organizations within the territory;

h) organizing the exchange of observers and guests on the occasion of important ecclesial convocations and similar events at the national or territorial levels;

i) informing the Bishops of the Conference and of the Synods about the developments of the dialogues taking place in the territory; sharing this information with the Pontifical Council for Promoting Christian Unity in Rome, so that mutual exchange of advice, experience and the results of dialogue can promote other dialogues on different levels of the life of the Church;

j) in general, maintaining relations in ecumenical matters between the Synods of the Eastern Catholic Churches or Episcopal Conferences and the Pontifical Council for Promoting Christian Unity in Rome, as well as with the ecumenical commissions of other territorial Conferences.

Ecumenical Structures within other Ecclesial Contexts

48. Supernational bodies which exist in various forms for assuring cooperation and assistance among Episcopal Conferences should also establish some structures for ensuring the ecumenical dimension of their work. The scope of their activities and the form these may take will be determined by the statutes and procedures of each of their bodies and the concrete possibilities of the territory.

49. Within the Catholic Church, certain communities and organizations exist which have a specific place in contributing to the apostolic life of the Church. While they do not immediately form part of the ecumenical structures described above, their work very frequently has an important ecumenical dimension which should be organized into adequate structures according to the fundamental purposes of the organization. Among these communities and organizations are found institutes of consecrated life, societies of apostolic life and various organizations of Catholic faithful.

Institutes of Consecrated Life and Societies of Apostolic Life

50. While the concern for restoring Christian unity involves the whole Church, clergy and laity alike,[55] religious orders and congregations and societies of apostolic life, by the very nature of their particular commitments in the Church and the contexts in which they live out these commitments, have significant opportunities of fostering ecumenical thought and action. In accordance with their particular charisms and constitutions — some of which antedate the divisions among Christians — and in the light of the spirit and aims of their institutes, they are encouraged to put into practice, within the concrete possibilities

and limits of their rules of life, the following attitudes and activities:

a) to foster an awareness of the ecumenical importance of their particular forms of life in as much as conversion of heart, personal holiness, public and private prayer and disinterested service to the Church and the world are at the heart of the ecumenical movement;

b) to contribute to an understanding of the ecumenical dimensions of the vocation of all Christians to holiness of life by offering occasions for developing spiritual formation, contemplation, adoration and praise of God and service to one's neighbour;

c) taking account of the circumstances of place and persons, to organise meetings among Christians of various Churches and ecclesial Communities for liturgical prayer, for recollection and spiritual exercises, and for a more profound understanding of Christian spiritual traditions;

d) to maintain relations with monasteries or communities of common life in other Christian Communions for an exchange of spiritual and intellectual resources, and experiences in apostolic life, since the growth of the religious charisms in these Communions can be a positive factor for the whole of the ecumenical movement. This can provide a fruitful spiritual emulation;

e) to conduct their many varied educational institutions with a view to ecumenical activity in accordance with the principles presented further on in this Directory;

f) to collaborate with other Christians in the areas of common work for social justice, economic development, progress in health and education, the safeguarding of creation, and for peace and reconciliation among nations and communities;

g) insofar as religious conditions permit, ecumenical action should be encouraged, so that, "while avoiding every form of indifferentism, or confusion and also senseless rivalry, Catholics might collaborate with their separated brethren, insofar as it is possible, by a common profession before the nations of faith in God and in Jesus Christ, and by a common, fraternal effort in social, cultural, technical and religious matters, in accordance with the Decree on Ecumenism. Let them cooperate, especially, because of Christ their common Lord. May his Name unite them!".[56]

In carrying out these activities, they will observe the norms for ecumenical work which have been established by the diocesan Bishop, the Synods of Eastern Catholic Churches or Episcopal Conferences as an element of their cooperation in the total apostolate of a given territory. They will maintain close contacts with the various dioceses or national ecumenical commissions and, where indicated, with the Pontifical Council for Promoting Christian Unity.

51. To assist this ecumenical activity, it is very opportune that the various institutes of consecrated life and societies of apostolic life establish, on the level of their central authorities, a delegate or a commission charged with promoting and assisting their ecumenical engagement. The function of these delegates or commissions will be to encourage the ecumenical formation of all the members, aid the specific ecumenical formation of those who have particular offices and act as advisors for ecumenical affairs to the various general and local authorities of the institutes and societies, especially for initiating or carrying forward the activities described above (n. 50).

Organizations of Faithful

52. Organizations of Catholic faithful in a particular territory or nation, as well as those of an international character having as their objectives, e.g., spiritual renewal, action for peace and social justice, education at various levels, economic aid to countries and institutions, etc., should develop the ecumenical aspects of their activities. They should see that the ecumenical dimensions of their work be given adequate attention and expression even, if necessary, in their statutes and structures. In carrying out their ecumenical activities, they should remain in contact with territorial and local ecumenical commissions and, where circumstances indicate it, with the Pontifical Council for Promoting Christian Unity for fruitful exchanges of experiences and advice.

The Pontifical Council for Promoting Christian Unity

53. At the level of the universal Church, the Pontifical Council for Promoting Christian Unity, a department of the Roman Curia, has the competence and the task of promoting full communion among all Christians. The Constitution *Pastor Bonus* (cf. n. 6 above) states that it promotes, on the one hand, the ecumenical spirit and action within the Catholic Church and, on the other hand, it cultivates relations with the other Churches and ecclesial Communities.

a) The Pontifical Council is concerned with the proper interpretation of the principles of ecumenism, and the means of putting them into effect; it implements the decisions of the Second Vatican Council with regard to ecumenism; it encourages and assists national or international groups which promote the unity of Christians and helps coordinate their work.

b) It organizes official dialogues with other Churches and ecclesial Communities on the international level; it delegates Catholic observers on the international level; it delegates Catholic observers to conferences or meetings of these bodies or of other ecumenical organizations and invites observers from them to meetings of the Catholic Church, whenever this is judged opportune.

54. To fulfil these functions, the Pontifical Council for Promoting Christian Unity at times issues directives and guidelines applicable to the entire Catholic Church. Furthermore, it maintains contacts with the Synods of Eastern Catholic Churches and Episcopal Conferences, with their ecumenical commissions, and with the Bishops and organizations within the Catholic Church. The coordination of the ecumenical activities of the entire Catholic Church requires that these contacts be reciprocal. It is therefore appropriate that the Council be informed of important initiatives taken at various levels of the life of the Church. This is necessary, in particular, when these initiatives have international implications such as when important dialogues are organized at a national or territorial level with other Churches and ecclesial Communities. The mutual exchange of information and advice will benefit ecumenical activities at the international level as well as those on every other level of the Church's life. Whatever facilitates a growth of harmony and of coherent ecumenical engagement also reinforces communion within the Catholic Church.

III. Ecumenical Formation in the Catholic Church

The Necessity and Purpose of Ecumenical Formation

55. "Concern for restoring unity pertains to the whole Church, faithful and clergy alike. It extends to everyone, according to the potential of each, whether it be exercised in daily Christian living or in theological and historical studies".[57] Bearing in mind the nature of the Catholic Church, Catholics will find, if they follow faithfully the indications of the Second Vatican Council, the means of contributing to the ecumenical formation, both of individuals and of the whole community to which they belong. Thus the unity of all in Christ will be the result of a common growth and maturing. For God's call to interior conversion[58] and renewal [59] in the Church, so fundamental to the quest for unity, excludes no one.

For that reason, all the faithful are called upon to make a personal commitment toward promoting increasing communion with other Christians. But there is a particular contribution that can be made to this by those members of the People of God who are engaged in formation — such as heads and staffs of colleges of higher and specialized education. Those who do pastoral work, and especially parish priests and other ordained ministers, also have their role to play in this matter. It is the responsibility of each Bishop, of Synods of Eastern Catholic Churches and of Episcopal Conferences to issue general directives relating to ecumenical formation.

Adaptation of Formation to the Concrete Situation of Persons

56. Ecumenism calls for renewal of attitudes and for flexibility of methods in the search for unity. Account must also be taken of the variety of persons, functions, situations

and even of the specific character of the particular Churches, and the communities engaged with them, in the search for unity. Consequently, ecumenical formation requires a pedagogy that is adapted to the concrete situation of the life of persons and groups, and which respects the need for gradualness in an effort of continual renewal and of change in attitudes.

57. Not only teachers, but all those who are involved in pastoral work will be progressively formed in accordance with the following principal orientations:

a) Knowledge of Scripture and doctrinal formation are necessary from the outset, together with knowledge of the history and of the ecumenical situation in the country where one lives.

b) Knowledge of the history of divisions and of efforts at reconciliation, as well as the doctrinal positions of other Churches and ecclesial Communities will make it possible to analyse problems in their socio-cultural context and to discern in expressions of faith what is legitimate diversity and what constitutes divergence that is incompatible with Catholic faith.

c) This perspective will take account of the results and clarifications coming from theological dialogues and scientific studies. It is even desirable that Christians should write together the history of their divisions and of their efforts in the search for unity.

d) In this way the danger of subjective interpretations can be avoided, both in the presentation of the Catholic faith and also in Catholic understanding of the faith and of the life of other Churches and ecclesial Communities.

e) In so far as it progresses well, ecumenical formation makes concern for the unity of the Catholic Church and concern for communion with other Churches and ecclesial Communities inseparable.

f) It is implicit in the concern for this unity and this communion that Catholics should be concerned to deepen relations both with Eastern Christians and Christians in communities issuing from the Reformation.

g) The method of teaching should allow for the necessity of progressing gradually. Such a method makes it possible to distinguish and distribute the questions to be studied and their respective contents in the various phases of doctrinal formation, taking account also of the ecumenical experience of the person concerned.

Thus, all those engaged in pastoral work will be faithful to the holy and living Tradition which is a source of initiative within the Church. They should be able to evaluate and welcome truth wherever it is found. "All truth, by whomsoever it is spoken, is of the Holy Spirit".[60]

A. Formation on all the Faithful

58. The concern for unity is fundamental to the understanding of the Church. The objective of ecumenical formation is that all Christians be animated by the ecumenical spirit, whatever their particular mission and task in the world and in society.

In the life of the faithful, imbued with the Spirit of Christ, the gift prayed for by Christ before his passion, the "grace of unity", is of primary importance. This unity is first of all unity with Christ in a single movement of charity extending both towards the Father and towards the neighbour. Secondly, it is a profound and active communion of the individual faithful with the universal Church within the particular Church to which he or she belongs.[61] And thirdly it is the fullness of visible unity which is sought with Christians of other Churches and ecclesial Communities.

The Means of Formation

59. *Hearing and studying the Word of God.* The Catholic Church has always considered Scriptures, together with Tradition, "as the supreme rule of faith"; they are for its children "the food of the soul, the pure and perennial source of spiritual life".[62] Our brothers and sisters of other Churches and ecclesial Communities have a deep love and reverence for the Holy Scriptures. This occasions their constant and deep study of the sacred books.[63] The Word of God, then, being one and the same for all Christians, will progressively strengthen the path towards unity insofar as it is approached with religious attention and loving study.

60. *Preaching.* Particular care must be taken with preaching, whether within or outside of liturgical worship as such. As Paul VI says: "As evangelizers, we must offer Christ's faithful not the image of a people divided and separated by unedifying quarrels, but the image of people who are mature in faith and capable of finding a meeting-point beyond the real tensions, thanks to a shared, sincere and disinterested search for truth".[64] The different parts of the liturgical year offer favourable opportunities for developing the themes of Christian unity, and for stimulating study, reflection and prayer.

Preaching should concern itself with revealing the mystery of the unity of the Church, and as far as possible promoting visibly the unity of Christians. In preaching, any improper use of Scripture must be avoided.

61. *Catechesis.* Catechesis is not only the teaching of doctrine, but initiation into the Christian life as a whole, with full participation in the sacraments of the Church. But, as shown in Pope John Paul II's Apostolic Exhortation *Catechesi Tradendae* (nn. 32-33), this teaching can help to form a genuine ecumenical attitude, by observing the following directives:

a) First, it should expound clearly, with charity and with due firmness the whole doctrine of the Catholic Church respecting in a particular way the order of the hierarchy of truths[65] and avoiding expressions and ways of presenting doctrine which would be an obstacle to dialogue.

b) When speaking of other Churches and ecclesial Communities, it is important to present their teaching correctly and honestly. Among those elements by which the Church itself is built up and given life, some — even many and very valuable ones — are to be found outside the visible limits of the Catholic Church.[66] The Spirit of Christ therefore does not refuse to use these communities as means of salvation. Doing this also puts in relief the truths of faith held in common by various Christian confessions. This will help Catholics both to deepen their own faith and to know and esteem other Christians, thus making easier the search in common for the path of full unity in the whole truth.[67]

c) Catechesis will have an ecumenical dimension if it arouses and nourishes a true desire for unity and still more if it fosters real effort, including efforts in humility to purify ourselves, so as to remove obstacles on the way, not by facile doctrinal omissions and concessions, but by aiming at that perfect unity which the Lord wills and by using the means that He wills.[68]

d) Catechesis will, moreover, have this ecumenical dimension if it sets out to prepare children and young people as well as adults to live in contact with other Christians, maturing as Catholics while growing in respect for the faith of others.[69]

e) It can do this by discerning the possibilities offered by the distinction between the truths of faith and their modes of expression;[70] by mutual striving to understand and esteem what is good in each other's theological traditions; by making clear that dialogue has created new relationships which, if they are well understood, can lead to collaboration and peace.[71]

f) The Apostolic Exhortation *Catechesi Tradendae* should be a point of reference in the elaboration of new catechisms which are prepared in local Churches under the authority of the Bishops.

62. *Liturgy.* Being "the primary and indispensable source from which the faithful are to derive the true Christian spirit",[72] liturgy makes an important contribution to the unity of all who believe in Christ; it is a celebration and an agent of unity; where it is fully understood and everybody fully participates in it, "it is (thus) the outstanding means by which the faithful can express in their lives, and manifest to others, the mystery of Christ and the real nature of the true Church".[73]

a) Since the holy Eucharist is "the wonderful sacrament ... by which the unity of the Church is both signified and brought about",[74] it is very important to see that it is celebrated well so that the faithful can participate in it, because "by offering the Immaculate Victim not only through the hands of the priest but also with him, they should learn to offer themselves too. Through Christ the Mediator they should be drawn day by day into ever closer union with God and with each other, so that finally God may be all in all".[75]

b) It would be good to foster fidelity to prayer for Christian unity, according to the indications of this Directory, whether at the times the liturgy indicates — as, for example, in celebrations of the Word or else at Eastern celebrations known as "Litia" and "Moleben"— or especially during Mass — in the prayer for the faithful or the "Ectenie" litanies, or also in celebration of the votive Mass for Unity of the Church, with the help of the appropriate formularies.

An efficacious formation can also be obtained by intensifying prayer for unity at special times, such as Unity Week (18-25 January) or the week between Ascension and Pentecost, so that the Holy Spirit may confirm the Church in its unity and in the apostolicity of its universal saving mission.

63. *The spiritual life.* In the ecumenical movement it is necessary to give priority to conversion of heart, spiritual life and its renewal. "This change of heart and holiness of life, along with public and private prayer for the unity of Christians, should be regarded as the soul of the whole ecumenical movement, and can rightly be called 'spiritual ecumenism' ".[76] Individual Christians, therefore, insofar as they live a genuine spiritual life with Christ the Saviour as its centre and the glory of God the Father as its goal, can always and everywhere share deeply in the ecumenical movement, witnessing to the Gospel of Christ with their lives.[77]

a) Catholics should also give value to certain elements and goods, sources of spiritual life, which are found in other Churches and ecclesial Communities, and which belong to the one Church of Christ: Holy Scripture, the sacraments and other sacred actions, faith, hope, charity and other gifts of the Spirit.[78] These goods have borne fruit for example in the mystical tradition of the Christian East and the spiritual treasures of the monastic life, in the worship and piety of Anglicans, in the evangelical prayer and the diverse forms of Protestant spirituality.

b) This appreciation should not remain merely theoretical; in suitable particular conditions, it should be completed by the practical knowledge of other traditions of spirituality. Therefore, sharing prayer and participating in some form of public worship or in devotional acts of other Christians can have a formative value when in accord with existing directives.[79]

64. *Other initiatives.* Collaboration in social and charitable initiatives in contexts such as schools, hospitals and prisons, has a proven formational value. So too has work for peace in the world or in particular regions where it is threatened, and for human rights and religious liberty.[80]

These activities, properly directed, can show the efficacy of the social application of the Gospel and the practical force of ecumenical sensitivity in various places. Periodic reflection on the Christian basis of such activities, testing their quality and their fruitfulness, while correcting their defects, will also be educative and constructive.

Suitable Settings for Formation

65. These are the places where human and Christian maturity, the sense of companionship and communion, grow step by step. Of particular importance in this connection are family, parish, school, different groups, associations and ecclesial movements.

66. *The family*, called the "domestic church" by the Second Vatican Council,[81] is the primary place in which

unity will be fashioned or weakened each day through the encounter of persons, who, though different in many ways, accept each other in a communion of love. It is also there that care must be taken not to entertain prejudices, but on the contrary to search for the truth in all things.

a) Awareness of its Christian identity and mission makes the family ready to be a community for others, a community not only open to the Church but also to human society, ready for dialogue and social involvement. Like the Church, it should be a setting in which the Gospel is transmitted and which radiates the Gospel; indeed *Lumen gentium* states that in the domestic church "parents should by their words and example be the first preachers of the faith to their children" (n. 11).

b) Mixed marriage families have the duty to proclaim Christ with the fullness implied in a common baptism, they have too the delicate task of making themselves builders of unity.[82] "Their common baptism and the dynamism of grace provide the spouses in these marriages with the basis and motivation for expressing their unity in the sphere of moral and spiritual values".[83]

67. *The parish,* as an ecclesial unity gathered around the Eucharist, should be, and proclaim itself to be the place of authentic ecumenical witness. Thus a great task for the parish is to educate its members in the ecumenical spirit. This calls for care with the content and form of preaching, especially of the homily, and with catechesis. It calls too for a pastoral programme which involves someone charged with promoting and planning ecumenical activity, working in close harmony with the parish priest; this will help in the various forms of collaboration with the corresponding parishes of other Christians. Finally it demands that the parish be not torn apart by internal polemics, ideological

polarization or mutual recrimination between Christians, but that everyone, according to his or her own spirit and calling, serve the truth in love.[84]

68. *The school,* of every kind and grade, should give an ecumenical dimension to its religious teaching, and should aim in its own way to train hearts and minds in human and religious values, educating for dialogue, for peace and for personal relationships.[85]

a) The spirit of charity, of respect, and of dialogue demands the elimination of language and prejudices which distort the image of other Christians. This holds especially for Catholic schools where the young must grow in faith, in prayer, in resolve to put into practice the Christian Gospel of unity. They should be taught genuine ecumenism, according to the doctrine of the Catholic Church.

b) Where possible, in collaboration with other teachers, different subjects, e.g. history and art, should be treated in a way that underlines the ecumenical problems in a spirit of dialogue and unity. To this end it is also desirable that teachers be correctly and adequately informed about the origins, history and doctrines of other Churches and ecclesial Communities especially those that exist in their region.

69. *Groups, associations, ecclesial movements.* Christian life, notably the life of particular Churches has been enriched throughout history by a variety of expressions, enterprises and spiritualities, according to the charisms given by the Spirit for the building up of the Church, revealing a clear distinction of tasks in the service of the community.

Those involved in such groups, movements and associations should be imbued with a solid ecumenical spirit, in living out their baptismal commitment in the world,[86] whether by seeking Catholic unity through dialogue and communion with similar movements and associations — or the wider communion with other Churches and ecclesial Communities and with the movements and groups inspired by them. These efforts should be carried out on the basis of a sound formation and in the light of Christian wisdom and prudence.

B. Formation of those engaged in Pastoral Work

1. Ordained Ministers

70. Among the principal duties of every future ordained minister is to shape his own personality, to the extent possible, in such a way as will serve his mission of helping others to meet Christ. In this perspective, the candidate for the ministry needs to develop fully those human qualities which make a person acceptable and credible among people, checking regularly his own language and capacity for dialogue so as to acquire an authentically ecumenical disposition. If this is essential for one who has the office of teacher and shepherd in a particular Church, like the Bishop, or one who as a priest takes care of souls, it is no less important for the deacon, and in a particular way for the permanent deacon, who is called to serve the community of the faithful.

71. In taking initiatives and promoting encounters, the minister must act clearly and with faithfulness to the Church, respecting the authority of others and following the disposition which the pastors of the Church are entitled to make for the ecumenical movement in the universal Church and in the single local Churches, to ensure that collaboration in the building-up of Christian unity shall be free of prejudice and ill-considered initiatives.

a) Doctrinal Formation

72. Episcopal Conferences should ensure that plans of study give an ecumenical dimension to each subject and provide specifically for the study of ecumenism. They should also ensure that plans of study are in conformity with the indications contained in this Directory.

a–1) The Ecumenical Dimension in the Different Subjects

73. Ecumenical activity "has to be fully and sincerely Catholic, that is, faithful to the truth we have received from the Apostles and the Fathers and consonant with the faith the Catholic Church has always professed".[87]

74. Students must learn to distinguish between on the one hand revealed truths, which all require the same assent of faith, and on the other hand the manner of stating those truths and theological doctrines.[88] As far as the formulation of revealed truths is concerned, account will be taken of what is said by, among others, the declaration of the Congregation for the Doctrine of the Faith's *Mysterium ecclesiae,* n. 5: "The truths which the Church intends actually to teach through its dogmatic formularies are, without doubt, distinct from the changing conceptions proper to a given age and can be expressed without them, but it can nonetheless happen that they will be expressed by the magisterium, in terms that bear traces of those conceptions. Account having been taken of these considerations, it must also be said that from the beginning the dogmatic formularies of the magisterium have always been appropriate for communicating revealed truth and that, remaining unchanged, they will always communicate it to those who interpret them properly".[89] Students should therefore learn to make the distinction between the "deposit of faith itself or the truths which are contained in our venerable doctrine",[90] and the way in which these truths are formu-

lated; between the truths to be proclaimed and the various ways of perceiving them and shedding light upon them; between the apostolic Tradition and strictly ecclesiastical traditions, and at the same time they should learn to recognize and respect the permanent value of dogmatic formulations. From the time of their philosophical formation, students should be prepared to appreciate the legitimate diversity in theology which derives from the different methods and language theologians use in penetrating the divine mysteries. From which it follows that different theological formulations are often more complementary than contradictory.

75. Moreover, the "hierarchy of truths" of Catholic doctrine should always be respected; these truths all demand due assent of faith, yet are not all equally central to the mystery revealed in Jesus Christ, since they vary in their connection with the foundation of the Christian faith.[91]

a–2) The Ecumenical Dimension of Theological Disciplines in general

76. Ecumenical openness is a constitutive dimension of the formation of future priests and deacons: "Sacred theology and other branches of knowledge, especially those of an historical nature, must be taught with due regard for the ecumenical point of view, so that they may correspond as exactly as possible with the facts".[92] The ecumenical dimension in theological formation should not be limited to different categories of teaching. Because we are talking about interdisciplinary teaching — and not only "pluridisciplinary" — this will involve cooperation between the professors concerned and reciprocal coordination. In each subject, even in those which are fundamental, the following aspects may be suitably emphasized:

a) the elements of the Christian patrimony of truth and holiness which are common to all Churches and ecclesial Communities, even though these are sometimes presented according to varying theological expressions;

b) the riches of liturgy, spirituality and doctrine proper to each communion, but which can help Christians towards a deeper knowledge of the nature of the Church;

c) points of disagreement on matters of faith and morals which can nonetheless encourage deeper exploration of the Word of God and lead to distinguishing real from apparent contradictions.

a–3) The Ecumenical Dimension of Individual Theological Disciplines

77. In every theological discipline an ecumenical approach should bring us to consider the link between the particular subject and the mystery of the unity of the Church. Moreover, the teacher should instil in his students fidelity to the whole authentic Christian Tradition in matters of theology, spirituality and ecclesiastical discipline. When students compare their own patrimony with the riches of the other Christian traditions of East and West, whether in their ancient or modern expression, they will become more deeply conscious of this fullness.[93]

78. This comparative study is important in all subjects: in the study of Scripture, which is the common source of faith for all Christians; in the study of the apostolic Tradition in the Fathers of the Church and in other church writers of East and West; of liturgy, where the various forms of divine worship and their doctrinal and spiritual importance are scientifically compared; in dogmatic and moral theology, especially in respect of problems arising from ecumenical dialogue; in church history, where there should

be a careful enquiry into the unity of the Church and into the causes of separation; in canon law, which must distinguish clearly between divine law and those ecclesiastical laws which can change with time, culture or local tradition; and finally, in pastoral and missionary training and sociological studies, which must pay attention to the conditions common to all Christians facing the modern world. Thus the fullness of Divine Revelation will be expressed in a better and more complete way, and we will better fulfil the mission for the world which Christ entrusted to his Church.

a–4) A Specific Course in Ecumenism

79. Even though an ecumenical dimension should permeate all theological formation, it is of particular importance that a course in ecumenism be given at an appropriate point in the first cycle. Such a course should be compulsory. In broad and adaptable terms, it might have the following content:

a) the notions of catholicity, of the visible and organic unity of the Church, of the *oecumene,* ecumenism; from their historical origins to the present meaning from the Catholic viewpoint;

b) the doctrinal basis of ecumenical activity with particular reference to the already existing bonds of communion between Churches and ecclesial Communities; [94]

c) the history of ecumenism, which includes that of the divisions and of the many attempts during the ages to reestablish unity, their achievements and failures, the present state of the search for unity;

d) the purpose and method of ecumenism, the various forms of union and of collaboration, the hope of re-establishing unity, the conditions of unity, the concept of full and perfect unity;

e) the "institutional" aspect and the contemporary life in the various Christian Communities: doctrinal tendencies, the real causes of separations, missionary efforts, spirituality, forms of worship, need for better knowledge of Eastern theology and spirituality; [95]

f) some more specific problems such as shared worship, proselytism and irenicism, religious freedom, mixed marriages, the role of the laity and, in particular, of women in the Church;

g) spiritual ecumenism, especially the significance of prayer for unity and other forms of tending towards the unity prayed for by Christ.

80. Studies might be organized on some plan such as this:

a) it would be good if a general introduction to ecumenism were offered fairly early so that the students could be sensitized, right from the beginning of their theological studies, to the ecumenical dimension of their studies.[96] This introduction would deal with the basic questions in ecumenism;

b) the specific part of the teaching on ecumenism would find its normal place towards the end either of the first cycle of theological studies or of the seminary course, so that the students in gaining a broad knowledge of ecumenism could make a synthesis of this with their theological formation;

c) text books and other aids should be carefully chosen: they should expound with fidelity the teaching of other Christians in history, theology and spirituality so as to permit honest and objective comparisons and to stimulate a further deepening of Catholic doctrine.

81. It would be useful to invite lecturers and experts of other traditions, in the context of the directives on collaboration between Catholic institutions and the centres under the auspices of other Christians.[97] In case of particular problems

arising in respect of a specific seminary or institute, it is up to the diocesan Bishop to decide, according to the norms established by the Episcopal Conference and after having ascertained the moral and professional qualities of prospective lecturers from other Churches and ecclesial Communities, which of the initiatives can be pursued under the specific responsibility of the academic authorities. In these cultural exchanges, the continuing Catholic character of the institution in question as well as its right and duty to form its own candidates and to teach Catholic doctrine according to the norms of the Church, should always be ensured.

b) Ecumenical Experience

82. In the formative period, in order that the approach to ecumenism is not cut off from life but rooted in the living experience of communities, encounters and discussions can usefully be organized with other Christians, at the universal and the local level, while observing the relative norms of the Catholic Church.

Representatives of other communities with a professional and religious preparation and the ecumenical spirit necessary for a sincere and constructive dialogue may be invited. Meetings with students of other Churches and ecclesial Communities can also be arranged.[98] Institutions for formation differ so much, however, that it is not possible to give uniform rules for this. As a matter of fact, reality allows for different nuances according to the diversity of nations and regions, as well as for difference of relations between the Catholic Church and the other Churches and ecclesial Communities on the level of ecclesiology, of collaboration and dialogue. Here also the necessity for gradualness and adaptation is very important and is unavoidable. Superiors must apply general principles and adapt these according to their particular situations and occasions.

2. Ministers and Collaborators not Ordained

a) Doctrinal Formation

83. Besides ordained ministers, there are other recognized collaborators in pastoral work — catechists, teachers and other lay helpers. Local Churches have institutes of religious science, pastoral institutes or other centres of formation or ?aggiornamento' for their formation. The same study programmes and norms as for the theological institutes apply here, but need to be adapted to the level of these participants and their studies.

84. More particularly, given the legitimate variety of charisms and of the work of monasteries, institutes of consecrated life, and societies of apostolic life, it is very important that "all communities should participate in the life of the Church. According to its individual character, each should make its own and foster in every possible way the enterprises and objectives of the Church", including the "ecumenical field".[99]

Formation here should start in the novitiate and continue through the further stages. The *Ratio formationis* of the various institutes should, in analogy with the curricula of the ordained ministers, stress both an ecumenical dimension in every subject and provide for a specific course of ecumenism appropriately adapted to the circumstances and local situations. At the same time, it is important that the competent authority of the institute see to the formation of specialists in ecumenism to serve as guides for the ecumenical commitment of the whole institute.

b) Ecumenical Experience

85. To translate study into experience, it is useful to encourage contacts and exchanges between Catholic

monasteries and religious communities and those of other Churches and religious Communities. These can take the form of exchanges of information, spiritual or occasionally even material help, or can be in the form of cultural exchanges.

86. Given the importance of the role of the laity in the Church and in society, laity with ecumenical responsibilities should be encouraged to develop contacts and exchanges with other Churches and ecclesial Communities, in accordance with the norms of this Directory.[100]

C. Specialized Formation

87. *The importance of formation for dialogue.* Taking account of the influence of higher cultural institutes, it is clear that ecclesiastical faculties and other institutes of higher education play a specially important part in the preparation for and conduct of ecumenical dialogue and for progress towards that Christian unity which dialogue itself helps Christians to attain. Pedagogical preparation for dialogue must meet the following requirements:

a) a sincere personal commitment, lived out in faith, without which dialogue is no longer a dialogue between brothers and sisters but rather a mere academic exercise;

b) the search for new ways and means for building up mutual relationships and re-establishing unity based on greater fidelity to the Gospel and on the authentic profession of the Christian faith, in truth and charity;

c) the conviction that ecumenical dialogue is not a purely private matter between persons or particular groups but that it takes place within the framework of the commitment of the whole Church and must in consequence be carried out in a way that is coherent with the teaching and the directives of its Pastors;

d) a readiness to recognize that the members of the different Churches and ecclesial Communities can help us better to understand and to expound accurately the doctrine and life of their Communities;

e) respect for the conscience and personal conviction of anyone who expounds an aspect or a doctrine of his or her own Church or its particular way of understanding Divine Revelation;

f) the recognition of the fact that not everybody is equally qualified to take part in dialogue, since there are various degrees of education, maturity of mind and spiritual progress.

The Role of the Ecclesiastical Faculties

88. The Apostolic Constitution *Sapientia Christiana* lays down that in the first cycle of the theology faculty, fundamental theology should be studied with reference also to ecumenical questions.[101]

In the second cycle too, "ecumenical questions should be carefully treated, as directed by competent ecclesiastical authority".[102]

In other words, it will be opportune to give courses of specialization in ecumenism which, besides the elements indicated above in n. 79, could also deal with:

a) the present state of relations between the Catholic Church and the other Churches and ecclesial Communities, based on study of the published results of dialogue;

b) the study of the patrimony and traditions of other Christians, Eastern and Western;

c) the importance in the ecumenical movement of the World Council of Churches and the present state of the Catholic Church's relations with the said Council;

d) the role of national and regional Councils of Churches, their achievements and difficulties.

It must also be remembered that the ecumenical dimension should also be present in theological teaching and research.

The Role of Catholic Universities

89. These too are called on to give sound ecumenical formation. Examples of the appropriate measures they may take are these:

a) to foster, when the subject calls for it, an ecumenical dimension to methods of teaching and research;

b) to organize discussions and study days on ecumenical questions;

c) to organize conferences and meetings for joint study, work and social activity, setting aside time for enquiry into Christian principles of social action and the means of putting them into practice. These occasions, whether involving only Catholics or bringing together Catholics and other Christians, should promote cooperation as far as possible with other advanced institutes in the area;

d) space could be given in university journals and reviews to reports on ecumenical events, and also to deeper ecumenical studies, with preference given to comments on the documents resulting from inter-church dialogue;

e) in academic halls of residence there is very much to recommend good relations between Catholics and other Christian students. With suitable guidance, they can learn, through these relations, to live together in a deeper ecumenical spirit and be faithful witnesses of their Christian faith;

f) it is important to give emphasis to prayer for unity, not only during the Week of Prayer for this purpose but also at other times during the year. Depending on circumstances of place and persons, and in conformity with the existing rules about shared worship, joint retreats under the guidance of a spiritual master, may also be envisaged;

g) there is a wide field of common witness in social or welfare works. Students should be trained and encouraged in this — not only theology students, but also those of other faculties, such as law, sociology and political science. By their contribution these students will help to promote and realize such initiatives;

h) chaplains, student counsellors and professors will have a particular concern to carry out their tasks in an ecumenical spirit, especially by organizing some of the initiatives indicated above. This obligation demands from them a deep knowledge of the doctrine of the Church, an adequate competence in academic subjects, unfailing prudence and a balanced attitude: all these qualities should enable them to help their students to harmonize their own life of faith with openness to others.

The Role of Specialized Ecumenical Institutes

90. To carry out its ecumenical task the Church needs a good number of experts in this matter — clerics, religious, lay men and women. These are necessary even in regions where Catholics are in the majority.

a) This calls for specialized institutes equipped with:

— adequate documentation on ecumenism, especially on existing dialogues and future programmes;

— and a staff of well-prepared and capable teachers both of Catholic doctrine and ecumenism.

b) These institutes should carry on ecumenical research in cooperation, as far as possible, with experts from other Christian traditions and their faithful; they should organize ecumenical meetings, such as conferences and congresses; and keep in touch with national ecumenical commissions and with the Pontifical Council for Promoting Christian Unity so as to be well informed and up to date with what is going on in interconfessional dialogue and with the progress accomplished.

c) Experts trained this way will supply personnel for the ecumenical task in order to promote the ecumenical movement in the Catholic Church, whether as members and directors of the responsible diocesan, national or international organisms, or as teachers of ecumenical subjects in institutes or ecclesiastical centres or as promoters of a genuine ecumenical spirit and action in their own surroundings.

D. Permanent Formation

91. Doctrinal formation and learning experience are not limited to the period of formation, but ask for a continuous "aggiornamento" of the ordained ministers and pastoral workers, in view of the continual evolution within the ecumenical movement.

Bishops and religious superiors, when organizing pastoral renewal programmes for clergy — through meetings, conferences, retreats, days of recollection or study of pastoral problems — should give careful attention to ecumenism along the following lines:

a) Systematic instruction of priests, religious, deacons and laity on the present state of the ecumenical movement, so that they may be able to introduce the ecumenical viewpoint into preaching, catechesis, prayer and Christian life in general. If it seems suitable and possible, it would be good to invite a minister of another Church to expound its tradition or speak on pastoral problems which are often common to all.

b) Where opportunity offers, and with the consent of the diocesan Bishop, Catholic clergy and those with pastoral responsibility in the diocese could take part in interconfessional meetings aimed at improving reciprocal relationships and at trying to resolve pastoral problems together. To give concrete form to these initiatives it might be useful to create local and regional clergy councils or associations, etc., or to join similar already existing societies.

c) Theology faculties and institutes of higher learning, as well as seminaries and other institutes of formation, can contribute to permanent formation, either by arranging courses for those involved in pastoral work, or by providing teachers or subsidies for the disciplines and courses organized by others.

d) Very useful also are the following: accurate information through the media of the local Church and, if possible, through the secular media; exchange of information with the media services of other Churches and ecclesial Communities; a permanent and systematic relationship with the diocesan and national ecumenical commission which will ensure precise and up to date documentation on ecumenical developments to all Catholics working in the field.

e) Full use should be made of the various kinds of spiritual meetings to explore those elements of spirituality which are held in common, as well as those which are particular.

These meetings provide an opportunity to reflect on unity and to pray for the reconciliation of all Christians. The participation of members of different Churches and ecclesial Communities at such meetings can help to foster mutual understanding and the growth of spiritual communion.

f) Finally, it is desirable that an evaluation of ecumenical activity be made periodically.

IV. Communion in Life and Spiritual Activity among the Baptized

A. The Sacrament of Baptism

92. By the sacrament of baptism a person is truly incorporated into Christ and into his Church and is reborn to a sharing of the divine life.[103] Baptism, therefore, constitutes the sacramental bond of unity existing among all who through it are reborn. Baptism, of itself, is the beginning, for it is directed towards the acquiring of fullness of life in Christ. It is thus ordered to the profession of faith, to the full integration into the economy of salvation, and to Eucharistic communion.[104] Instituted by the Lord himself, baptism, by which one participates in the mystery of his death and resurrection, involves conversion, faith, the remission of sin, and the gift of grace.

93. Baptism is conferred with water and with a formula which clearly indicates that baptism is done in the name of the Father, Son and Holy Spirit. It is therefore of the utmost importance for all the disciples of Christ that baptism be administered in this manner by all and that the various Churches and ecclesial Communities arrive as closely as possible at an agreement about its significance and valid celebration.

94. It is strongly recommended that the dialogue concerning both the significance and the valid celebration of baptism take place between Catholic authorities and those of other Churches and ecclesial Communities at the diocesan or Episcopal Conference levels. Thus it should be possible to arrive at common statements through which they express mutual recognition of baptisms as well as procedures for considering cases in which a doubt may arise as to the validity of a particular baptism.

95. In arriving at these expressions of common agreement, the following points should be kept in mind:

a) Baptism by immersion, or by pouring, together with the Trinitarian formula is, of itself, valid. Therefore, if the rituals, liturgical books or established customs of a Church or ecclesial Community prescribe either of these ways of baptism, the sacrament is to be considered valid unless there are serious reasons for doubting that the minister has observed the regulations of his/her own Community or Church.

b) The minister's insufficient faith concerning baptism never of itself makes baptism invalid. Sufficient intention in a minister who baptizes is to be presumed, unless there is serious ground for doubting that the minister intended to do what the Church does.

c) Wherever doubts arise about whether, or how water was used,[105] respect for the sacrament and deference towards these ecclesial Communities require that serious investigation of the practice of the Community concerned be made before any judgment is passed on the validity of its baptism.

96. According to the local situation and as occasion may arise, Catholics may, in common celebration with other

Christians, commemorate the baptism which unites them, by renewing the engagement to undertake a full Christian life which they have assumed in the promises of their baptism, and by pledging to cooperate with the grace of the Holy Spirit in striving to heal the divisions which exist among Christians.

97. While by baptism a person is incorporated into Christ and his Church, this is only done in practice in a given Church or ecclesial Community. Baptism, therefore, may not be conferred jointly by two ministers belonging to different Churches or ecclesial Communities. Moreover, according to Catholic liturgical and theological tradition, baptism is celebrated by just one celebrant. For pastoral reasons, in particular circumstances the local Ordinary may sometimes permit, however, that a minister of another Church or ecclesial Community take part in the celebration by reading a lesson, offering a prayer, etc. Reciprocity is possible only if a baptism celebrated in another Community does not conflict with Catholic principles or discipline.[106]

98. It is the Catholic understanding that godparents, in a liturgical and canonical sense, should themselves be members of the Church or ecclesial Community in which the baptism is being celebrated. They do not merely undertake a responsibility for the Christian education of the person being baptized (or confirmed) as a relation or friend; they are also there as representatives of a community of faith, standing as guarantees of the candidate's faith and desire for ecclesial communion.

a) However, based on the common baptism and because of ties of blood or friendship, a baptized person who belongs to another ecclesial Community may be admitted as a witness to the baptism, but only together with a Catholic godparent.[107] A Catholic may do the same for a person being baptized in another ecclesial Community.

b) Because of the close communion between the Catholic Church and the Eastern Orthodox Churches, it is permissible for a just cause for an Eastern faithful to act as godparent; together with a Catholic godparent, at the baptism of a Catholic infant or adult, so long as there is provision for the Catholic education of the person being baptized, and it is clear that the godparent is a suitable one.

A Catholic is not forbidden to stand as godparent in an Eastern Orthodox Church, if he/she is so invited. In this case, the duty of providing for the Christian education binds in the first place the godparent who belongs to the Church in which the child is baptized.[108]

99. Every Christian has the right for conscientious religious reasons, freely to decide to come into full Catholic communion.[109] The work of preparing the reception of an individual who wishes to be received into full communion with the Catholic Church is of its nature distinct from ecumenical activity.[110] The Rite of Christian Initiation of Adults provides a formula for receiving such persons into full Catholic communion. However, in such cases, as well as in cases of mixed marriages, the Catholic authority may consider it necessary to inquire as to whether the baptism already received was validly celebrated. The following recommendations should be observed in carrying out this inquiry.

a) There is no doubt about the validity of baptism as conferred in the various Eastern Churches. It is enough to establish the fact of the baptism. In these Churches the sacrament of confirmation (chrismation) is properly administered by the priest at the same time as baptism. There it often happens that no mention is made of confirmation in the canonical testimony of baptism. This does not give grounds for doubting that this sacrament was also conferred.

b) With regard to Christians from other Churches and ecclesial Communities, before considering the validity of baptism of an individual Christian, one should determine whether an agreement on baptism (as mentioned above, n. 94) has been made by the Churches and ecclesial Communities of the regions or localities involved and whether baptism has in fact been administered according to this agreement. It should be noted, however, that the absence of a formal agreement about baptism should not automatically lead to doubt about the validity of baptism.

c) With regard to these Christians, where an official ecclesiastical attestation has been given, there is no reason for doubting the validity of the baptism conferred in their Churches and ecclesial Communities unless, in a particular case, an examination clearly shows that a serious reason exists for having a doubt about one of the following: the matter and form and words used in the conferral of baptism, the intention of an adult baptized or the minister of the baptism.[111]

d) If, even after careful investigation, a serious doubt persists about the proper administration of the baptism and it is judged necessary to baptize conditionally, the Catholic minister should show proper regard for the doctrine that baptism may be conferred only once by explaining to the person involved, both why in this case he is baptizing conditionally and what is the significance of the rite of conditional baptism. Furthermore, the rite of conditional baptism is to be carried out in private and not in public.[112]

e) It is desirable that Synods of Eastern Catholic Churches and Episcopal Conferences issue guidelines for the reception into full communion of Christians baptized into other Churches and ecclesial Communities. Account is to be taken of the fact that they are not catechumens and of the degree of knowledge and practice of the Christian faith which they may have.

100. According to the Rite of Christian Initiation of Adults, those adhering to Christ for the first time are normally baptized during the Paschal Vigil. Where the celebration of this Rite includes the reception into full communion of those already baptized, a clear distinction must be made between them and those who are not yet baptized.

101. In the present state of our relations with the ecclesial Communities of the Reformation of the 16th century, we have not yet reached agreement about the significance or sacramental nature or even of the administration of the sacrament of Confirmation. Therefore, under present circumstances, persons entering into full communion with the Catholic Church from one of these Communities are to receive the sacrament of Confirmation according to the doctrine and rite of the Catholic Church before being admitted to Eucharistic communion.

B. Sharing Spiritual activities and resources

General Principles

102. Christians may be encouraged to share in spiritual activities and resources, i.e., to share that spiritual heritage they have in common in a manner and to a degree appropriate to their present divided state.[113]

103. The term "sharing in spiritual activities and resources" covers such things as prayer offered in common,

sharing in liturgical worship in the strict sense, as described below in n. 116, as well as common use of sacred places and of all necessary objects.

104. The principles which should direct this spiritual sharing are the following:

a) In spite of the serious difficulties which prevent full ecclesial communion, it is clear that all those who by baptism are incorporated into Christ share many elements of the Christian life. There thus exists a real, even if imperfect, communion among Christians which can be expressed in many ways, including sharing in prayer and liturgical worship,[114] as will be indicated in the paragraph which follows.

b) According to Catholic faith, the Catholic Church has been endowed with the whole of revealed truth and all the means of salvation as a gift which cannot be lost.[115] Nevertheless, among the elements and gifts which belong to the Catholic Church (e.g.; the written Word of God, the life of grace, faith, hope and charity etc.) many can exist outside its visible limits. The Churches and ecclesial Communities not in full communion with the Catholic Church have by no means been deprived of significance and value in the mystery of salvation, for the Spirit of Christ has not refrained from using them as means of salvation.[116] In ways that vary according to the condition of each Church or ecclesial Community, their celebrations are able to nourish the life of grace in their members who participate in them and provide access to the communion of salvation.[117]

c) The sharing of spiritual activities and resources, therefore, must reflect this double fact:

1) the real communion in the life of the Spirit which already exists among Christians and is expressed in their prayer and liturgical worship;

2) the incomplete character of this communion because of differences of faith and understanding which are incompatible with an unrestricted mutual sharing of spiritual endowments.

d) Fidelity to this complex reality makes it necessary to establish norms for spiritual sharing which take into account the diverse ecclesial situations of the Churches and ecclesial Communities involved, so that, as Christians esteem and rejoice in the spiritual riches they have in common, they are also made more aware of the necessity of overcoming the separations which still exist.

e) Since Eucharistic concelebration is a visible manifestation of full communion in faith, worship and community life of the Catholic Church, expressed by ministers of that Church, it is not permitted to concelebrate the Eucharist with ministers of other Churches or ecclesial Communities.[118]

105. There should be a certain "reciprocity" since sharing in spiritual activities and resources, even with defined limits, is a contribution, in a spirit of mutual good will and charity, to the growth of harmony among Christians.

106. It is recommended that consultations on this sharing take place between appropriate Catholic authorities and those of other Communions to seek out the possibilities for lawful reciprocity according to the doctrine and traditions of different Communities.

107. Catholics ought to show a sincere respect for the liturgical and sacramental discipline of other Churches and ecclesial Communities and these in their turn are asked to show the same respect for Catholic discipline. One of the objectives of the consultation mentioned above should be a

greater mutual understanding of each other's discipline and even an agreement on how to manage a situation in which the discipline of one Church calls into question or conflicts with the discipline of another.

Prayer in Common

108. Where appropriate, Catholics should be encouraged, in accordance with the Church's norms, to join in prayer with Christians of other Churches and ecclesial Communities. Such prayers in common are certainly a very effective means of petitioning for the grace of unity, and they are a genuine expression of the ties which still bind Catholics to these other Christians.[119] Shared prayer is in itself a way to spiritual reconciliation.

109. Prayer in common is recommended for Catholics and other Christians so that together they may put before God the needs and problems they share — e.g., peace, social concerns, mutual charity among people, the dignity of the family, the effects of poverty, hunger and violence, etc. The same may be said of occasions when, according to circumstances, a nation, region or community wishes to make a common act of thanksgiving or petition to God, as on a national holiday, at a time of public disaster or mourning, on a day set aside for remembrance of those who have died for their country, etc. This kind of prayer is also recommended when Christians hold meetings for study or common action.

110. Shared prayer should, however, be particularly concerned with the restoration of Christian unity. It can centre, e.g. on the mystery of the Church and its unity, on baptism as a sacramental bond of unity, or on the renewal of personal and community life as a necessary means to

achieving unity. Prayer of this type is particularly recommended during the "Week of Prayer for Christian Unity" or in the period between Ascension and Pentecost.

111. Representatives of the Churches, ecclesial Communities or other groups concerned should cooperate and prepare together such prayer. They should decide among themselves the way in which each is to take part, choose the themes and select the Scripture readings, hymns and prayers.

a) In such a service there is room for any reading, prayer and hymn which manifest the faith or spiritual life shared by all Christian people. There is a place for an exhortation, address or biblical meditation drawing on the common Christian inheritance; and able to promote mutual good will and unity.

b) Care should be taken that the versions of Holy Scripture used be acceptable to all and be faithful translations of the original text.

c) It is desirable that the structure of these celebrations should take account of the different patterns of community prayer in harmony with the liturgical renewal in many Churches and ecclesial Communities, with particular regard being given to the common heritage of hymns, of texts taken from lectionaries and of liturgical prayers.

d) When services are arranged between Catholics and those of an Eastern Church, particular attention should be given to the liturgical discipline of each Church, in accordance with n. 115 below.

112. Although a church building is a place in which a community is normally accustomed to celebrating its own liturgy, the common services mentioned above may be celebrated in the church of one or other of the communities

concerned, if that is acceptable to all the participants. Whatever place is used should be agreeable to all, be capable of being properly prepared and be conducive to devotion.

113. Where there is a common agreement among the participants, those who have a function in a ceremony may use the dress proper to their ecclesiastical rank and to the nature of the celebration.

114. Under the direction of those who have proper formation and experience, it may be helpful in certain cases to arrange for spiritual sharing in the form of days of recollection, spiritual exercises, groups for the study and sharing of traditions of spirituality, and more stable associations for a deeper exploration of a common spiritual life. Serious attention must always be given to what has been said concerning the recognition of the real differences of doctrine which exist, as well as to the teaching and discipline of the Catholic Church concerning sacramental sharing.

115. Since the celebration of the Eucharist on the Lord's Day is the foundation and centre of the whole liturgical year,120 Catholics — but those of Eastern Churches according to their own Law121 — are obliged to attend Mass on that day and on days of precept.[122] It is not advisable therefore to organize ecumenical services on Sundays, and it must be remembered that even when Catholics participate in ecumenical services or in services of other Churches and ecclesial Communities, the obligation of participating at Mass on these days remains.

Sharing in Non-Sacramental Liturgical Worship

116. By liturgical worship is meant worship carried out according to books, prescriptions and customs of a Church

or ecclesial Community, presided over by a minister or delegate of that Church or Community. This liturgical worship may be of a non-sacramental kind, or may be the celebration of one or more of the Christian sacraments. The concern here is non-sacramental worship.

117. In some situations, the official prayer of a Church may be preferred to ecumenical services specially prepared for the occasion. Participation in such celebrations as Morning or Evening Prayer, special vigils, etc., will enable people of different liturgical traditions — Catholic, Eastern, Anglican and Protestant — to understand each other's community prayer better and to share more deeply in traditions which often have developed from common roots.

118. In liturgical celebrations taking place in other Churches and ecclesial Communities, Catholics are encouraged to take part in the psalms, responses, hymns and common actions of the Church in which they are guests. If invited by their hosts, they may read a lesson or preach.

119. Regarding assistance at liturgical worship of this type, there should be a meticulous regard for the sensibilities of the clergy and people of all the Christian Communities concerned, as well as for local customs which may vary according to time, place, persons and circumstances. In a Catholic liturgical celebration, ministers of other Churches and ecclesial Communities may have the place and liturgical honors proper to their rank and their role, if this is judged desirable. Catholic clergy invited to be present at a celebration of another Church or ecclesial Community may wear the appropriate dress or insignia of their ecclesiastical office, if it is agreeable to their hosts.

120. In the prudent judgment of the local Ordinary, the funeral rites of the Catholic Church may be granted

to members of a non-Catholic Church or ecclesial
Community, unless it is evidently contrary to their will
and provided that their own minister is unavailable,[123] and
that the general provisions of Canon Law do not forbid it.[124]

121. Blessings ordinarily given for the benefit of Catholics may also be given to other Christians who request them,
according to the nature and object of the blessing. Public
prayer for other Christians, living or dead, and for the needs
and intentions of other Churches and ecclesial Communities and their spiritual heads may be offered during the litanies and other invocations of a liturgical service, but not
during the Eucharistic Anaphora. Ancient Christian liturgical and ecclesiological tradition permits the specific
mention in the Eucharistic Anaphora only of the names of
persons who are in full communion with the Church celebrating the Eucharist.

Sharing in Sacramental Life, especially the Eucharist

*a) Sharing in Sacramental Life with members of the various
Eastern Churches*

122. Between the Catholic Church and the Eastern
Churches not in full communion with it, there is still a very
close communion in matters of faith.[125] Moreover, "through
the celebration of the Eucharist of the Lord in each of these
Churches, the Church of God is built up and grows in
stature" and "although separated from us, these Churches
still possess true sacraments, above all — by apostolic succession — the priesthood and the Eucharist ... ".[126] This offers
ecclesiological and sacramental grounds, according to the
understanding of the Catholic Church, for allowing and even
encouraging some sharing in liturgical worship, even of the
Eucharist, with these Churches, "given suitable circum-

stances and the approval of church authorities".[127] It is recognized, however, that Eastern Churches, on the basis of their own ecclesiological understanding, may have more restrictive disciplines in this matter, which others should respect. Pastors should carefully instruct the faithful so that they will be clearly aware of the proper reasons for this kind of sharing in liturgical worship and of the variety of discipline which may exist in this connection.

123. Whenever necessity requires or a genuine spiritual advantage suggests, and provided that the danger of error or indifferentism is avoided, it is lawful for any Catholic for whom it is physically or morally impossible to approach a Catholic minister, to receive the sacraments of penance, Eucharist and anointing of the sick from a minister of an Eastern Church.[128]

124. Since practice differs between Catholics and Eastern Christians in the matter of frequent communion, confession before communion and the Eucharistic fast, care must be taken to avoid scandal and suspicion among Eastern Christians through Catholics not following the Eastern usage. A Catholic who legitimately wishes to communicate with Eastern Christians must respect the Eastern discipline as much as possible and refrain from communicating if that Church restricts sacramental communion to its own members to the exclusion of others.

125. Catholic ministers may lawfully administer the sacraments of penance, Eucharist and the anointing of the sick to members of the Eastern Churches, who ask for these sacraments of their own free will and are properly disposed.

In these particular cases also, due consideration should be given to the discipline of the Eastern Churches for their own faithful and any suggestion of proselytism should be avoided.[129]

126. Catholics may read lessons at a sacramental liturgical celebration in the Eastern Churches if they are invited to do so. An Eastern Christian may be invited to read the lessons at similar services in Catholic churches.

127. A Catholic minister may be present and take part in the celebration of a marriage being properly celebrated between Eastern Christians or between a Catholic and an Eastern Christian in the Eastern church, if invited to do so by the Eastern Church authority and if it is in accord with the norms given below concerning mixed marriages, where they apply.

128. A member of an Eastern Church may act as bridesmaid or best man at a wedding in a Catholic church; a Catholic also may be bridesmaid or best man at a marriage properly celebrated in an Eastern church. In all cases this practice must conform to the general discipline of both Churches regarding the requirements for participating in such marriages.

b) Sharing Sacramental Life with Christians of Other Churches and Ecclesial Communities

129. A sacrament is an act of Christ and of the Church through the Spirit.[130] Its celebration in a concrete community is the sign of the reality of its unity in faith, worship and community life. As well as being signs, sacraments — most specially the Eucharist — are sources of the unity of the Christian community and of spiritual life, and are means for building them up. Thus Eucharistic communion is inseparably linked to full ecclesial communion and its visible expression.

At the same time, the Catholic Church teaches that by baptism members of other Churches and ecclesial Communities are brought into a real, even if imperfect communion, with the Catholic Church[131] and that "baptism, which constitutes the sacramental bond of unity existing among all who through it are reborn ... is wholly directed toward the acquiring of fullness of life in Christ".[132] The Eucharist is, for the baptized, a spiritual food which enables them to overcome sin and to live the very life of Christ, to be incorporated more profoundly in Him and share more intensely in the whole economy of the Mystery of Christ.

It is in the light of these two basic principles, which must always be taken into account together, that in general the Catholic Church permits access to its Eucharistic communion and to the sacraments of penance and anointing of the sick, only to those who share its oneness in faith, worship and ecclesial life.[133] For the same reasons, it also recognizes that in certain circumstances, by way of exception, and under certain conditions, access to these sacraments may be permitted, or even commended, for Christians of other Churches and ecclesial Communities.[134]

130. In case of danger of death, Catholic ministers may administer these sacraments when the conditions given below (n. 131) are present. In other cases, it is strongly recommended that the diocesan Bishop, taking into account any norms which may have been established for this matter by the Episcopal Conference or by the Synods of Eastern Catholic Churches, establish general norms for judging situations of grave and pressing need and for verifying the conditions mentioned below (n. 131).[135] In accord with Canon Law,[136] these general norms are to be established only after consultation with at least the local competent authority of the other interested Church or ecclesial Community. Catholic ministers will judge individual cases and administer these sacraments only in accord with these

established norms, where they exist. Otherwise they will judge according to the norms of this Directory.

131. The conditions under which a Catholic minister may administer the sacraments of the Eucharist, of penance and of the anointing of the sick to a baptized person who may be found in the circumstances given above (n. 130) are that the person be unable to have recourse for the sacrament desired to a minister of his or her own Church or ecclesial Community, ask for the sacrament of his or her own initiative, manifest Catholic faith in this sacrament and be properly disposed.[137]

132. On the basis of the Catholic doctrine concerning the sacraments and their validity, a Catholic who finds himself or herself in the circumstances mentioned above (nn. 130 and 131) may ask for these sacraments only from a minister in whose Church these sacraments are valid or from one who is known to be validly ordained according to the Catholic teaching on ordination.

133. The reading of Scripture during a Eucharistic celebration in the Catholic Church is to be done by members of that Church. On exceptional occasions and for a just cause, the Bishop of the diocese may permit a member of another Church or ecclesial Community to take on the task of reader.

134. In the Catholic Eucharistic Liturgy, the homily which forms part of the liturgy itself is reserved to the priest or deacon, since it is the presentation of the mysteries of faith and the norms of Christian living in accordance with Catholic teaching and tradition.[138]

135. For the reading of Scripture and preaching during other than Eucharistic celebrations, the norms given above (n. 118) are to be applied.

136. Members of other Churches or ecclesial Communities may be witnesses at the celebration of marriage in a Catholic church. Catholics may also be witnesses at marriages which are celebrated in other Churches or ecclesial Communities.

Sharing Other Resources for Spiritual Life and Activity

137. Catholic churches are consecrated or blessed buildings which have an important theological and liturgical significance for the Catholic community. They are therefore generally reserved for Catholic worship. However, if priests, ministers or communities not in full communion with the Catholic Church do not have a place or the liturgical objects necessary for celebrating worthily their religious ceremonies, the diocesan Bishop may allow them the use of a church or a Catholic building and also lend them what may be necessary for their services. Under similar circumstances, permission may be given to them for interment or for the celebration of services at Catholic cemeteries.

138. Because of developments in society, the rapid growth of population and urbanization, and for financial motives, where there is a good ecumenical relationship and understanding between the communities, the shared ownership or use of church premises over an extended period of time may become a matter of practical interest.

139. When authorization for such ownership or use is given by the diocesan Bishop, according to any norms which may be established by the Episcopal Conference or the Holy See, judicious consideration should be given to the reservation of the Blessed Sacrament, so that this question is resolved on the basis of a sound sacramental theology with the respect that is due, while also taking account of the

sensitivities of those who will use the building, e.g., by constructing a separate room or chapel.

140. Before making plans for a shared building, the authorities of the communities concerned should first reach agreement as to how their various disciplines will be observed, particularly in regard to the sacraments. Furthermore, a written agreement should be made which will clearly and adequately take care of all questions which may arise concerning financial matters and the obligations arising from church and civil law.

141. In Catholic schools and institutions, every effort should be made to respect the faith and conscience of students or teachers who belong to other Churches or ecclesial Communities. In accordance with their own approved statutes, the authorities of these schools and institutions should take care that clergy of other Communities have every facility for giving spiritual and sacramental ministration to their own faithful who attend such schools or institutions. As far as circumstances allow, with the permission of the diocesan Bishop these facilities can be offered on the Catholic premises, including the church or chapel.

142. In hospitals, homes for the aged and similar institutions conducted by Catholics, the authorities should promptly advise priests and ministers of other Communities of the presence of their faithful and afford them every facility to visit these persons and give them spiritual and sacramental ministrations under dignified and reverent conditions, including the use of the chapel.

C. Mixed Marriages

143. This section of the Ecumenical Directory does not attempt to give an extended treatment of all the pastoral and canonical questions connected with either the actual celebration of the sacrament of Christian marriage or the pastoral care to be given to Christian families, since such questions form part of the general pastoral care of every Bishop or regional Conference of Bishops. What follows below focuses on specific issues related to mixed marriages and should be understood in that context. The term "mixed marriage" refers to any marriage between a Catholic and a baptized Christian who is not in full communion with the Catholic Church.[139]

144. In all marriages, the primary concern of the Church is to uphold the strength and stability of the indissoluble marital union and the family life that flows from it. The perfect union of persons and full sharing of life which constitutes the married state are more easily assured when both partners belong to the same faith community. In addition, practical experience and the observations obtained in various dialogues between representatives of Churches and ecclesial Communities indicate that mixed marriages frequently present difficulties for the couples themselves, and for the children born to them, in maintaining their Christian faith and commitment and for the harmony of family life. For all these reasons, marriage between persons of the same ecclesial Community remains the objective to be recommended and encouraged.

145. In view, however, of the growing number of mixed marriages in many parts of the world, the Church includes within its urgent pastoral solicitude couples preparing to enter, or already having entered, such marriages. These

marriages, even if they have their own particular difficulties, "contain numerous elements that could well be made
good use of and develop both for their intrinsic value and
for the contribution they can make to the ecumenical movement. This is particularly true when both parties are faithful
to their religious duties. Their common baptism and the
dynamism of grace provide the spouses in these marriages
with the basis and motivation for expressing unity in the
sphere of moral and spiritual values".[140]

146. It is the abiding responsibility of all, especially
priests and deacons and those who assist them in pastoral
ministry, to provide special instruction and support for the
Catholic party in living his or her faith as well as for the
couples in mixed marriages both in the preparation for the
marriage, in its sacramental celebration and for the life
together that follows the marriage ceremony. This pastoral
care should take into account the concrete spiritual condition of each partner, their formation in their faith and their
practice of it. At the same time, respect should be shown for
the particular circumstances of each couple's situation, the
conscience of each partner and the holiness of the state of
sacramental marriage itself. Where judged useful, diocesan
Bishops, Synods of Eastern Catholic Churches or Episcopal
Conferences could draw up more specific guidelines for this
pastoral care.

147. In fulfilling this responsibility, where the situation
warrants it, positive steps should be taken, if possible, to
establish contacts with the minister of the other Church or
ecclesial Community, even if this may not always prove
easy. In general, mutual consultation between Christian
pastors for supporting such marriages and upholding their
values can be a fruitful field of ecumenical collaboration.

148. In preparing the necessary marriage preparation programmes, the priest or deacon, and those who assist him, should stress the positive aspects of what the couple share together as Christians in the life of grace, in faith, hope and love, along with the other interior gifts of the Holy Spirit.[141] Each party, while continuing to be faithful to his or her Christian commitment and to the practice of it, should seek to foster all that can lead to unity and harmony, without minimizing real differences and while avoiding an attitude of religious indifference.

149. In the interest of greater understanding and unity, both parties should learn more about their partner's religious convictions and the teaching and religious practices of the Church or ecclesial Community to which he or she belongs. To help them live the Christian inheritance they have in common, they should be reminded that prayer together is essential for their spiritual harmony and that reading and study of the Sacred Scriptures are especially important. In the period of preparation, the couple's effort to understand their individual religious and ecclesial traditions, and serious consideration of the differences that exist, can lead to greater honesty, charity and understanding of these realities and also of the marriage itself.

150. When, for a just and reasonable cause, permission for a mixed marriage is requested, both parties are to be instructed on the essential ends and properties of marriage which are not to be excluded by either party. Furthermore, the Catholic party will be asked to affirm, in the form established by the particular law of the Eastern Catholic Churches or by the Episcopal Conference, that he or she is prepared to avoid the dangers of abandoning the faith and to promise sincerely to do all in his/her power to see that the

children of the marriage be baptized and educated in the Catholic Church. The other partner is to be informed of these promises and responsibilities.[142] At the same time, it should be recognized that the non-Catholic partner may feel a like obligation because of his/her own Christian commitment. It is to be noted that no formal written or oral promise is required of this partner in Canon Law.

Those who wish to enter into a mixed marriage should, in the course of the contacts that are made in this connection, be invited and encouraged to discuss the Catholic baptism and education of the children they will have, and where possible come to a decision on this question before the marriage.

In order to judge the existence or otherwise of a "just and reasonable cause" with regard to granting permission for this mixed marriage, the local Ordinary will take account, among other things, of an explicit refusal on the part of the non-Catholic party.

151. In carrying out this duty of transmitting the Catholic faith to the children, the Catholic parent will do so with respect for the religious freedom and conscience of the other parent and with due regard for the unity and permanence of the marriage and for the maintenance of the communion of the family. If, notwithstanding the Catholic's best efforts, the children are not baptized and brought up in the Catholic Church, the Catholic parent does not fall subject to the censure of Canon Law.[143] At the same time, his/her obligation to share the Catholic faith with the children does not cease. It continues to make its demands, which could be met, for example, by playing an active part in contributing to the Christian atmosphere of the home; doing all that is possible by word and example to enable the other members of the

family to appreciate the specific values of the Catholic tradition; taking whatever steps are necessary to be well informed about his/her own faith so as to be able to explain and discuss it with them; praying with the family for the grace of Christian unity as the Lord wills it.

152. While keeping clearly in mind that doctrinal differences impede full sacramental and canonical communion between the Catholic Church and the various Eastern Churches, in the pastoral care of marriages between Catholics and Eastern Christians, particular attention should be given to the sound and consistent teaching of the faith which is shared by both and to the fact that in the Eastern Churches are to be found "true sacraments, and above all, by apostolic succession, the priesthood and the Eucharist, whereby they are still joined to us in closest intimacy".[144] If proper pastoral care is given to persons involved in these marriages, the faithful of both communions can be helped to understand how children born of such marriages will be initiated into and spiritually nourished by the sacramental mysteries of Christ. Their formation in authentic Christian doctrine and ways of Christian living would, for the most part, be similar in each Church. Diversity in liturgical life and private devotion can be made to encourage rather than hinder family prayer.

153. A marriage between a Catholic and a member of an Eastern Church is valid if it has taken place with the celebration of a religious rite by an ordained minister, as long as any other requirements of law for validity have been observed. For lawfulness in these cases, the canonical form of celebration is to be observed.[145] Canonical form is required for the validity of marriages between Catholics and Christians of Churches and ecclesial Communities.[146]

154. The local Ordinary of the Catholic partner, after having consulted the Local Ordinary of the place where the marriage will be celebrated, may for grave reasons and without prejudice to the law of the Eastern Churches,[147] dispense the Catholic partner from the observance of the canonical form of marriage.[148] Among these reasons for dispensation may be considered the maintaining of family harmony, obtaining parental consent to the marriage, the recognition of the particular religious commitment of the non-Catholic partner or his/her blood relationship with a minister of another Church or ecclesial Community. Episcopal Conferences are to issue norms by which such a dispensation may be granted in accordance with a common practice.

155. The obligation imposed by some Churches or ecclesial Communities for the observance of their own form of marriage is not a motive for automatic dispensation from the Catholic canonical form. Such particular situations should form the subject of dialogue between the Churches, at least at the local level.

156. One must keep in mind that, if the wedding is celebrated with a dispensation from canonical form, some public form of celebration is still required for validity.[149] To emphasize the unity of marriage, it is not permitted to have two separate religious services in which the exchange of consent would be expressed twice, or even one service which would celebrate two such exchanges of consent jointly or successively.[150]

157. With the previous authorisation of the local Ordinary, and if invited to do so, a Catholic priest or deacon may attend or participate in some way in the celebration of mixed marriages, in situations where the dispensation from

canonical form has been granted. In these cases, there may be only one ceremony in which the presiding person receives the marriage vows. At the invitation of this celebrant, the Catholic priest or deacon may offer other appropriate prayers, read from the Scriptures, give a brief exhortation and bless the couple.

158. Upon request of the couple, the local Ordinary may permit the Catholic priest to invite the minister of the party of the other Church or ecclesial Community to participate in the celebration of the marriage, to read from the Scriptures, give a brief exhortation and bless the couple.

159. Because of problems concerning Eucharistic sharing which may arise from the presence of non-Catholic witnesses and guests, a mixed marriage celebrated according to the Catholic form ordinarily takes place outside the Eucharistic liturgy. For a just cause, however, the diocesan Bishop may permit the celebration of the Eucharist.[151] In the latter case, the decision as to whether the non-Catholic party of the marriage may be admitted to Eucharistic communion is to be made in keeping with the general norms existing in the matter both for Eastern Christians [152] and for other Christians,[153] taking into account the particular situation of the reception of the sacrament of Christian marriage by two baptized Christians.

160. Although the spouses in a mixed marriage share the sacraments of baptism and marriage, Eucharistic sharing can only be exceptional and in each case the norms stated above concerning the admission of a non-Catholic Christian to Eucharistic communion,[154] as well as those concerning the participation of a Catholic in Eucharistic communion in another Church,[155] must be observed.

V. Ecumenical Cooperation Dialogue
and Common Witness

161. When Christians live and pray together in the way described in Chapter IV, they are giving witness to the faith which they share and to their baptism, in the name of God, the Father of all, in his Son Jesus, the Redeemer of all, and in the Holy Spirit who transforms and unites all things through the power of love. Based on this communion of life and spiritual gifts, there are many other forms of ecumenical cooperation that express and promote unity and enhance the witness to the saving power of the Gospel that Christians give to the world. When Christians cooperate in studying and propagating the Bible, in liturgical studies, in catechesis and higher education, in pastoral care, in evangelization and in their service of charity to a world that is struggling to realize its ideals of justice and peace and love, they are putting into practice what was proposed in the Decree on Ecumenism:

"Before the whole world, let all Christians profess their faith in God, one and three, in the incarnate Son of God, our Redeemer and Lord. United in their efforts, and with mutual respect, let them bear witness to our common hope, which does not play us false. Since in our times cooperation in social matters is very widely practiced, all without exception are summoned to united effort. Those who believe in God have a stronger summons, but the strongest claims are laid on Christians, since they have been sealed with the name of Christ. Cooperation among all Christians vividly expresses that bond which already unites them, and it sets in clearer relief the features of Christ the Servant".[156]

162. Christians cannot close their hearts to the crying needs of our contemporary world. The contribution they are able to make to all the areas of human life in which the need for salvation is manifested will be more effective when they make it together, and when they are seen to be united in making it. Hence they will want to do everything together that is allowed by their faith. The absence of full communion between different Churches and ecclesial Communities, the divergences that still exist in teaching regarding both faith and morals, the wounded memories and the heritage of a history of separation — each of these set limits to what Christians can do together at this time. Their cooperation can help them to overcome the barriers to full communion and at the same time to put together their resources for building Christian life and service and the common witness that it gives, in view of the mission which they share:

"In this unity in mission, which is decided principally by Christ himself, all Christians must find what already unites them even before their full communion is achieved."[157]

Forms and Structures of Ecumenical Cooperation

163. Ecumenical collaboration can take the form of participation by different Churches and ecclesial Communities in programmes already set up by one of their number. Or there may be a coordination of independent actions, with consequent avoidance of duplication and of the unnecessary multiplication of administrative structures. Or there may be joint initiatives and programmes. Various kinds of councils or committees may be set up, in more or less permanent form, to facilitate relations between Churches and ecclesial Communities and to promote cooperation and common witness among them.

164. Catholic participation in all forms of ecumenical meetings and cooperative projects should respect the norms established by the local ecclesiastical authority. Ultimately, it is for the diocesan Bishop, taking account of what has been decided at the regional or national level, to judge the acceptability and appropriateness of all forms of local ecumenical action. Bishops, Synods of Eastern Catholic Churches and Episcopal Conferences should act in accord with the directives of the Holy See and in a special way with those of the Pontifical Council for Promoting Christian Unity.

165. Meetings of authorized representatives of Churches and ecclesial Communities that occur periodically or on special occasions can help greatly to promote ecumenical cooperation. As well as being themselves an important witness to the commitment of those who participate in the promotion of Christian unity, they can give the stamp of authority to the cooperative efforts of members of the Churches and ecclesial Communities they represent. They may also provide the occasion for examining what specific questions and tasks of ecumenical cooperation need to be addressed and for taking necessary decisions about the setting up of working groups or programmes to deal with them.

Councils of Churches and Christian Councils

166. Councils of Churches and Christian Councils are among the more permanent structures that are set up for promoting unity and ecumenical cooperation. A Council of Churches is composed of Churches[158] and is responsible to the Churches that set it up. A Christian Council is composed of other Christian groups and organizations as

well as Churches. There are also other institutions for cooperation similar to these Councils but having other titles. Generally, Councils and similar institutions seek to enable their members to work together, to engage in dialogue, to overcome divisions and misunderstandings, to engage in prayer and work for unity, and to give, as far as possible, a common Christian witness and service. They are to be evaluated according to their activities and to the self-understanding set out in their constitutions. They have only the authority accorded to them by their constituent members. As a rule, they do not have responsibility for negotiations directed to the union of Churches.

167. Since it is desirable for the Catholic Church to find the proper expression for various levels of its relation with other Churches and ecclesial Communities, and since Councils of Churches and Christian Councils are among the more important forms of ecumenical cooperation, the growing contacts which the Catholic Church is having with Councils in many parts of the world are to be welcomed.

168. The decision to actually join a Council is the responsibility of the Bishops in the area served by the Council who also have responsibility for overseeing the Catholic participation in these Councils. For national Councils, that will generally be the Synod of Eastern Catholic Churches or the Episcopal Conference (except where there is only one diocese in a nation). In considering the question of membership of a Council, the appropriate authorities should be in touch during the preparation of the decision with the Pontifical Council for Promoting Christian Unity.

169. The pastoral advisability of joining a Council is one of the many factors that are to be taken into account in

taking such a step. It must also be clear that participation in the life of the Council can be compatible with the teaching of the Catholic Church, and does not blur its unique and specific identity. The first concern should be that of doctrinal clarity, especially as far as ecclesiology is concerned. Councils of Churches and Christian Councils do not in fact contain either within themselves or among themselves the beginning of a new Church which could replace the communion that now exists in the Catholic Church. They are not to proclaim themselves Churches or to claim for themselves an authority which would permit them to confer a ministry of Word or Sacrament.[159] Careful attention should be given to the Council's system of representation and voting rights, to its decision-making processes, to its manner of making public statements and to the degree of authority attributed to such statements. Clear and precise agreement on these matters should be reached before membership is taken up.[160]

170. Catholic membership of a local, national or regional Council is a quite distinct matter from the question of the relationship between the Catholic Church and the World Council of Churches. The World Council may, indeed, invite selected Councils "to enter into working relationships as associated Councils", but it does not have any authority or control over these Councils or their member Churches.

171. Joining a Council ought to be seen as undertaking serious responsibilities. The Catholic Church should be represented by well-qualified and committed persons. In the exercise of their mandate, they should be clearly aware of the limits beyond which they cannot commit the Church without referring the matter to the authority that has

appointed them. The more attentively the work of these Councils is followed by their member Churches, the more important and efficacious will be the Councils' contribution to the ecumenical movement.

Ecumenical Dialogue

172. Dialogue is at the heart of ecumenical cooperation and accompanies all forms of it. Dialogue involves both listening and replying, seeking both to understand and to be understood. It is a readiness to put questions and to be questioned. It is to be forthcoming about oneself and trustful of what others say about themselves. The parties in dialogue must be ready to clarify their ideas further, and modify their personal views and ways of living and acting, allowing themselves to be guided in this by authentic love and truth. Reciprocity and mutual commitment are essential elements in dialogue, as is also a sense that the partners are together on an equal footing.[161] Ecumenical dialogue allows members of different Churches and ecclesial Communities to get to know one another, to identify matters of faith and practice which they share and points on which they differ. They seek to understand the roots of such differences and assess to what extent they constitute a real obstacle to a common faith. When differences are recognised as being a real barrier to communion, they try to find ways to overcome them in the light of those points of faith which they already hold in common.

173. The Catholic Church may engage in dialogue at a diocesan level, at the level of Episcopal Conferences or Synods of Eastern Catholic Churches, and at the level of the universal Church. Its structure, as a universal communion in faith and sacramental life, allows it to present a consistent and united position on each of these levels. Where

there is just one partner Church or Community in the dialogue, it is called bilateral; when there are several it is described as multilateral.

174. On the local level there are countless opportunities for exchanges between Christians, ranging from informal conversations that occur in daily life to sessions for the common examination in a Christian perspective of issues of local life or of concern to particular professional groups (doctors, social workers, parents, educators) and to study groups for specifically ecumenical subjects. Dialogues may be carried on by groups of lay people, by groups of clergy, by groups of professional theologians or by various combinations of these. Whether they have official standing (as a result of having been set up or formally authorized by ecclesiastical authority) or not, these exchanges must always be marked by a strong ecclesial sense. Catholics who take part in them will feel the need to be well informed about their faith and to deepen their living of it, and they will be careful to remain in communion of thought and desire with their Church.

175. The participants in certain dialogues are appointed by the hierarchy to take part not in a personal capacity, but as delegated representatives of their Church. Such mandates can be given by the local Ordinary, the Synod of Eastern Catholic Churches or the Episcopal Conference within its territory, or by the Holy See. In these cases, the Catholic participants have a special responsibility towards the authority that has sent them. The approval of that authority is also needed before any results of the dialogue engage the Church officially.

176. Catholic participants in dialogue follow the principles about Catholic doctrine set down by *Unitatis redintegratio*:

"The manner and order in which Catholic belief is expressed should in no way become an obstacle to dialogue with our brethren. It is, of course, essential that the doctrine be clearly presented in its entirety. Nothing is so foreign to the spirit of ecumenism as a false conciliatory approach which harms the purity of Catholic doctrine and obscures its assured genuine meaning.

At the same time, Catholic belief needs to be explained more profoundly and precisely, in ways and in terminology which our separated brethren too can easily understand.

Furthermore, Catholic theologians engaged in ecumenical dialogue, while standing fast by the teaching of the Church and searching together with separated brethren into the divine mysteries, should act with love for truth, with charity, and with humility. When comparing doctrines they should remember that in Catholic teaching there exists an order or 'hierarchy' of truths, since they vary in their relationship to the foundation of the Christian faith. Thus the way will be opened for this kind of fraternal rivalry to incite all to a deeper realization and a clearer expression of the unfathomable riches of Christ".[162]

The question of the hierarchy of truths is also taken up in the document *Reflections and Suggestions Concerning Ecumenical Dialogue:*

"Neither in the life nor in the teaching of the whole Church is everything presented on the same level. Certainly all revealed truths demand the same acceptance of faith, but according to the greater or lesser proximity that they have to the basis of the revealed mystery, they are variously placed with regard to one another and have varying connections among themselves".[163]

177. The subject of dialogue may be a broad range of doctrinal issues covered over an extended period of time, or

a single issue dealt with in a definite time framework; or it may be a pastoral or missionary problem about which the Churches wish to find a common position in order to eliminate conflicts that arise between them and to promote mutual help and common witness. For some questions a bilateral dialogue may be found more effective, for others multilateral dialogue gives better results. Experience shows that the two forms of dialogue complement one another in the complex task of promoting Christian unity. The results of a bilateral dialogue should be promptly communicated to all other interested Churches or ecclesial Communities.

178. A commission or committee set up to engage in dialogue on behalf of two or more Churches or ecclesial Communities may reach various degrees of agreement about the subject assigned to it and formulate their conclusions in a statement. Even before such agreement is reached, it may sometimes be judged useful by a commission to issue a statement or report that marks the convergencies that have been established, that identifies the problems that remain and suggests the direction that future dialogue might take. All statements or reports of dialogue commissions are submitted to the Churches concerned for assessment. Statements produced by dialogue commissions have intrinsic weight because of the competence and status of their authors. They are not, however, binding on the Catholic Church until they have been approved by the appropriate ecclesiastical authorities.

179. When the results of a dialogue are considered by proper authorities to be ready for submission for evaluation, the members of the People of God, according to their role or charism, must be involved in this critical process. The faithful, as a matter of fact, are called to exercise: "the supernatural appreciation of the faith (*sensus fidei*) of the

whole people, when 'from the Bishops to the last of the faithful' they manifest a universal consent in matters of faith and morals. By this appreciation of the faith, aroused and sustained by the Spirit of truth, the People of God, guided by the sacred teaching authority (*magisterium*), and obeying it, receives not the mere word of men, but truly the Word of God,[164] the faith once for all delivered to the saints.[165] The people unfailingly adheres to this faith, penetrates it more deeply with right judgment, and applies it more fully in daily life".[166]

Every effort should be made to find appropriate ways of bringing the results of dialogues to the attention of all members of the Church. In so far as possible, an explanation should be provided in respect of new insights into the faith, new witnesses to its truth, new forms of expression developed in dialogue — as well as with regard to the extent of the agreements being proposed. This will allow for an accurate judgment being made in respect of the reactions of all concerned as they assess the fidelity of these dialogue results to the Tradition of faith received from the Apostles and transmitted to the community of believers under the guidance of their authorized teachers. It is to be hoped that this manner of proceeding would be adopted by each Church or ecclesial Community that is partner to the dialogue and indeed by all Churches and ecclesial Communities that are hearing the call to unity. Cooperation between the Churches in this effort is most desirable.

180. The life of faith and the prayer of faith, no less than reflection on the doctrine of faith, enter into this process of reception, by which the whole Church, under the inspiration of the Holy Spirit "who distributes special graces among the faithful of every rank" [167] and guides in a special way the ministry of those who teach, makes its own the fruits of a

dialogue, in a process of listening, of testing, of judging and of living.

181. In assessing and assimilating new forms of expression of the faith, which may appear in statements issued from ecumenical dialogue, or even ancient expressions which have been taken up again in preference to certain more recent theological terms, Catholics will bear in mind the distinction made in the Decree on Ecumenism between "the way that Church teaching has been formulated" and "the deposit of faith itself".[168] They will take care however to avoid ambiguous expressions especially in the search for agreement on points of doctrine that are traditionally controversial. They will also take account of the way in which the Second Vatican Council itself applied this distinction in its own formulation of Catholic faith; they must also allow for the "hierarchy of truths" in Catholic doctrine noted by the Decree on Ecumenism.[169]

182. The process of reception includes theological reflection of a technical nature on the Tradition of faith, as well as on the contemporary liturgical and pastoral reality of the Church. Important contributions to this process come from the specific competence of theological faculties. The whole process is guided by the official teaching authority of the Church which has the responsibility of making the final judgment about ecumenical statements. The new insights that are thus accepted enter into the life of the Church, renewing in a certain way that which fosters reconciliation with other Churches and ecclesial Communities.

Common Bible Work

183. The Word of God that is written in the Scriptures nourishes the life of the Church in manifold ways [170] and is "a precious instrument in the mighty hand of God for

attaining to that unity which the Saviour holds out to all men".[171] Veneration of the Scriptures is a fundamental bond of unity between Christians, one that holds firm even when the Churches and Communities to which they belong are not in full communion with each other. Everything that can be done to make members of the Churches and ecclesial Communities read the Word of God, and to do that together when possible (e.g., Bible Weeks), reinforces this bond of unity that already unites them, helps them to be open to the unifying action of God and strengthens the common witness to the saving Word of God which they give to the world. The provision and diffusion of suitable editions of the Bible is a prerequisite to the hearing of the Word. While the Catholic Church continues to produce editions of the Bible that meet its own specific standards and requirements, it also cooperates willingly with other Churches and ecclesial Communities in the making of translations and in the publication of common editions in accordance with what was foreseen by the Second Vatican Council and is provided for in the Code of Canon Law.[172] It sees ecumenical cooperation in this field as a valuable form of common service and common witness in the Church and to the world.

184. The Catholic Church is involved in this cooperation in many ways and at different levels. The Pontifical Council for Promoting Christian Unity was involved in the setting up, in 1969, of the World Catholic Federation for the Biblical Apostolate (now *"Catholic Biblical Federation)"*, as an international Catholic organization of a public character to further the pastoral implementation of *Dei Verbum,* ch. VI. In accordance with this objective, whenever local circumstances allow, collaboration at the level of local Churches as well as at regional level, between the ecumen-

ical officer and the local sections of the Federation should be strongly encouraged.

185. Through the General Secretariat of the Catholic Biblical Federation, the Pontifical Council for Promoting Christian Unity maintains and develops relations with the United Bible Societies, an international Christian organization which has published jointly with the Secretariat *"Guidelines for Interconfessional Cooperation in Translating the Bible"*.[173] This document sets out the principles, methods and concrete orientations of this special type of collaboration in the biblical field. This collaboration has already yielded good results. Similar contacts and cooperation between institutions devoted to the publication and use of the Bible are encouraged on all levels of the life of the Church. They can help cooperation between the Churches and ecclesial Communities in missionary work, catechetics and religious education, as well as in common prayer and study. They can often result in the joint production of a Bible that may be used by several Churches and ecclesial Communities in a given cultural area, or for specific purposes such as study or liturgical life.[174] Cooperation of this kind can be an antidote to the use of the Bible in a fundamentalist way or for sectarian purposes.

186. Catholics can share the study of the Scriptures with members of other Churches and ecclesial Communities in many different ways and on many different levels. This sharing goes from the kind of work that can be done in neighbourhood or parochial groups to that of scholarly research among professional exegetes. In order to have ecumenical value, at whatever level it is done, this work needs to be grounded on faith and to nourish faith. It will often bring home to the participants how the doctrinal positions of different Churches and ecclesial Communities, and

differences in their approaches to the use and exegesis of the Bible, lead to different interpretations of particular passages. It is helpful for Catholics when the editions of the Scriptures that they use actually draw attention to passages in which the doctrine of the Church is at issue. They will want to face up to any difficulties and disagreements that come from the ecumenical use of the Scriptures with an understanding of and a loyalty to the teaching of the Church. But this need not prevent them from recognizing how much they are at one with other Christians in the interpretation of the Scriptures. They will come to appreciate the light that the experience and traditions of the different Churches can throw on parts of the Scriptures that are especially significant for them. They will become more open to the possibility of finding new starting points in the Scriptures themselves for discussion about controversial issues. They will be challenged to discover the meaning of God's Word in relation to contemporary human situations that they share with their fellow Christians. Moreover, they will experience with joy the unifying power of God's Word.

Common Liturgical Texts

187. Churches and ecclesial Communities whose members live within a culturally homogeneous area should draw up together, where possible, a text of the most important Christian prayers (the Lord's Prayer, Apostles' Creed, Nicene-Constantinopolitan Creed, a Trinitarian Doxology, the Glory to God in the Highest). These would be for regular use by all the Churches, and ecclesial Communities or at least for use when they pray together on ecumenical occasions. Agreement on a version of the Psalter for liturgical use, or at least of some of the more frequently used psalms would also be desirable; a similar agreement for

common Scriptural readings for liturgical use should also be explored. The use of liturgical and other prayers that come from the period of the undivided Church can help to foster an ecumenical sense. Common hymn books, or at least common collections of hymns to be included in the hymn books of the different Churches and ecclesial Communities, as well as cooperation in developing liturgical music, are also to be recommended. When Christians pray together, with one voice, their common witness reaches to heaven as well as being heard on earth.

Ecumenical Cooperation in Catechesis

188. To complement the normal catechesis that Catholics must receive in any event, the Catholic Church recognizes that, in situations of religious pluralism, cooperation in the field of catechesis can enrich its own life as well as that of other Churches and ecclesial Communities. It can also strengthen their ability to give a common witness to the truth of the Gospel, in so far as this is possible. The basis of this cooperation, its conditions and its limits are set out in the Apostolic Exhortation *Catechesi Tradendae:*

"Such experiences have a theological foundation in the elements shared by all Christians. But the communion of faith between Catholics and other Christians is not complete and perfect; in certain cases there are even profound divergences. Consequently, this ecumenical collaboration is by its very nature limited; it must never mean a 'reduction' to a common minimum. Furthermore, catechesis does not consist merely in the teaching of doctrine; it also means initiating into the whole of Christian life, bringing full participation in the sacraments of the Church. Therefore, where there is an experience of ecumenical collaboration in the field of catechesis, care must be taken that the education of Catholics in the Catholic Church should be well ensured in matters of doctrine and of Christian living".[175]

189. In some countries a form of Christian teaching common to Catholics and other Christians is imposed by the state or by particular circumstances, with text-books and the content of the course all laid down. In such cases, we are not dealing with true catechesis nor with books that can be used as catechisms. But such teaching, when it presents elements of Christian doctrine loyally, has authentic ecumenical value. In these cases, while appreciating the potential value of such teaching, it still remains indispensable to provide a specifically Catholic catechesis for Catholic children.

190. When the teaching of religion in schools is done in collaboration with members of religions other than Christian, a special effort should be made to ensure that the Christian message is presented in a way that highlights the unity of faith that exists between Christians about fundamental matters, while at the same time explaining the divisions that do exist and the steps that are being taken to overcome them.

Cooperation in Institutes of Higher Studies

191. There are many opportunities for ecumenical cooperation and common witness in the scientific study of theology and the branches of learning associated with it. Such cooperation contributes to theological research. It improves the quality of theological education by helping teachers to provide that attention to the ecumenical aspect of theological issues that is required in the Catholic Church by the conciliar decree *Unitatis redintegratio*.[176] It facilitates the ecumenical formation of pastoral agents (see above chapter III). It helps Christians to address together the

great intellectual issues that face men and women today from a shared fund of Christian wisdom and expertise. Instead of accentuating their difference they are able to give due preference to the profound harmony of faith and understanding that can exist within the diversity of their theological expressions.

In Seminaries and Undergraduate Studies.

192. Ecumenical cooperation in study and teaching is already desirable in programmes of the first stages of theological education, such as are given in seminaries and in first cycles of theological faculties. This cannot yet be done in the same way as is possible at the level of research and among those who have already completed their basic theological formation. An elementary requirement for ecumenical cooperation at those higher levels — to be dealt with in nn. 196-203 -, is that the participants be well formed in their faith and in the tradition of their own Church. Theological education in seminaries and first-cycle courses is directed to giving students this basic formation. The Catholic Church, like other Churches and ecclesial Communities, plans the programmes and courses that it considers appropriate for this purpose and selects suitably qualified directors and professors. The rule is that professors of the doctrinal courses should be Catholics. Thus the elementary principles of initiation into ecumenism and ecumenical theology, which is a necessary part of basic theological formation, are given by Catholic teachers.[177] Once these fundamental concerns of the Church about the purpose, values and requirements of initial theological training—which are understood and shared by many other Churches and ecclesial Communities — are respected, students and

teachers from Catholic seminaries and theological faculties can cooperate ecumenically in various ways.

193. The norms for promoting and regulating cooperation between Catholics and other Christians at the level of seminary and first cycle theological studies are to be determined by Synods of Eastern Catholic Churches and Episcopal Conferences, particularly in so far as they affect the education of candidates for ordination. The appropriate ecumenical commission should be heard on the subject. The relevant guidelines should be included in the Programme of Training for Priesthood that is drawn up in accordance with the Decree on the Training of Priests *Optatam Totius*. Since institutes for training members of religious orders may also be involved in this kind of ecumenical cooperation in theological education, major superiors or their delegates should contribute towards drawing up rules, in keeping with the Conciliar Decree *Christus Dominus*.[178]

194. Catholic students may attend special courses given at institutes, including seminaries, of Christians of other Churches and ecclesial Communities, in accordance with the general criteria for the ecumenical formation of Catholic students, and subject to any norms that may have been laid down by the Synod of Eastern Catholic Churches or the Episcopal Conference. When a decision has to be taken about whether or not they should actually attend special courses, attention will be paid to the usefulness of the course in the general context of their training, the quality and ecumenical attitude of the professor, the level of previous preparation of the pupils themselves, as well as their spiritual and psychological maturity. The more closely the lectures or courses bear on doctrinal subjects, the more

care will be needed in coming to a decision regarding the participation of the students. The formation of students and the development of their ecumenical sense is to be undertaken by a gradual process.

195. In the second and third cycles of faculties and in seminaries after the students have received basic formation, professors from other Churches and ecclesial Communities may be invited to give lectures on the doctrinal positions of the Churches and Communities they represent, in order to complete the ecumenical formation the students are already receiving from their Catholic professors. Such professors may also provide courses of a technical nature, as for example, language courses, instruction on communication media, religious sociology, etc. In laying down norms to regulate this matter, Synods of Eastern Catholic Churches and Episcopal Conferences will bear in mind the degree of development reached by the ecumenical movement in their country and the state of relationship between Catholics and other Churches and ecclesial Communities.[179] They will specifically determine how Catholic criteria concerning the qualifications of professors, the period of their teaching and their accountability for the content of courses [180] are to be applied in their region. They will also give directives about how the teaching received by Catholic students in such lectures can be integrated into their complete programme. Professors so invited will be classified as "visiting lecturers". When necessary, Catholic institutions will organize seminars or courses to put into context the teaching given by lecturers from other Churches and ecclesial Communities. Catholic professors invited to lecture in corresponding circumstances in the seminaries and theological schools of other Churches and ecclesial

Communities will gladly do so under the same conditions. Such an exchange of professors, that respects the concerns of each Church and ecclesial Community for the basic theological formation of its members, and especially of those who are called to be its ministers, is an effective form of ecumenical collaboration and gives an appropriate witness to Christian concern for sound teaching in the Church of Christ.

In Theological Research and Post-Graduate Studies.

196. A wider field of ecumenical collaboration is open to those who are engaged in theological research and teaching on a post-graduate level than is possible on the level of seminary or undergraduate (institutional) teaching. The maturity of the participants (research workers, professors, students) and the advanced levels of study already attained in the faith and theology of their own Church brings a special security and richness to their cooperation, such as could not be expected from those who are still engaged in undergraduate or seminary formation.

197. Cooperation in higher studies is practised by experts who consult and share their research with experts from other Churches and ecclesial Communities. It is practised by ecumenical groups and associations of experts set up for the purpose. It is to be found in a special way within various forms of relationships that are entered into between institutions for the study of theology that belong to different Churches and ecclesial Communities. Such relationships and the cooperation they facilitate can help to give an ecumenical character to all the work of the participating institutions. They can provide for a sharing of personnel, library, courses, premises and other resources, to

the considerable advantage of researchers, professors and students.

198. Ecumenical cooperation is particularly indicated in the interest of those institutes that are set up within existing faculties of theology for research and specialized formation in ecumenical theology or for the pastoral practice of ecumenism; it can similarly benefit those independent institutes that are set up for the same purpose. Although these latter may belong to particular Churches or ecclesial Communities, they will be more effective when they cooperate actively with similar institutes that belong to other Churches. It may be useful from an ecumenical point of view if such institutes have members of other Churches and ecclesial Communities on their staff and in their student body.

199. The setting up and administration of institutions and structures for ecumenical collaboration in the study of theology should normally be entrusted to those who conduct the institutions involved, and to those who work within them in a spirit of legitimate academic freedom. Their ecumenical effectiveness requires that they operate in close relationship with the authorities of the Churches and ecclesial Communities to which their members belong. When the institute involved in such cooperative structures is part of a faculty of theology that already belongs to the Catholic Church, or is set up by it as a separate institution under its authority, its relationship to Church authorities in ecumenical activity will be defined in the articles of agreement on cooperation.

200. Interconfessional institutes, set up and administered jointly by several Churches and ecclesial Communities, are especially effective in dealing with topics of

common concern to all Christians. Joint study of certain questions will indeed contribute to the solution of problems and to the approval of suitable policies, thus contributing to the advancement of Christian unity. Among such questions the following may be mentioned: mission work, relations with non–Christian religions, atheism and unbelief, the use of social communications media, architecture and sacred art, theological subjects as the explanation of Holy Scripture, salvation history and pastoral theology. The responsibility of such institutes towards the authorities of the Churches and ecclesial Communities concerned is to be defined clearly in their statutes.

201. Associations or institutes may be set up for the joint study of theological and pastoral questions by ministers of different Churches and ecclesial Communities. Under the guidance and with the help of experts in various fields, these ministers discuss and analyse together the theoretical and practical aspects of their ministry within their own Communities, in its ecumenical dimensions and in its contribution to common Christian witness.

202. The field of study and research in institutes for ecumenical activity and cooperation can cover the whole ecumenical reality, or it can be limited to particular questions that are studied in depth. When institutes specialize in the study of one area of ecumenism (the Orthodox tradition, Protestantism, the Anglican Communion, as well as the kind of questions mentioned in n. 200), it is important that they should deal with that study within the context of the whole ecumenical movement and all the other questions that are connected with the subject under consideration.

203. Catholic institutions are encouraged to become members of ecumenical associations designed to promote improvement in the standard of theological education, better training of those intended for pastoral ministry and better cooperation between institutions for advanced learning. They will be also open to proposals that are being put forward with increasing frequency today by the authorities of public and non-denominational universities to bring together for the study of religion different institutes that are connected with them. Membership of such ecumenical associations and participation in the teaching of associated institutes must respect the legitimate autonomy of Catholic institutes in matters of the programme of studies, of the doctrinal content of subjects to be taught, and of the spiritual and priestly training of students destined for ordination.

Pastoral Cooperation in Special Situations

204. While each Church and ecclesial Community takes pastoral care of its own members and is built up in an irreplaceable way by the ministers of its local communities, there are certain situations in which the religious need of Christian people may well be served more effectively when pastoral agents, ordained or lay, from different Churches and ecclesial Communities work together. This kind of ecumenical collaboration can be practised with success in the pastoral care of those who are in hospitals, prisons, the armed forces, universities, and large industrial complexes. It is also effective in bringing a Christian presence into the world of the social communications media. Care should be taken to coordinate these special ecumenical ministries with the local pastoral structures of each Church. That will be more readily achieved when those structures are them-

selves imbued with the ecumenical spirit and practise ecumenical cooperation with corresponding local units of other Churches or ecclesial Communities. Liturgical ministry, especially that of the Eucharist and of the other sacraments, is provided in such cooperative situations according to the norms that each Church or ecclesial Community lays down for its own members, which for Catholics are those stated in chapter IV of this Directory.

Cooperation in Missionary Activity

205. The common witness given by all forms of ecumenical cooperation is already missionary. The ecumenical movement has, in fact, gone hand in hand with a new discovery by many communities of the missionary nature of the Church.

Ecumenical cooperation shows to the world that those who believe in Christ and live by his Spirit, being thus made children of God who is Father of all, can set about over coming human divisions, even about such sensitive matters as religious faith and practice, with courage and hope. The divisions that exist among Christians are certainly a major obstacle to the successful preaching of the Gospel.[181] But the efforts being made to overcome them do much to offset the scandal and to give credibility to Christians who proclaim that Christ is the one in whom all things and people are gathered together into unity:

"As evangelizers we must offer Christ's faithful not the image of people divided and separated by unedifying quarrels, but the image of people who are mature in faith and capable of finding a meeting-point beyond the real tensions, thanks to a shared, sincere and disinterested search for truth. Yes, the destiny of evangelization is certainly bound up with the witness of unity given by the

Church. This is a source of responsibility and also of comfort".[182]

206. Ecumenical witness can be given in missionary activity itself. For Catholics, the basis for ecumenical cooperation with other Christians in mission is "the foundation of baptism and the patrimony of faith which is common to us".[183] Other Churches and ecclesial Communities which draw people to faith in Christ the Saviour and to baptism in the name of the Father, Son and Holy Spirit draw them into the real though imperfect communion that exists between them and the Catholic Church. Catholics would want all who are called to Christian faith to join with them in that fullness of communion they believe to exist in the Catholic Church, yet they recognize that in the Providence of God some will live out their Christian lives in Churches and ecclesial Communities that do not provide such full communion. They should be careful to respect the lively faith of other Churches and ecclesial Communities which preach the Gospel, and rejoice in the grace of God that is at work among them.

207. Catholics can join with other Churches and ecclesial Communities — provided there is nothing sectarian or deliberately anti-Catholic about their work of evangelization — in organizations and programmes that give common support to the missionary activities of all the participating Churches. A special subject of such cooperation will be to ensure that the human, cultural and political factors that were involved in the original divisions between the Churches, and have marked the historical tradition of separation, will not be transplanted into areas where the Gospel is being preached and Churches are being founded. Those who have been sent by missionary institutes to help

in the foundation and growth of new Churches, will be especially sensitive to this need. Bishops will give special attention to it. It is for the Bishop to determine when it becomes necessary to insist in a special way on points of doctrine and morality about which Catholics differ from other Churches and ecclesial Communities. These latter may find it necessary to do the same in relation to Catholicism. But all this must be done, not in a contentious or sectarian spirit, but with mutual respect and love.[184] New converts to the faith should be carefully nourished in the ecumenical spirit, "so that, while avoiding every form of indifferentism or confusion and also senseless rivalry, Catholics might collaborate with their separated brethren, insofar as it is possible, by a common profession before the nations of faith in God and in Jesus Christ, and by a common, fraternal effort in social, cultural, technical and religious matters".[185]

208. Ecumenical cooperation is particularly necessary in the mission to the de-Christianized masses of our contemporary world. The ability of Christians, though still divided, to bear common witness, even now, to central truths of the Gospel [186] can be a powerful invitation to a renewed appreciation of Christian faith in a secularized society. A common evaluation of the forms of atheism, secularization and materialism that are at work in the world of today, and a shared strategy to deal with them would greatly benefit the Christian mission to the contemporary world.

209. There should be a special place for cooperation between members of the different Churches and ecclesial Communities in the reflection constantly needed on the meaning of Christian mission, on the manner of engaging in

the dialogue of salvation with the members of other religions and on the general question of the relationship between the preaching of the Gospel of Christ and the cultures and way of thinking of the contemporary world.

Ecumenical Cooperation in the Dialogue with Other Religions

210. There are increasing contacts in today's world between Christians and persons of other religions. These contacts differ radically from the contacts between the Churches and ecclesial Communities, which have for their object the restoration of the unity Christ willed among all his disciples and are properly called ecumenical. But in practice they are deeply influenced by, and in turn influence ecumenical relationships. Through them Christians can deepen the level of communion existing among themselves, and so they are to be considered an important part of ecumenical cooperation. This is particularly true for all that is done to develop the specially privileged religious relationship that Christians have with the Jewish people.

For Catholics, directives about relationships with the Jewish people are guided by the Commission for Religious Relations with the Jews. Relations with the members of other religions are guided by the Pontifical Council for Inter-Religious Dialogue. In working out religious relationships with Jews and in their relations with members of other religions, in accordance with appropriate directives, Catholics can find many opportunities for collaboration with members of other Churches and ecclesial Communities. There are many areas where Christians can work together in fostering dialogue and common action with the Jews, as for example in struggling together against anti-Semitism, religious fanaticism and sectarianism. Collaboration with other believers can take place in promoting religious perspectives on issues of justice and peace, support for family life, respect for minority communities, and such cooperation can also address the many new questions of the present age. In these interreligious contacts, Christians can appeal together to their common biblical and theological sources, thereby bringing Christian insights to this broader context, in a way that fosters Christian unity as well.

Ecumenical Cooperation in Social and Cultural Life

211. The Catholic Church considers ecumenical collaboration in social and cultural life to be an important aspect of working towards unity. The Decree on Ecumenism sees such cooperation as a clear expression of the bond that unites all the baptized.[187] For this reason, it encourages and supports very concrete forms of collaboration:

"Such cooperation which has already begun in many countries, should be ever increasingly developed, particularly in regions where a social and technical evolution is taking place. It should contribute to a just appreciation of the dignity of the human person, the promotion of the blessings of peace, the application of Gospel principles to social life, and advancement of the arts and science in a Christian spirit. Christians should also work together in the use of every possible means to relieve the afflictions of our times such as famine and national disasters, illiteracy and poverty, lack of housing, and the unequal distribution of wealth".[188]

212. As a general principle, ecumenical collaboration in the social and cultural life ought to be carried out within the overall context of the search for Christian unity. When it is not accompanied by other forms of ecumenism, especially by prayer and spiritual sharing, it can easily be confused with ideological and merely political interests and thus become an

obstacle to the progress toward unity. Like all forms of ecumenism, it should be carried out under the supervision of the local Ordinary, the Episcopal Conference or the Synod of the Eastern Catholic Churches.

213. Through such cooperation, all believers in Christ are able to learn easily how they can understand each other better and esteem each other more, and so prepare the way for the unity of Christians.[189] On a number of occasions, Pope John Paul II has affirmed the commitment of the Catholic Church to ecumenical collaboration.[190] The same affirmation was expressed in the common declaration between Cardinal Johannes Willebrands and Dr. Philip Potter, General Secretary of the World Council of Churches, on the occasion of the Holy Father's visit to the World Council of Churches' headquarters in Geneva in 1984.[191] It is in view of this that the Ecumenical Directory offers some examples of collaboration at various levels without these pretending to be exhaustive in any way.[192]

a) Cooperation in common studies of social and ethical questions

214. Regional or national Episcopal Conferences, in collaboration with other Churches and ecclesial Communities, as well as with Councils of Churches, could set up groups to give common expression to basic Christian and human values.

This kind of shared discernment will help to provide a significant starting point for an ecumenical address to questions of a social and ethical nature; it will open up the moral and social dimension of the partial communion that Christians of different Churches and ecclesial Communities already enjoy.

The purpose of a common study of this kind is the promotion of a Christian culture, a "civilization of love" —

the Christian humanism often spoken of by Pope Paul VI and Pope John Paul II. To construct this culture, we must clearly establish the values that form part of it as well as the things that threaten it. Clearly, therefore, the study will involve for example a Christian appreciation of the value of life, the meaning of human work, questions of justice and peace, religious liberty, human rights and land rights. It will likewise focus on the factors in society that threaten basic values, such as poverty, racism, consumerism, terrorism, and indeed all that threatens human life at whatever stage of its development. The long tradition of Catholic social teaching will provide considerable guidance and inspiration for this kind of collaboration.

b) Cooperation in the field of development, human need and stewardship of creation

215. There is an intrinsic connection between development, human need and the stewardship of creation. For experience has taught us that development in response to human needs cannot misuse or overuse natural resources without serious consequences.

The responsibility for the care of creation, which in itself has a particular dignity, is given by the Creator himself to all people, in so far as they are to be stewards of creation.[193] Catholics are encouraged to enter, at various levels, into joint initiatives aimed at study and action on issues that threaten the dignity of creation and endanger the whole human race. Other topics for such study and action could include, for example, certain forms of uncontrolled rapid industrialization and technology that cause pollution of the natural environment with serious consequences to the ecological balance, such as destruction of forests, nuclear testing and the irrational use or misuse of both renewable and unrenewable natural resources. An important aspect of joint action in this field is in the area of education of people in the use of resources as well as in the planned use of them and in the care of creation.

The field of development, which is basically a response to human needs, offers a variety of possibilities for collaboration between the Catholic Church and Churches and ecclesial Communities at regional, national and local levels. Such collaboration would include, among other things, working for a more just society, for peace, for promotion of the rights and dignity of women, and for a more equitable distribution of resources. In this sense, it would be possible to provide joint services for the poor, the sick, the handicapped, the aged and all who suffer because of unjust "structures of sin".[194] Cooperation in this field is encouraged particularly in places where there is high concentration of population with serious consequences for housing, food, water, clothing, sanitation and medical care. An important aspect of collaboration in this field would be in dealing with the problem of migrants, refugees, and victims of natural catastrophes. In the event of world emergencies, the Catholic Church encourages the pooling of resources and services with the international organizations of Churches and ecclesial Communities, for reasons of efficiency and to reduce costs. It likewise encourages ecumenical collaboration with international organizations that specialize in these concerns.

c) Cooperation in the field of medicine

216. The whole area of health care constitutes a very important challenge for ecumenical collaboration. In some countries ecumenical collaboration by the Churches in health care programmes is vital if adequate health care is to be provided. Increasingly, moreover, collaboration in this whole area, be it at the level of research, or at the level of

practical health care, raises questions of medical ethics which are both a challenge and an opportunity for ecumenical collaboration. The task mentioned earlier of identifying basic values that are integral to Christian life is especially urgent, given the rapid developments in areas such as genetics. In this context, the indications of the 1975 document on ecumenical collaboration [195] are especially pertinent: "Particularly where ethical norms are concerned, the doctrinal stand of the Catholic Church has to be made clear and the difficulties which this can raise for ecumenical collaboration faced honestly and with loyalty to Catholic teaching".

d) *Cooperation in Social Communications Media*

217. It is possible to cooperate in this matter, in understanding the nature of modern media and particularly the challenges it offers to Christians today. Collaboration in this area could include ways of infusing Christian principles into communications media and study of problems encountered in this field, as well as education of the people on critical use of the media. Interconfessional groups can be especially effective as advisory bodies to the secular media, particularly as to the way in which they deal with religious affairs. This can be particularly useful in countries where the majority of viewers, listeners, or readers are from one particular Church or ecclesial Community. "There is almost no end to the opportunities for such collaboration. Some are obvious: joint programmes on radio and television; educational projects and services, especially for parents and young people; meetings and discussions between professionals on an international level; recognition of achievement in these fields by annual awards; cooperation in research in the media field and especially in professional training and education".[196] Where interconfessional structures with full Catholic partic-

ipation already exist, they should be strengthened, particularly for the use of radio and television, and for publishing and audio-visual work. At the same time, each participating body should be given the opportunity to enunciate its own doctrine and practice.[197]

218. It would be important at times to work in mutual cooperation; either by having Catholic communicators take part in the initiatives of other Churches and ecclesial Communities, or by having communicators from these latter to participate in Catholic initiatives. Ecumenical collaboration could include exchanges between International Catholic Organizations and the communications organizations of other Churches and ecclesial Communities (as, for example, in keeping the World Day for Social Communications). The common use of satellites and cable television networks offers practical opportunities for ecumenical collaboration.[198] Clearly, at the regional level, this kind of collaboration should take place with reference to ecumenical commissions and, internationally, with reference to the Pontifical Council for Promoting Christian Unity. The formation of Catholic communicators should include a serious ecumenical preparation.

On March 25th, 1993, His Holiness Pope John Paul II approved this Directory, confirmed it by his authority and ordered that it be published. Anything to the contrary notwithstanding.

Vatican City
March 25th, 1993

Edward Idris Cardinal Cassidy
President
+ **Pierre Duprey**
Tit. Bishop of Thibar
Secretary

Notes

[1] Secretariat for Promoting Christian Unity (SPCU), *Ecumenical Directory, Ad Totam Ecclesiam, AAS* 1967, 574-592; *AAS* 1970, 705-724.

[2] *Address* of Pope John Paul II to the Plenary Session of the Secretariat for Promoting Christian Unity, February 6, 1988, *AAS* 1988, 1203.

[3] Among these are the Motu Proprio *Matrimonia Mixta, AAS* 1970, 257-263; *Reflections and Suggestions concerning Ecumenical Dialogue,* SPCU, *Information Service* (IS) 12, 1970, pp. 5-11; the *Instruction on Admitting Other Christians to Eucharistic Communion in the Catholic Church, AAS* 1972, 518-525; a *Note about certain interpretations* of the *Instruction concerning particular cases when other Christians may be admitted to Eucharist communion in the Catholic Church, AAS* 1973, 616-619; the document on *Ecumenical Collaboration at the Regional, National and Local Levels,* SPCU, IS 29, 1975, pp. 8-31; Pope Paul VI, Apostolic Exhortation *Evangelii Nuntiandi* (EN), 1975; John Paul II Apostolic Constitution *Sapientia Christiana* (SapC) on Ecclesiastical Universities and Faculties, 1979; John Paul II Apostolic Exhortation *Catechesi Tradendae,* 1979; and the *Relatio Finalis* of the Extraordinary Synod of Bishops, 1985; *Ratio Fundamentalis Institutionis Sacerdotalis* of the Congregation for Catholic Education, Rome, 1985; the Apostolic Constitution *Ex Corde Ecclesiae, AAS* 1990, 1475-1509.

[4] *AAS* 1988, 1204.

[5] Cf. *CIC,* can. 755; *CCEO,* can. 902 and 904, 1. In this Directory the adjective *catholic* refers to the faithful and to the Churches that are in full communion with the Bishop of Rome.

[6] See Nos. 35-36 below.

[7] Apostolic Constitution *Pastor Bonus* states:

"Art. 135: The function of the Council is to concentrate in an appropriate way on initiatives and ecumenical activities for the restoration of unity among Christians.

Art. 136: (1) It sees that the decrees of the Second Vatican Council which pertain to ecumenical matters are put into practice. It deals with the correct interpretation of the principles of ecumenism and mandates their execution. (2) It fosters, brings together, and coordinates national and international Catholic organizations promoting the unity of Christians, and it is watchful over their initiatives. (3) After having first consulted with the Supreme Pontiff, it looks after relations with Christians of Churches and ecclesial Communities which do not yet have full com-

munion with the Catholic Church, and especially establishes dialogues and talks for promoting unity with them, carrying out the work with trained experts of proven theological doctrine. It deputes Catholic observers for Christian meetings and invites observers from other Churches and ecclesial Communities to Catholic gatherings whenever it seems appropriate.
Art. 137: (1) Since the matters dealt with by this department often by their nature touch on questions of faith, it must proceed in close connection with the Congregation for the Doctrine of the Faith, especially when it is a matter of publishing public documents and declarations. (2) In carrying out matters of major importance, however, which concern the separated Eastern Churches, it must first consult the Congregation for the Eastern Churches.

[8] Unless otherwise indicated, the term *particular Church* is used throughout this Directory to indicate a diocese, eparchy or equivalent ecclesiastical territory.
[9] *John* 17:21; cf. *Eph* 4:4.
[10] Dogmatic Constitution *Lumen gentium* (LG), n. 1.
[11] Cf. *LG* 1-4 and also Conciliar Decree on Ecumenism *Unitatis redintegratio* (UR), n. 2.
[12] Cf. *UR*, n. 2.
[13] *LG*, nn. 2 and 5.
[14] *UR*, n. 2; cf. *Eph* 4:12.
[15] *LG* Chapter III.
[16] *Acts* 2:42.
[17] *Relatio Finalis* of the Extraordinary Synod of Bishops in 1985, "The ecclesiology of communion is the central and fundamental idea of the Council's document" (C,1). Cf. Congregation for the Doctrine of the Faith, *Letter to the Bishops of the Catholic Church on certain aspects of the Church as Communion* (28th May 1992).
[18] Cf. *LG*, n. 14.
[19] Conciliar Decree on the Pastoral Office of Bishops in the Church, *Christus Dominus* (CD), n. 11.
[20] Cf. *LG*, n. 22.
[21] *Jn*, 17:21.
[22] *LG*, n. 8.
[23] *LG*, n. 9.
[24] Cf. *UR*, nn. 3 and 13.
[25] Cf. *UR*, n. 3: "Without doubt, the differences that exist in varying degrees between them (other believers in Christ) and the Catholic Church — whether in doctrine and sometimes in discipline, or concerning the structure of the Church — do indeed create many obstacles, sometimes

serious ones, to full ecclesial communion. The ecumenical movement is striving to overcome these obstacles." Such divergences continue to have their influence and sometimes they create new divisions.

[26] *UR*, n. 3.

[27] *UR*, n. 4.

[28] Cf. *UR*, nn. 14-18. Those to whom the term *"Orthodox"* is generally applied are those Eastern Churches which accept the decisions of the Councils of Ephesus and Chalcedon. In recent times, however, it has also been applied, for historical reasons, to those Churches which did not accept the dogmatic formulae of one or other of these Councils (cf. *UR*, n. 13). To avoid confusion, the general term *"Eastern Churches"* will be used throughout this Directory to designate all of those Churches of the various Eastern traditions which are not in full communion with the Church of Rome.

[29] Cf. *UR*, nn. 21-23.

[30] *Ibidem*, n. 3.

[31] Cf. *ibidem*, n. 4.

[32] *UR*, n. 2; *LG*, n. 14; *CIC*, can. 205; *CCEO*, can. 8.

[33] Cf. *UR*, nn. 4 and 15-16.

[34] *Relatio Finalis* of the Extraordinary Synod of Bishops, 1985, C. 7.

[35] Cf. *Jn* 17:21.

[36] Cf. *Rom* 8:26-27.

[37] Cf. *UR*, n. 5.

[38] Cf. nn. 92-101 below.

[39] In this Directory, when, the term *Local Ordinary* is used, it also refers to *local hierarchies of Eastern Churches* in accordance with the terminology in *CCEO*.

[40] The term *Synods of Eastern Catholic Churches* refers to the higher authorities of Eastern Catholic Churches sui juris as found in *CCEO*.

[41] Cf. Conciliar Declaration *Dignitatis Humanae* (DH), n. 4: "In spreading religious belief and in introducing religious practices everybody must at all times avoid any action which seems to suggest coercion or dishonest or unworthy persuasion especially when dealing with the uneducated or the poor". At the same time the Declaration affirms that "religious communities have the further right not to be prevented from publicly teaching and bearing witness to their beliefs by the spoken or written word" *(ibidem)*.

[42] Cf. *UR*, nn. 9-12; 16-18.

[43] *UR*, n. 8.

[44] *1 Cor* 13:7.

[45] Cf. *UR*, n. 3.

[46] Cf *LG*, n. 23; *CD*, n. 11; *CIC*, can. 383, 3 and *CCEO*, can. 192, 2.

[47] Cf. *CIC*, can. 755, 1; *CCEO*, cann. 902 and 904, 1.

[48] Cf. *CIC*, cann. 216 and 212; *CCEO*, cann. 19 and 15.

[49] Cf. *Sects or New Religious Movements: A Pastoral Challenge;* an interim Report based on the responses (about 75) and the documentation received up until the 30th of October, 1985 from regional or national Episcopal Conferences, SPCU, *IS* 1986, n. 61, pp. 144-154.

[50] Cf. nn. 166-171 below.

[51] *UR*, n. 4.

[52] Cf. *CCEO*, can. 904, 1; *CIC*, can. 755, 2.

[53] Cf. *UR*, nn. 9 and 11 and *Reflections and Suggestions Concerning Ecumenical Dialogue,* op.cit.

[54] Cf. *UR*, n. 12; Conciliar Decree on the Church's Missionary Activity *Ad Gentes* (AG), n. 12, and *Ecumenical Collaboration at the Regional, National and Local Levels,* op. cit., n. 3.

[55] Cf. *UR*, n. 5.

[56] Cf. *AG*, n. 15; see also *ibidem,* nn. 5 and 29; cf. *EN,* nn. 23, 28, 77; see also below, nn. 205-209.

[57] *UR*, n. 5.

[58] Cf. *ibidem,* n. 7.

[59] *Ibidem,* n. 6.

[60] Ambrosiaster, *PL* 17, 245.

[61] Cf. *CIC*, can. 209, 1; *CCEO*, can. 12, 1.

[62] Dogmatic Constitution on Divine Revelation *Dei Verbum* (DV), n. 21.

[63] Cf. *UR*, n. 21.

[64] *EN,* n. 77.

[65] Cf. *UR*, n. 11; *AG,* n. 15. For these considerations, cf. *General Catechetical Directory,* nn. 27, 43, and cf. below nn. 75 and 176.

[66] Cf. *UR*, nn. 3-4.

[67] Cf. *CT*, n. 3 and *CCEO*, can. 625.

[68] Cf. *CT*, n. 32.

[69] Cf. *ibidem.*

[70] Cf. *UR*, n. 6 and Pastoral Constitution on the Church in the Modern World *Gaudium et Spes* (GS), n. 62.

[71] Concerning ecumenical collaboration in the field of catechesis, see *CT*, n. 33 and also nn. 188-190 below.

[72] See Constitution on the Sacred Liturgy *Sacrosanctum Concilium* (SC), n. 14.

[73] *Ibidem,* n. 2.

[74] *UR*, n. 2.

[75] *SC*, n. 48.

[76] *UR*, n. 8.

[77] Cf. *ibidem,* n. 7.

[78] Cf. *LG*, n. 15 and *UR*, n. 3.

[79] Cf. nn. 102-142 below.

[80] Cf. nn. 161-218 below.

[81] *LG*, n. 11.

[82] Cf. *EN*, n. 71; see also nn. 143-160 below.

[83] Pope John Paul II, Apostolic Exhortation *Familiaris Consortio* (FC), n. 78.

[84] Cf. *CIC*, can. 529, 2.

[85] Cf. Conciliar Declaration *Gravissimum Educationis* (GE), nn. 6-9.

[86] Cf. *LG*, n. 31.

[87] *UR*, n. 24.

[88] Cf. *GS*, n. 62, 2; *UR*, n. 6; Congregation for the Doctrine of the Faith *Mysterium Ecclesiae* (ME), n. 5.

[89] *ME*, n. 5.

[90] *Ecumenical Directory, AAS* 1970, n. 74.

[91] Cf. *ME*, n. 4; see also nn. 61a and 176.

[92] *UR*, n. 10; cf. *CIC*, can. 256, 2; *CCEO*, cann. 350, 4 and 352, 3.

[93] Cf. *UR*, nn. 14-17.

[94] Cf. *UR*, chap. I.

[95] Cf. *ibidem*, chap. III.

[96] Cf. nn. 76-80 above.

[97] Cf. nn. 194-195 below.

[98] Cf. nn. 192-194 below.

[99] Conciliar Decree *Perfectae Caritatis* (PC), n. 2.

[100] Cf. nn. 50-51 above.

[101] Cf. *SapC*, Practical Norms, art 51, 1, b.

[102] *SapC*, n. 69.

[103] Cf. *UR*, n. 22.

[104] Cf. *ibidem*, n. 22.

[105] With regard to all Christians, consideration should be given to the danger of invalidity when baptism is administered by sprinkling, especially of several people at once.

[106] Cf. *Ecumenical Directory* (1967).

[107] Cf. *CIC*, can. 874, 2. According to the explanation given by the *Acta Commissionis (Communicationes* 5, 1983, p. 182), the wording "communitas ecclesialis" does not include the Eastern Orthodox Churches not in full communion with the Catholic Church ("Notatur insuper Ecclesias Orientales Orthodoxas in schemate sub nomine communitatis ecclesialis non venire").

[108] Cf. *Ecumenical Directory* (1967), n. 48; *CCEO*, can. 685, 3.

[109] Cf. *UR*, n. 4; *CCEO*, cann. 896-901.

[110] Cf. *UR*, n. 4.

[111] Cf. *CIC*, can. 869, 2, and n. 95 above.

[112] Cf. *CIC*, can. 869, 1 and 3.

[113] Cf. *UR*, n. 8.

[114] Cf. *UR*, nn. 3 and 8; see also n. 116 below.

[115] Cf. *LG*, n. 8; *UR*, n. 4.

[116] Cf. *UR*, n. 3.

[117] Cf. *UR*, nn. 3, 15, 22.

[118] Cf. *CIC*, can. 908; *CCEO*, can. 702.

[119] Cf. *UR*, n. 8.

[120] Cf. *SC*, n. 106.

[121] Cf. *CCEO*, can. 881, 1; *CIC*, can. 1247.

[122] Cf. *CIC*, can. 1247; *CCEO*, can. 881, 1.

[123] Cf. *CIC*, can. 1183, 3; *CCEO*, can. 876, 1.

[124] Cf. *CIC*, can. 1184; *CCEO*, can. 887.

[125] Cf. *UR*, n. 14.

[126] *Ibidem*, n. 15.

[127] *Ibidem*.

[128] Cf. *CIC*, can. 844, 2 and *CCEO*, can. 671, 2.

[129] Cf. *CIC*, can. 844, 3 and cf. n. 106 above.

[130] Cf. *CIC*, can. 840 and *CCEO*, can. 667.

[131] Cf. *UR*, n. 3.

[132] *UR*, n. 22.

[133] Cf. *UR*, n. 8; *CIC*, can. 844, 1 and *CCEO*, can. 671, 1.

[134] Cf. *CIC*, can. 844, 4 and *CCEO*, can. 671, 4.

[135] For the establishing of these norms we refer to the following documents: *On Admitting Other Christians to Eucharistic Communion in the Catholic Church* (1972) and *Note Interpreting the "Instruction on Admitting Other Christians to Eucharistic Communion Under Certain Circumstances"* (1973).

[136] Cf. *CIC*, can. 844, 5 and *CCEO*, can. 671, 5.

[137] Cf. *CIC*, can. 844, 4 and *CCEO*, can. 671, 4.

[138] Cf. *CIC*, can. 767 and *CCEO*, can. 614, 4.

[139] Cf. *CIC*, can. 1124 and *CCEO*, can. 813.

[140] Cf. *FC*, n. 78.

[141] Cf. *UR*, n. 3.

[142] Cf. *CIC*, cann. 1125, 1126 and *CCEO*, cann. 814, 815.

[143] Cf. *CIC*, can. 1366 and *CCEO*, can. 1439.

[144] Cf. *UR*, n. 15.

[145] Cf. *CIC*, can. 1127, 1 and *CCEO*, can. 834, 2.

[146] Cf. *CIC*, can. 1127, 1 and *CCEO*, can. 834, 1.

[147] Cf. *CCEO*, can. 835.

[148] Cf. *CIC*, can. 1127, 2.

[149] Cf. *CIC*, can. 1127, 2.

[150] Cf. *CIC*, can. 1127, 3 and *CCEO*, can. 839.

[151] *Ordo celebrandi Matrimonium*, n. 8.

[152] Cf. n. 125 above.

[153] Cf. nn. 129-131 above.

[154] Cf. nn. 125, 130 and 131 above.

[155] Cf. n. 132 above.

[156] *UR*, n. 12.

[157] Pope John Paul II, Encyclical Letter *Redemptoris Hominis* (RH), n. 12.

[158] In this context the term Church is generally to be understood in the sociological rather than in the strictly theological sense.

[159] SPCU, *Ecumenical Collaboration at the Regional, National and Local Levels*, op.cit., n. 4 A.c.

[160] Episcopal Conferences and Synods of Eastern Catholic Churches should take care not to authorize Catholic participation in Councils of Churches in which groups are present who are not really considered to be ecclesial Communities.

[161] Cf. *UR*, n. 9.

[162] *UR*, n. 11; cf. *Eph* 3:8.

[163] *Reflections and Suggestions* [...], op. cit. n. 4,b; cf. also *UR*, n. 11 and *ME*, n. 4. See also nn. 61a, 74-75 above and 181 below.

[164] Cf. *1 Thess.* 2:13.

[165] Cf. *Jude* 3.

[166] *LG*, n. 12.

[167] *Ibidem*.

[168] Cf. *UR*, n. 6 and *GS*, n. 62.

[169] Cf. *UR*, n. 11.

[170] Cf. *DV*, chapter VI.

[171] *UR*, n. 21.

[172] Cf. *CIC*, can. 825, 2 and *CCEO*, can. 655, 1.

[173] New revised edition 1987 of the first 1968 version. Published in *IS* of the Secretariat for Promoting Christian Unity, N 65 (1987) pp. 140-145.

[174] In accordance with the norms laid down in *CIC*, cann. 825-827, 838 and in *CCEO*, cann. 655-659 and the *Decree* of the Sacred Congregation for the Doctrine of the Faith *Ecclesiae Pastorum* de Ecclesiae pastorum vigilantia circa Libros (19.3.1975) in *AAS* 1975, 281-184.

[175] N. 33.

[176] Cf. *UR*, nn. 10-11.

[177] Cf. n. 72 above and Circular Letter of the SPCU on Ecumenical Teaching, n. 6, in *IS*, n. 62 (1986), p. 196.

[178] Cf. *CD*, n. 35, 5-6.

[179] Cf. SPCU, *Circular Letter on Ecumenical Teaching*, 10a, op. cit., p. 197.

[180] Cf. *Ibidem*.
[181] Cf. *UR*, n. 1.
[182] *EN*, n. 77.
[183] *Ibidem*.
[184] Cf. *AG*, n. 6.
[185] *Ibidem*, n. 15.
[186] Cf. *RH*, n. 11.
[187] Cf. *UR*, n. 12
[188] *Ibidem*.
[189] Cf. *Ibidem*.
[190] Cf. Pope John Paul II, *Address* to the Roman Curia, 28 June 1985, *AAS* 1985, 1148-1159; cf. idem Encyclical Letter *Sollicitudo Rei Socialis* (SRS), n. 32.
[191] Cf. SPCU, *IS*, 55, 1984, pp. 42-43.
[192] *Ecumenical Collaboration [...]*, op.cit. n. 3.
[193] *RH*, nn. 8, 15, 16; *SRS*, nn. 26, 34.
[194] *SRS*, n. 36.
[195] Cf. *op. cit.*, n. 3 g.
[196] Pontifical Council for Social Communications, Pastoral Instruction *Communio et Progressio*, n. 99, *AAS* 1971, 593-656.
[197] Cf. *Ecumenical Collaboration [...]*, op cit., 3, f.
[198] Cf. Pontifical Council for Social Communications, *Criteria for Ecumenical and Interreligious Cooperation in Communications*, nn. 11 and 14, 1989, *Origins*, 1989, n. 23, 375-377.

Printed in the United States
67452LVS00004B/1-21